LOCAL SERVICES OF AEROFLOT N

The local service points on this map tot
number accounts for about 60% of all points served
because of map scale limitations. Transcontinental,
inter-city trunk, and intra-regional routes are excluded.

AEROFLOT:
AN AIRLINE AND ITS AIRCRAFT

An Illustrated History of the World's Largest Airline

OTHER BOOKS BY R.E.G. DAVIES

A History of the World's Airlines
Airlines of the United States Since 1914
Airlines of Latin America Since 1919
Continental Airlines — the First Fifty Years
Rebels and Reformers of the Airways
Pan Am: An Airline and Its Aircraft
Lufthansa: An Airline and Its Aircraft
Delta: An Airline and Its Aircraft

AEROFLOT: AN AIRLINE AND ITS AIRCRAFT
АЭРОФЛОТ

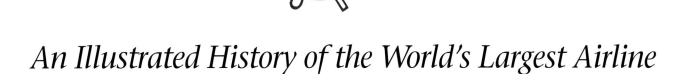

An Illustrated History of the World's Largest Airline

By R.E.G. Davies
Illustrated by Mike Machat

PALADWR PRESS

DEDICATION

With the support of his dear wife, Patricia, John Stroud
has devoted a lifetime of painstaking work to the cause of air
transport. He has researched, written, and meticulously
edited countless books, many of which are of such renown
that they are referred to simply as 'Stroud'. I have been
inspired by John's zeal, integrity, and enthusiasm.
In dedicating this book to him, I hope also that I shall come
up to his own exacting standards.

Published by Paladwr Press, P.O. Box 1467P, Rockville, MD 20850, USA

Manufactured in Hong Kong

Designed by R.E.G. Davies

Artwork by Mike Machat

Edited and Produced by John Wegg

Typesetting/Layout by Fisher & Day, San Francisco

Prepress and Press Management by The Drawing Board

ISBN Ø-9626483-1-Ø

First Edition

CONTENTS

Introduction

Father of Russian Aviation — The Constructor

No book on Russian aviation is complete without reference to the inventor **Aleksander Fedorovich Mozhaisky** (1825-1890). He began to study bird flight when aged 31, and during the next 20 years, experimented with models. He flew kites and designed propellers. In 1876 he himself flew in a large kite, towed by a team of three horses.

In 1877, the War Ministry granted 3,000 rubles for further tests, and on 23 March 1878 Mozhaisky outlined an ambitious `large apparatus' able to lift a man. Granted a further 2,000 rubles, he traveled to England in 1880 to obtain, from R. Baker, Son, and Hemkiens, two small steam engines, one of 20hp, the other of ten. On 3 November 1981, he received a `Privilege' to build his flying machine.

Parts were constructed at the Baltiisky factory at St Petersburg and assembled at the Krasny Selo military field. On 31 January 1883, he approached the Russian Technical Society with a request to demonstrate his apparatus. By the end of the year, it was moving under its own power, at least on the ground.

The fuselage and the tail, as well as the $353m^2$ (3,800sq ft) square planform wing, were built of wood, with steel angle brackets, and covered with varnished silk fabric, as were the three four-bladed propellers, the center one of which was 8.75m (28ft 7in) in diameter.

Some time in 1884, an unknown pilot attempted to fly Mozhaisky's apparatus. He was launched down a sloping ramp, but failed to take to the air because of inadequate power. Mozhaisky ordered more powerful engines from the Obukhovsky steelworks, but died before the work was completed.

Other Russian scientists and inventors, such as S.I. Chernov, K.Ye. Isiolkovsky, and S.A. Chaplygin, all made considerable contributions to aeronautical knowledge during the 1890s.

Father of Russian Aviation — The Scientist

It was left to a notable scholar of the next generation to examine the scientific principles of flight and to publish analyses of his research. **Nikolai Yegorovich Zhukovskiy** (1847-1921) is recognized in Russia as the founder of modern aerodynamics and hydrodynamics.

Zhukovskiy graduated at Moscow University in 1868, taught at the Moscow Higher Technical School (M.V.T.U.) from 1872, and, from 1886, simultaneously at the University. He continued teaching in Moscow, and supervised the construction of his first wind tunnel in 1902, founded Europe's first aerodynamic institute in 1904, and M.V.T.U.'s own aerodynamics laboratory in 1910.

His continued studies led to the publication of the law governing lift in 1906, profiles of aerofoils and propellers in 1910-11, and analyses of propeller tip vortices in 1912-13. He published many important monographs on aerodynamic theory.

In 1918, Nikolai Zhukovskiy was chosen to head the prestigious Central Aero-Hydrodynamics Institute (TsAGI). He died in 1921, but such was his stature that TsAGI became known as the Zhukovskiy Institute.

Acknowledgements

The compilation of this book would not have been possible without the cordial cooperation of the International Commercial Department of **Aeroflot**, under the direction of **Vladimir Tikhonov**, and with the supervision of **Vladimir Masenkov**, who assembled a team to provide data essential for the work. The team consisted of **Vadim Suvarov**, veteran pilot of the Great Patriotic War; **Boris Urenovsky**, Professor of the Civil Aviation Institute in Moscow; and **Tatiana Vinogradova**, once a senior flight attendant (she flew on the Tupolev Tu-114 to Havana and to Tokyo). Together the team helped to ensure that errors in early drafts were corrected and accuracy ensured.

Much of the Russian documentation was translated by **Alex Kampf**, an enthusiastic student of Aeroflot history. In Moscow, I received great support from my good friend **Yuri Salnikov**, television director of aviation documentaries and author of magazine articles on famous Soviet airmen. He introduced me to **Vladimir Samoroukov**, who examined my credentials and first approved the book project.

Vasily Karpy, editor of *Vozduzhny Transport*, proof-read the text and gave valuable advice. He also introduced me to **Boris Vdovienko**, photographer par excellence, from whose magnificent collection I was able to draw. Veteran pioneer pilot, **General Georgy Baidukov**, Valery Chkalov's right hand on his epic 1937 polar crossing, gave me a personal insight into the workings of the old Aeroflot, and a first-hand account of the historic meeting with Josef Stalin in 1936.

I received generous help from many others. In **Leningrad/St Petersburg**, I was hosted by the Academy of Civil Aviation, where Professor-Director Georgy Kryzhanovsky, Deputy Director Anatoly Khvostovsky, Nina Nekrasovich, Irene Volkova, Vitaly Khalikov, and the Academy's librarian, Natella Safronova, were most helpful. In **Novgorod**, thanks to the Chief of the Sub-Region, Anatoli Golovanov, and Deputy Chief Vladimir Bolovsky, I was able to sample the crop-spraying versatility of the remarkable Antonov An-2. In **Khabarovsk**, the *Vozduzhny Transport* correspondent, **Oleg Borisov**, has been a catalyst for some thrilling research. Through the courtesy of **Vladimir Skripnik**, Director of the Far Eastern Region of Aeroflot, I learned much about the airline's provincial operations, including a demonstration of the acrobatic prowess of the An-2. At **Nikolayevsk-na-Amure**, **Valery Dolmatov**, Head of the Nikolayevsk station and also a deputy to the Russian Parliament in Moscow, afforded me the extraordinary privilege of making a helicopter pilgrimage to the dignified monument on Chkalov (formerly Udd) Island; and I met **Vadim Romanuk**, local helicopter mechanic and historian, who inspired the erection of the monument. Later, **Leonid Nagorny**, who succeeded Skripnik in 1991 (and whose 50th birthday party I shall long remember), Vladimir Lenuk, Aleksander Glushko, and Vladimir Kuznetzov, also gave me much assistance. In **Tyumen**, Director Vladimir Illarionov and especially **Mikhail Ponomarev** opened my eyes to the helicopter capital of the world. At **Krasnoyarsk**, Deputy Director Boris Kovchenkov was most hospitable, as was Nikolei Klimenko at **Yeneseisk**. At **Irkutsk**, Vladimir Sokolnikov and Peter Osharov were generous hosts, and my guide to the excellent museum there was **Professor-Doctor Yvgeny Altunin**, aviation historian and author from Irkutsk University. Similarly, at **Yakutsk**, General Director, Vitaly Pinaev, Mikhail Vasilev and others introduced me to the special problems of operations in Yakutia, and to aviation historians Ivan Nygenblya and Vladimir Pesterev.

Back in **Moscow**, I was able to meet **Genrikh Novozhilov**, Igor Katyrev, Aleksander Shakhnovich, and Georgy Sheremetev, of the **Ilyushin Design Bureau**; Yuri Popov, Gleb Mahetkin, and Sergei Agavilyan, of **Tupolev**; and Aleksander Domdukov and Evegeny Tarassov, of **Yakovlev**. I interviewed veteran Aeroflot pilots such as Constantin Sepulkin and Aleksander Vitkovsky. Tatiana Vinogradova, Vasily Karpy, Yuri Salnikov, and **Viktor Temichev** arranged the programs of visits — no easy task during often-congested traveling schedules.

I must not forget the eminent British writers who have contributed so much to the annals of Soviet aviation history during times when information was most difficult to obtain. Veteran author and authority **John Stroud**, airline chronicler **Klaus Vomhof**, and technical specialist **Bill Gunston** have all produced pioneering works that have become standard references (see bibliography) for latterday writers such as myself. **Bob Ruffle**, stalwart of Air-Britain's Russian Aviation Research Group, generously supplied pre-war fleet data and scrutinized the text. **Carl Bobrow** and **Harry Woodman** provided expertise on the Il'ya Muromets and **Paul Duffy's** camera work and information bulletins on post-U.S.S.R. developments (not to mention his scoop in ascertaining the Lisunov Li-2 production total) have been invaluable.

Author

This book started a long time ago. In the late 1950s, when I was researching material for my *History of the World's Airlines*, I was fascinated by the Soviet airline that seemed to be performing an enormous task, but of which little was known. An almost impenetrable curtain shrouded all but a trickle of information from Moscow. Travel was severely restricted, and even in the decades that followed, was scanty and sporadic, to selected tourist destinations. In 1988, however, when Mikhail Gorbachev drew aside the curtain, an opportunity seemed at last to be in sight, and I once again approached the Soviet Embassy for permission to visit Aeroflot.

In 1990, I made the first reconnaissance to Moscow, and asked to see the workings of the secondary, feeder, and bush services of the vast domestic network. The International Department responded admirably. I visited the Far Eastern Division, flew in the Antonov An-2 and An-24, and, in a Mil Mi-2, made a pilgrimage to the dignified monument to the Chkalov crew on the former Udd Island. I began to feel the pulse of Aeroflot, to meet its pilots, its managers, and its staff, and to realize that this huge airline was as dedicated to its task as any other airline of world stature.

Returning to Moscow, I was privileged to sit at the desks of the late Andrei Tupolev and Sergei Ilyushin, and to visit the museums of the great design bureaux. Welcomed everywhere with courtesy and enthusiasm, my appetite was whetted for more.

In 1991, I continued the mission. I visited the Leningrad Aviation Academy, did some simulated crop-dusting at Novgorod, and rounded off a round-the-world trip (all on Aeroflot) by visiting old friends in Khabarovsk. On the return to the U.S., I made the decision to begin this book.

In 1992, I made a whistle-stop tour of Siberia (by this time the Soviet Union had become the CIS) and gained first-hand knowledge of the array of different roles played by Aeroflot, in agriculture, forestry, fishing patrol, ambulance and emergency work, and construction, especially in oilfields, pipelines, power lines, and railroads. Everywhere, I enjoyed visits to museums. Every region of Aeroflot has its historians, justly proud of their heritage.

Telling the story, and meeting some of the people who have contributed to it, has been an exciting and stimulating exercise. Finally, I must record the great pleasure of working once again with the `Old Firm' who produced the previous books in the series: *Pan Am*, *Lufthansa*, and *Delta*. To consult, to review, to plan, and to organize — and yes, sometimes to argue — with my good friends artist **Mike Machat** and producer/editor **John Wegg** has been a rewarding, (if at times strenuous), and totally fulfilling experience. — *R.E.G. Davies*.

Artist

As with previous books in this series, Machat's Law has been a constant and often unwelcome companion. The Law states (as some readers will know) that for any single type of airliner, no two individual aircraft are painted exactly the same; and very few carry their original paint scheme for the whole of their lives.

In recent years, Aeroflot's enormous fleet of front-line aircraft — I exclude the feeder types, whose color schemes are legion — have carried more or less standardized markings. But this was not the case in years gone by, when Soviet aircraft design bureaux seemed to delight in individualism. Dozens of lettering styles were used for the word AEROFLOT, and I have identified a host of different versions of the airline's logo. Fortunately (and unlike its U.S. counterpart) the Soviet flag remained constant.

In the size comparisons, I have used the Ilyushin Il-86, Aeroflot's largest wide-bodied aircraft, roughly comparable with the McDonnell Douglas DC-10. — *Mike Machat.*

Producer/Editor

This book is designed according to the successful formula set by its predecessor volumes on Pan American World Airways, Lufthansa, and Delta Air Lines. The same standards of accuracy, relevance, and balance have been set, but inevitably, some problems arose.

With the aircraft specifications, we have been conscious of the dangers of misrepresenting performance by associating, for example, the maximum range with maximum passenger and/or cargo load. The term normal, where used, therefore, is not a retreat to a broad generalization, but normality correctly expressed. A Tupolev Tu-114, for example, could fly 10,000km (6,000mi), but could not do so with a full payload.

Spelling presented real difficulties. Transliteration from the Russian, a language with vowel and consonant sounds different from most others, has been and still is interpreted in English in several ways. Aeroflot's predecessor airline has been spelled Dobroliot, Dobrolyot, Dobriolot, and the generally accepted Dobrolet, which latter, in fact, is misleading, because it omits the y sound. We have done our best to be consistent.

Some place names have changed according to political decree, and several major cities, Leningrad, Kuibyshev, and Sverdlovsk, for example, changed back to their pre-Revolution names (St Petersburg, Samara, and Ekaterinberg, respectively) even while this book was being written. We have attempted, in the text, the tables, and the maps, to be contemporarily correct.

With a current fleet alone in the region of 11,000 aircraft, it was impossible to attempt to include individual aircraft details as in the previous volumes—even if they were available. Instead, emphasis has been placed on the pre-war non-Soviet aircraft, and selected post-war types where the listing did not preclude essential text, photographs, drawings, or other tabular data.

The computerized layout of the text and final design according to Ron Davies's original plan was fashioned and polished by Kimberley Fisher, of Fisher & Day; and Paladwr Press is much indebted to her and Brian Day for their enthusiastic support and professional advice. Printing, once again, was accomplished under the professional direction of Scott Piazza of The Drawing Board. — *John Wegg.*

The People's Airline

Aeroflot traces its direct ancestry back to 1923, but its mission began in 1930, with the proclamation of the first Soviet Five Year Plan, which, among other objectives, charged the airline with providing an air service for all the people, an obligation as essential as public housing, public utilities, or an urban subway system. Profit-making was irrelevant. Aeroflot received its aircraft, fuel, airport facilities, and ground services from the State; and in return it performed a public service for the State.

Business travel no longer existed as there were no private businesses. First-class service was therefore not required. Indeed, it was politically undesirable, although senior officials usually received preferential treatment. As Aeroflot grew, it was able to offer extremely cheap travel to tens of millions of Soviet people, in the equivalent of America's Greyhound Bus, and just as affordable for the ordinary citizen.

Such a true People's Airline, with fares set low, with passengers paying only for the transport, not for meals and amenities, has been alien to the minds of many western commentators. In the West, air travel was at first the privilege of the rich, with very high fares, and only filtered down to economy-class and group travel levels in later years. In the Soviet Union, the reverse was the case. Only when the airline expanded its horizons into the western world, mainly during the past three decades, did it need to cope with first-class cabin standards. But the people's airbus service, for politicians and peasants alike, Aeroflot has done its job superbly.

Aeroflot Director-Generals

1930-33 B.I. Baranov	1957-59 P.F. Shigarev
1933-35 I.S. Unshlikht	1959-70 Ye.F. Loginov
1935-38 I.F. Tkachev	1970-87 B.P. Bugaev
1938-42 V.S. Molokov	1987-90 A.N. Volkov
1942-47 F.A. Astakhov	1990-91 B.Ye. Paniokov
1947-49 G.F. Baidukov	1991-92 A.A. Larin
1949-57 S.F. Zhavaronkov	

Prelude to Air Transport

Igor Sikorsky — Aviation Genius

For many years during the early development of the commercial airliner, little notice was taken of, or little credit given to, the remarkable achievements of the Russian designer, **Igor Sikorsky**. Less than ten years after the historic flight of the Wright brothers on 17 December 1903, and while designers in other countries were still dabbling with single-engined light aircraft, Sikorsky built a multi-engined giant that began to carry respectable loads of passengers, in acceptable comfort, on demonstrations and test flights over the city of St Petersburg.

Born in Kiev in 1889, Sikorsky was the son of a professor at the Imperial University of St Vladimir, and was fortunate in being able to study at Kiev Polytechnic Institute and also in Paris. He quickly embraced the science of aeronautics, then in its embryo stage and, early in 1912, was able to propose the idea of a multi-engined aircraft to **Mikhail Shidlovsky**, chairman of the Russo-Baltic Wagon Company at St Petersburg. Sikorsky advocated more than one engine because of the notorious unreliability of power plants at that time. Shidlovsky was impressed, and authorized construction of the world's first four-engined aircraft on 30 August 1912.

Development of a Magnificent Machine

On 15 March 1913 (Julian calendar — add 13 days to convert to the modern, Gregorian, calendar — same as western calendar from 1 January 1918) the Sikorsky *Le Grand* made its maiden flight at the Komendantsky airfield. Built of wood and fabric by skilled carpenters, it would eventually weigh 4,200kg (9,240lb) and carry a load of 700kg (1,600lb) at 80km/h (50mph). Because of its — for the time — awesome size, and with two extra engines fitted in tandem, it was soon called the *Bolshoi Baltiskiy (Great Baltic)*. During that summer, the extra engines were moved to line abreast along the wing, and it was again renamed the *Russkiy vityaz (Russian Knight)*. First flown in that form on 23 July (Julian), it was inspected by Tsar Nicholas II. Re-designed, the **Il'ya Muromets**, with four tractor engines mounted in line along the wings, first flew in October 1913 (Julian).

By February 1914, the four-engined giant was able to carry 11 tons — at that time more than any other aircraft's total weight; in June, it stayed aloft for 61 hours, with six passengers aboard. The Il'ya Muromets was named after a legendary Russian folk hero, but it deserves an heroic place in the reality of aviation's Hall of Fame.

The cabin of the Il'ya Muromets was as comfortable as those of many a post-World War I passenger aircraft. It was adequately furnished, and featured electric lighting and a toilet in the rear. (photo: United Technologies)

The Myth

While reports of these events were published, so that the Il'ya Muromets was well known in Russia, the western European countries seemed not to believe the bulletins. The aircraft was even regarded as something of a freak, only one or two were thought to have been built, and that they were unsuccessful. While the French, German, and British aircraft manufacturers, engulfed in the demands of the Great War, paid little attention to the obvious potential of the multi-engined aircraft so ably demonstrated in St Petersburg, Sikorsky forged ahead, and continuously improved the breed. Far from being a transitory experiment, as many liked to think, the **Il'ya Muromets** was the greatest advance in aircraft technology since the Wrights; records indicate that at least 80 aircraft, and possibly more, came off the `production line'.

The Great Flight

The pictures taken of the Il'ya Muromets in 1914 necessarily show the aircraft at low altitude, because few other aircraft could position themselves to match the Sikorsky giant at 1,800m (6,000ft), an altitude already achieved by the summer. Any doubts about its performance, however, were quickly dispelled. On 30 June of that year, the Il'ya Muromets, with a crew of three as well as Sikorsky in command, flew from St

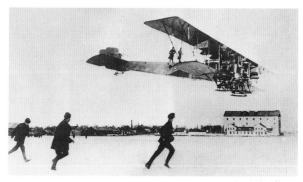

The famous picture of the Il'ya Muromets — probably the Russian Knight prototype — flying low over the airfield at St Petersburg in 1913 or 1914. (photo: United Technologies)

Petersburg to Kiev, with only one stop, to refuel, at Orsha. Taking off at 1.00 a.m. from Korpusnoi airfield, the crew arrived triumphantly at Kiev in the early afternoon of the next day. On 12 July, they returned to St Petersburg, this time covering the 1,060km (660mi) in only 13 hours.

But a month later, the Lights Went Out in Europe, and Russia was swept into the Great War. The Sikorsky aircraft were put into production, to be used for reconnaissance and for bombing, and gave a good account of themselves.

THE EPIC FLIGHT OF THE Il'ya Muromets 30 June-12 July 1914

St Petersburg
Orsha
Kiev

SCALE
Kilometers
Statute Miles

Il'ya Muromets

6 SEATS ■ 80km/h (50mph)

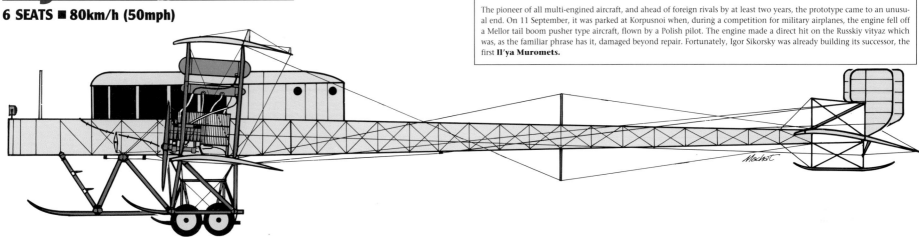

The pioneer of all multi-engined aircraft, and ahead of foreign rivals by at least two years, the prototype came to an unusual end. On 11 September, it was parked at Korpusnoi when, during a competition for military airplanes, the engine fell off a Mellor tail boom pusher type aircraft, flown by a Polish pilot. The engine made a direct hit on the Russkiy vityaz which was, as the familiar phrase has it, damaged beyond repair. Fortunately, Igor Sikorsky was already building its successor, the first **Il'ya Muromets.**

Argus (4 x 100hp) ■ MTOW 4,200kg (9,260lb) ■ Normal Range 170km (105mi)

The Russo-Baltic Works

In 1838, in Riga under Tsarist Russia, in the area known as Courland, but now the capital of Latvia — the **Russko-Baltiski Vagoni Zavod (R-BVZ)**, the Russo-Baltic Wagon Works, was founded. It became the largest builder of railroad cars in Russia which, during the nineteenth century, built up an extensive rail network, mainly in Europe, but extending, from 1891 to 1904, to the Pacific Ocean via the Trans-Siberian Railway. In 1905, the R-BVZ started to build motor cars, producing the Russobalts, some of which were purchased by the Tsar. The Riga works also turned out farm machinery and tramcars. It was a company of considerable stature in the Russian industrial world.

In 1910, it widened its horizons further by forming an aeronautical division, building French aircraft, mainly those designed by Roger Sommer. Such progressive flexibility was inspired by the remarkable general director of R-BVZ, **Mikhail V. Shidlovsky**, who decided to move the aeronautical division to St Petersburg in 1912, to occupy some old factory buildings on the north bank of the Neva River. His attention was drawn to the creative talents of a young man from Kiev, and on the advice of Baron General Kaulbars, **Igor Sikorsky** became the chief designer of R-BVZ's aircraft works in St Petersburg. He was not yet 23 years old.

Le Grand

Early in 1912, Sikorsky had, with the help of friends from the Kiev Polytechnic, built, after earlier experimental types, the **S-6B** biplane, powered by a 100hp German Argus engine, a type favored by Sikorsky until the Great War cut off supplies. On 14 March he established a record by carrying four passengers at a speed of 106km/(65mph). The S-6B then won a competition against seven other aircraft, including foreign entries; but Sikorsky decided to eliminate the ever-present danger of disaster through engine failure, simply by having more than one. On 17 September 1912, he persuaded Shidlovsky (who, in turn, persuaded the R-BVZ board and the Russian Army) to allow him to build a twin-engined version of the S-6B.

This aircraft, which was to become **Le Grand**, was built by master carpenters. Its fuselage was

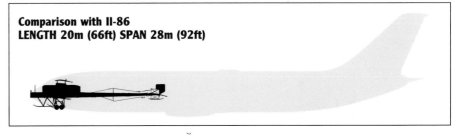

Comparison with Il-86
LENGTH 20m (66ft) SPAN 28m (92ft)

made of four main ash longerons, framed by transverse and vertical members of pinewood, braced with piano wire and additional pine tie-rods, covered with a skin of 4mm (0.15in) Kostovich Arborit, a Russian patented plywood. The doped fabric-covered wings had the high aspect ration of 12-1. Sixteen Nieuport IV wheels, in eight pairs were used for the landing gear. The most remarkable feature was the cabin, which featured wicker armchairs, a table, electric lights, curtained windows, glass paneled doors between the cabin and thecockpit, and even a toilet in the rear.

The Big Baltic

The twin-engined aircraft made its first flight on 15 March 1913 (Julian) (see opposite page), and then, with two extra engines, mounted in tandem, and renamed the **Bolshoi Baltiskiy (Big Baltic)** it made an impressive demonstration on 13 May 1913 at the Korpusnoi military airfield. The flight lasted 20 minutes and Sikorsky was carried shoulder-high in triumph by the awaiting crowd that had assembled.

The next step was to rearrange the engines, in line abreast rather than in tandem; and this became the basic design for all subsequent versions of the big aircraft. Again renamed, this time as the **Russkiy vityaz (Russian Knight)** it first flew on 23 July 1913, and on 2 August set a world record by carrying seven passengers for 1hr 54min.

The First Multi-engined Transport

Aircraft Variant		Date of First Flight	Engines			Remarks	No. Built
Type	Name (if any)		No.	Type	H.P. ea.		
—	Grand: *Bolshoi Baltiskiy* (*Great Baltic*)	March 1913	2	Argus	100	Original prototype, 2 engines	1
		April 1913	4	Argus	100	Same aircraft, with 4 engines paired in tandem	
	Grand: *Russkiy vityaz* (*Russian Knight*)	July 1913	4	Argus	100	Same aircraft, with 4 engines on leading edge. Set a world record by carrying 7 passengers for 1 hour, 54 minutes	
—	Il'ya Muromets	October 1913	4	Argus	100	Also flown as floatplane, with 2x115hp Argus + 2x200 Salmson engines	1
A	Kievsky (prototype military conversion)	Spring 1914	2 / 2	Argus / Argus	100 / 125	Made the epic long distance flight, St. Petersburg-Kiev (750 miles), and back, with Igor Sikorsky and crew of three, 30 June 1914	1
B(Beh)	(Series production of military conversion)		4 / 4	Argus or Salmson	140 / 140	Five aircraft adapted for military use. Some, used only for training, had only two engines	5
B(Veh)	Kievsky II (military version)	1914	2 / 2	Argus / Argus	140 / 125	Military version, with special modifications and aerodynamic improvements. "Kievsky II" was squadron name	1
B(Veh)		1914	4	Sunbeam	150	Production version of Type B(Veh)	36
D 1	DIM (IM = Il'ya Muromets)	1915	4	Sunbeam	150	Smaller and lighter model, with detachable wings, for ease of rail transport 3 rudders. First 2 had engines in tandem	13
D 2		1916	4	Sunbeam	150	Improved version of D1. Center rudder removed to install tail gun	
B(Veh)	Modified as prototype for the G series	1915	4	Sunbeam	150	Advanced military version, with larger wing.Crew of six.	1
G 1	Familiarly known as "Russovalts" or "Renobalts" according to the engine type used (R-BVZ or Renault, respectively)	1915	2 / 2	Renault R-BVZ	220 / 150	Production version of G series	24
G 2		1916		various: R-BVZ, Renault, Argus, Hall-Scott,		Strengthened wing, tailgun with trolley access. One G2 with Beardmore engines, attained a height of 17,000ft.	
G 3		1917				Bigger load, more defensive power	
G 4		1917	4	Renault	220	Used in 1921 for first commercial air route in Soviet Union, Moscow-Nizhne Novgorod (later Gorky, until 1992)	8
E(Ye-1)		1916-1918	4	Renault	220	Largest and most advanced of all the Il'ya Muromets types, with increased bomb load and as many as 8 machine guns. Crew of eight.	
E(Ye-2)							
TOTAL, all multi-engined types							**91**

The numbers built include all airframes constructed. Some of these never flew, because engines were unavailable.
A few sub-assemblies were never put together.
All information based on original research and detailed data compiled by Carl J. Bobrow and Harry Woodman

Ploughshares into Swords

Just before the first Il'ya Muromets made its historic round-trip from St Petersburg to Kiev (page 8), on 28 June the Austrian Archduke Ferdinand was assassinated in Sarajevo and Austria declared war on Serbia a month later. On 1 August Germany declared war on Russia, which had decided, on 25 July, to support Serbia. Amid frantic mobilization for war, Sikorsky's plans for his fine machine came to an end, at least for commercial purposes.

The E.V.K.

But the ability of the Il'ya Muromets to carry heavy loads over long distances was noted by many military minds. The Russo-Baltic Works chairman, Mikhail Shidlovsky, convinced the Russian High Command, the Stavka, that it had military applications, and in December 1914 he was instructed to create the **Escadra vozduzhnykh karablei (E.V.K.)**, or the **Squadron of Flying Ships**, to perform flying duties on the Eastern Front, where Russia was engaged in a life-or-death struggle with the Central Powers, and had already suffered a massive defeat at the Battle of Tannenburg at the end of August 1914.

By 1915, the first units were deployed at Jablonna, near Warsaw, and in Galicia. Sikorsky then began to install different engines: French Renaults, British Sunbeams, the home-built R-BVZs, and other types. On 24 January 1915, he demonstrated Il'ya Muromets performance by climbing to 2,500m (8,000ft) in 49 minutes, and then climbing to 3,300m (11,000ft). The E.V.K. carried out bombing missions, with bomb loads of up to and even exceeding 680kg (1,500lb); yet the reception by the front-line commanders was lukewarm, at a time when the cry should have been ``send us more Sikorskys.''

This picture of the Il'ya Muromets shows the engine mountings, gravity-feed fuel tanks, and the excellent visibility of the cabin. (photo: United Technologies)

A Country In Chaos

Had civil war not intervened in Russia, Irgor Sikorsky's Il'ya Murometsy might have put his country in the forefront of air transport in Europe. But as the map shows, the massive foreign invasion after the Bolshevik Revolution postponed any development in this direction.

Revolution

The Great War did not go well for Russia. Although possessing far superior numbers, its armies lacked good logistics, and were generally badly led. By the time the infrastructure of armaments, food, and clothing supplies were showing signs of improvement, the administration of the Tsarist government had collapsed. Of several political parties, one, the **Bolshevik**, succeeded in mounting a coup in Petrograd (the new westernized name for St Petersburg) and the **October Revolution** of 24-26 October 1917 changed the course of history. The autocratic monarchy was replaced by an idealistic but ruthless ruling class.

Brest-Litovsk

One of the Bolshevik policies had been, effectively, `peace at any price'. When it signed the **Treaty of Brest Litovsk** on 3 March 1918, Russia lost all the western provinces as, one after another, independent republics were formed (see map). The Bolshevik leader **Vladimir I. Lenin**, was forced to surrender territory as the price of peace — territory that **Josef Stalin** was to regain (Finland and Poland excepted) after World War II.

Siege and Counter-Attack

The agony was not yet over. In April 1918, a contingent of British troops had landed at Murmansk, at first in support of its Russian ally, but quickly becoming part of an international alliance of intervention whose objective was to destroy the threat of a communist Russian state. As the map shows, the intervention was widespread, encircling the besieged Bolsheviks with a ring of opposing forces that became known as **The Whites**, to distinguish them from the Bolshevik Reds. The British in the North, at Murmansk and Archangelsk, were joined by the troops and naval forces of many nations, both on land and in the Black Sea. Many Russians themselves, with their Slavic cousins in the Ukraine, Byelo-Russia, and Poland, took up arms in a bloody civil war. In the east, a makeshift army including Czech prisoners-of-war, under the leadership of Admiral Kolchak, actually set up a Government of West Siberia at Omsk on 1 July 1918, and changed its name to the All-Russian Government on 18 November 1918. On 8 August of that year, British and French troops landed at Vladivostok, to be joined by the Japanese on 12 August and the Americans on 15 August. By 6 September, the British and Japanese had reached Chita, in a westward march to outflank the Russians.

But the tide turned. Just as the British troops in the north, reinforced by White Russians, reached the shores of Lake Onega, posing a threat to Petrograd, the Red Army, under the direction of **Leon Trotsky**, counter-attacked in the east on 28 April 1919, repulsing the Czechs, who had reached the Volga at Samara. In October, the Red Army went on to the offensive against General Denikin in the Ukraine and against General Yudenich on the Baltic front. During the next year, the Bolshevik forces steadily re-occupied the lost territories, meeting, however, stiff resistance from the Poles, who won a great victory under General Pilsudski, with considerable losses on the Russian side. But by the end of 1920, it was all over. The White forces under General Wrangel evacuated southern Russia, and the **Peace of Riga** on 18 March 1921 ended the war with Poland.

Lost Opportunity

One of the casualties in the terrible conflict had been the dismemberment of the **Escadra vozduzhnykh korablei E.V.K.** (see page 10), and the destruction of many of the Il'ya Muromets aircraft. A few were assembled near Moscow and in spring 1920, were sent to the western and southern fronts. The Russo-Baltic Works ceased production. **Igor Sikorsky** himself was on the wrong side, and, like thousands of other educated technicians and scholars, he fled to the West, arriving in New York on 30 March 1919.

The First Soviet Air Services

An Embryo Organization

The Bolshevik leaders, now beginning to call themselves Soviet, recognized the importance of aviation as a new industry. V.I. Lenin supported aviation and agreed to its receiving priority. Before the Revolution, there were 27 aircraft factories and seven more were being built. Tsarist Russia had been far from backward in the new science.

As early as 10 November 1917, two weeks after the Ten Days That Shook The World, a **Bureau of Commissars for Aviation and Aeronautics** was formed, to review the aviation assets of the country, with a view to creating a Soviet Air Force. The first Soviet detachment, with a modest contingent of twelve crews, was formed to defend Petrograd against General Krasnov's forces. Then on 29 December 1917, the Bureau became the **All-Russian Collegium for the Administration of the Air Fleet**, widening its scope to cover all facets of aviation and aeronautics. Then again, on 24 May 1918, the Collegium was replaced by the **Main Directorate of Workers and Peasants of the Red Army Air Force (Glavvozdykhoflot)**, at first headed by M.A. Solovov and A.S. Vorodnikof. This Directorate was charged with uniting all air units ``in the interests of protecting the Soviet Motherland.''

Building a Technical Base

All this took place before the official establishment of the Russian Soviet Federated Socialist Republic (R.S.F.S.R.) in July 1918. And in spite of the chaotic conditions inflicted by the waging of civil war, the nucleus of an aviation industry was taking shape. On 1 December 1918, the **Centralyni Aero Gydrodynamichesky Institut (TsAGI)** or **Central Aerodynamics and Hydrodynamics Institute** was established under the direction of **Nikolai E. Zhukovskiy**; his deputy was Andrei N. Tupolev. On 13 September 1919, Zhukovskiy formed the **Moscow Technical Aviation College**, later reorganized as the **Institute of Engineers of the Red Air Force**, and known familiarly as the **Zhukovskiy Academy**. On 3 December 1920, by a decree signed by Lenin, this man was named The Father of Russian Aviation for his outstanding efforts.

An Historic Airfield

On 21 September 1919, an airfield was opened at **Khodinka**, only 6km (4mi) to the northwest of Moscow's Red Square, where, in March 1918, the Bolshevik party had established its capital in the Kremlin, to replace St Petersburg/Petrograd. It is still the site of Aeroflot's central bus terminal and design bureaux of Ilyushin, Yakovlev, and Sukhoi are adjacent to it.

Civil Aviation Begins

On 17 January 1921, Lenin signed a decree to regulate travel in the airspace over Soviet territory. On 26 January a further decree set aside 3 million gold rubles for an aviation development program under the jurisdiction of Glavvozdykhoflot. The terrible civil war between the Reds and the Whites was over; the Peace Treaties had been signed; the new Soviet Russia was ready to go to work.

The First Commercial Air Service

The successor to the Tsarist E.V.K., the **D.V.K. (Divisionye Vozdushniy Korablei** or Flying Ships Division) had a small part to play in this revival of activity. On 1 May 1921, three converted Sikorsky **Il'ya Muromets** four-engined bombers of the 2nd Otryad (Detachment), commanded by A.K. Tumanskiy, carried the first official mail and passengers from Moscow to Kharkov, via Orel. The frequency was two or three services per week, and a total of 43 flights were made over a period of five months. Sixty passengers and six tons of mail were carried altogether, before the service ended on 11 October.

In spring 1920, **KOMTA (Kommassiy po Tyazheloi Aviatsiy**, or commission for heavy aviation) had been formed under the chairmanship of Zhukovskiy, and a six-/eight-passenger twin-engined triplane, called Komta (Comet), was completed in March 1922. It proved almost incapable of flight, and the design was abandoned.

Deruluft

Resulting from Lenin's advocacy, Soviet Russia adopted, by decree, on 9 August 1921, the **New Economic Policy (N.E.P.)** that broadened the base of commerce and trade, to allow limited participation by private firms or individuals. The country needed help badly, in all sectors of the economy, and one sequel was the establishment, in March 1922, of the American Relief Administration, under the direction of Herbert Hoover, to help to relieve the great famine of 1922.

Another manifestation of this widening scope was the formation of a joint Soviet-German airline on 24 November 1921. Most of the aircraft used were German, and so was most of the organization and administration, at least until the 1930s; and the airline was known everywhere by its German name, the **Deutsch-Russische Luftverkehrs A.G.**, or **Deruluft**. (Its history is related in *Lufthansa: An Airline and Its Aircraft*, a companion volume to this book.)

On 16 April 1922, Germany signed the **Treaty of Rapallo**, interpreted — correctly — by historians as a device to evade the harsh conditions of the Peace Treaty imposed on Germany on 7 May 1919. Germany recognized the Soviet Union, although it was not yet officially in existence. Almost two years were to follow before any other nation recognized the Soviet Union — Great Britain was next, on 1 February 1924.

Deruluft opened its first service to Moscow from Königsberg (later Kaliningrad) on 1 May 1922, started a new route via Tallinn (Reval) to Leningrad (renamed from Petrograd on 22 April 1920) on 6 June 1928, and maintained both routes until 31 March 1937.

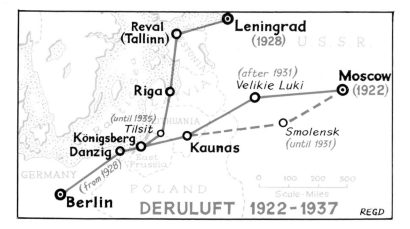

Fokker F.III

DERULUFT FOKKER F.IIIs

Regn.	MSN	In Service	Remarks
RR 1		4/22-26	
RR 2	1653	4/22-26	Rebuilt as Grulich V1, to D 902
RR 3		4/22-5/28	to D 1389
RR 4		4/22-26	to D 904
RR 5		8/22-30	Rebuilt as Grulich V1, V1a
RR 6	1656	5/22-26	to D 906
RR 7		5/22-26	
RR 8	1658	8/22-26	to D 200
RR 9		5/22-26	
RR 10	1660	7/22-26	to D 910 *Zugspitze*
	1530		ex H-NABR
	1531		ex H-NABS, to D 180

Notes: Deruluft also operated Fokker F.V RR 13 (2050), ex H-NABW;
Fokker F.VII RR 21 (4845), to H-NACR; LVG C.VI RR 11 (46443),
ex D 123; Albatross L.76a D 1127 (10101); and at least one Polikarpov PM-1.
F.111s RR 3, RR 5, RR 6, & RR 10 to Ukrvozdukhput.

A Fokker F.III of Deruluft. The pilot was seated on the port side of the engine, in front of the passenger cabin. (photo: Lufthansa)

Aero-Union

The Russian aircraft industry had been severely handicapped by the ravages of the Great War. Most aircraft factories were in ruins and even the **Il'ya Murometsy** survived only in small numbers. A few were produced in the early 1920s but only the **AK-1** and the **ANT-2** (page 18) were suitable for air transport.

German airlines sprang up in a profusion of interlocking relationships, involving shipping lines, aircraft manufacturers, and states or cities which sponsored the many small companies. One of these was **Aero-Union**, direct descendant of Deutsche Luft Reederei, backed by the A.E.G. company, and the first post-war scheduled airline in the world. When Deruluft was founded on 24 November 1921, its first aircraft were acquired through the 50% shareholding held by Aero-Union.

Deruluft's First Aircraft

Deruluft began services on 1 May 1922 from Konigsberg, East Prussia, to Moscow (see map, opposite page). Its first aircraft were Dutch-built **Fokker F.IIIs**, third in the line of famous early transport aircraft, with wood-covered tubular steel-framed fuselages, and the characteristically thick wooden wing construction of Fokker aircraft. At first, Deruluft carried only mail and officials, but on 27 August 1922, the service was opened to the public. The large **Lloyd** group, backed by the Nord-Deutscher Lloyd shipping line, took over Aero-Union on 6 February 1923, and in turn, its shares were acquired by **Deutsche Luft Hansa** when all the German airlines were amalgamated on 6 January 1926. But Deruluft, with its joint ownership with the Soviet Union, remained legally independent. In practice, however, there were close links with the German flag carrier. Ten Fokker F.IIIs were leased by D.L.H. to Deruluft from 1922.

Fokker F.III RR 5 was converted by Deutscher Aero Lloyd at Berlin-Staaken (directed by technical manager Dr Ing Karl Grulich), with a revised fuselage, tail unit, cockpit, and landing gear, and — later — a Bristol Jupiter radial engine. In this guise, it was designated Grulich V1a. (photo: Lufthansa)

Formation of Dobrolet

Russian Aviation Recovery

By 1922, aviation in Russia was slowly recovering. The service to Berlin (pages 12-13) carried 400 passengers and 18 tons of mail. And some progress was being made elsewhere. On 8 July 1922 in Moscow, for example, the first experimental flight was made spraying insecticide from the air, as a prelude to developing aviation for agricultural use (page 82). Aerial photography was quickly recognized to be ideal for mapping

Russia's vast eastern expanses, almost totally devoid of surface transport north of the trans-Siberian Railway.

Other than Deruluft, another small air transport service, the All-Russian, was offered in 1922. On 1 August, flights began between Moscow and Nizhne Novgorod, in conjunction with the annual fair. The aircraft used were **Junkers-F 13s**, lent by the German Junkers firm, which was planning to establish an assembly plant in Moscow (see opposite). The service operated until 25 September, and 57 flights were made, carrying 209 passengers and 2,600kg (5,800lb) of freight over the 420km (260mi) distance.

As a result, the Russian authorities ordered 20 Junkers-F 13s for future use, and the national budget for aviation purposes was raised to 35 million rubles. During 1922 also, the first Soviet-built aircraft made its debut in Leningrad. It was a small training model, designated the U-1, and named Red Pilot. Some 700 are reported to have been built, as well as 120 of the Mu-1 floatplane version. The U-2 was built in 1928.

Formation of the U.S.S.R.

Political consolidation was delayed until the end of 1922, when the Far Eastern Republic, which had declared independence during the turmoil of the Revolution, finally agreed to merge with the Russian S.F.S.R. On 30 December 1922, the 10th All-Russian Congress of the Soviets (and the First All-Union Congress) officially declared the formation of the **Union of Socialist Soviet Republics (U.S.S.R.)**, consisting of Russia, the Ukraine, Byelorussia (White Russia), and Transcaucasia. Russia effectively controlled central Asia, but the republics in that region did not become part of the Soviet Union until 1924.

A Civil Aviation Administration

On 23 November 1922, the Institute of Engineers of the Red Air Force (page 12) in Moscow became the **Academy of the Air Force**, which was also named after its driving personality, **Nikolai Zhukovskiy**. On 1 December, as the threat of war receded, the Revolutionary War Soviet of the Republic, under the Chief Directorate of the Workers and Peasants of the Red Army Air Force (**Glavvozdykhoflot**) was charged with the responsibility of inspecting all civil aviation and overseeing its technical activities. Simply put, this Inspectorate of the Civil Air Fleet was akin to the U.S. Civil Aeronautics Authority, and it paved the way for the establish-

ment of civil air transport. On **9 February 1923**, the Soviet Council of Labour and Defence issued a decree whereby the establishment of airlines was entrusted to Glavvozdykhoflot, through the Inspectorate of the Air Fleet. With the support of the post office and other government agencies, the operation was, in turn, placed under a full-time Civil Aviation Board (or Council) and this event is recognized as the **official birth date of Aeroflot.**

Formation of Dobrolet

On 8 March 1923, an important meeting was held by the Obshestvo Druzhny Vozduzhnovo Flota (Society of Friends of the Air Fleet). This influential body was patronized at this meeting by senior party members such as Frunze, Dzerzhinsky, and by Lenin himself. The result was the organization, on 14 March 1923, of the All-Russian Volunteer Air Fleet, or **Rossiskoye Obshestvo Dobrovolnogo Vozduzhnogo Flota (Dobrolet)**, with a capital of 500,000 rubles. Its first chairman was Krasnoschekov, who was also chairman of the Russian Mercantile Trading Bank.

Echoing the Junkers service of the previous year, Dobrolet started a short-lived service from Moscow to Nizhne Novgorod, and carried 229 passengers and 1,900kg (4,200lb) of freight. The Red Air Fleet lent various makeshift types imported from overseas: de Havilland D.H.9s, Vickers Vimys, and Junkers. Dobrolet's capital was increased in 1923 to 2 million rubles.

Except for this brief interlude, only a few other flights were made, from Moscow to Leningrad, Kazan, Kursk, and Kharkov, but these were neither regular nor open to the public. But on 19 October 1923, the Council for Labour and Defence established a three-year program to expand air travel, not only within European Russia, but also to Turkestan, and ambitiously, to Mongolia.

Poster advertising the Junkers 'Aviakultura' flights between Moscow and Nizhne Novogorod in 1922.

Junkers-F 13fe RR 38 of Deruluft. (photo: Lufthansa)

Junkers-F 13

4 SEATS ■ 165km/h (105mph)

A Great Airliner

To the relief of the whole of Europe, the Armistice of 11 November 1918 brought an end to the Great War, **Professor Junkers** drew on the experience of building military aircraft almost entirely of metal, and designed one of the most successful transport aircraft of the 1920s, and one of the great airliners of all time.

Designated the **Junkers-F 13** — defying superstition — it first went into service in Germany in 1919, and the last F 13 in scheduled service retired in Brazil in 1948. Constructed of corrugated light-weight aluminum, it easily outlived the wood-and-fabric steel-framed aircraft of the time, few of which survived for more than two or three years — and would not have lasted long in northern Russia or Siberia.

Restrictive Practices

The F 13s were, like all German aircraft, handicapped by severe restrictions imposed by the victorious Allies. In May 1920, all German aircraft were confiscated by the occupying powers, and under the terms of the `London Ultimatum' of 5 May 1921, these were enforced with even more severity. Not until 14 April 1922 was the ban on aircraft construction finally lifted, albeit with limitations on engine power and load carrying.

German companies evaded the letter — and the intent — of the law by setting up production in other countries. It also sponsored the formation of airlines in those countries which had no aircraft industries of their own (and even one or two that had) by setting up joint ventures. The host country supplied the infrastructure of installations, airfields, and administrative staff; Junkers supplied the aircraft and technical support.

The little four-passenger F 13 carried its customers in a comfortable cabin, in comfortable seats; however, the two crew sat in a semi-open cockpit. Altogether, over 300 F 13s were built, an astonishing production performance for the period, and the F 13 formed the basis for later types such as the W 33, and ultimately the Ju 52/3m. The F 13s were to be seen all over Europe, in South America, and in other countries such as Persia and South Africa.

The F 13 in Russia

Junkers leaped at the chance of taking advantage of the **Treaty of Rapallo**, signed on 16 April 1922, and in which Germany became the first country to recognize the Soviet Union. A production line was set up at Fili, a suburb of

Moscow, where a factory had been built in 1916 to produce the Il'ya Muromets. The Fili-built F 13s were designated **Ju 13s**.

During 1923, under the title of **Junkers Luftverkehr Russland**, Ju 13s operated a trunk route from Moscow to Baku, on the Caspian Sea, and center of the new oil industry. It thus provided a westbound airlink, via Moscow, with Berlin, via Deruluft; and a potential eastbound connection to Persia — an intriguing aerial variant of the *Drag Nacht Oosten* movement that had, in 1889, seen the sponsorship of the Baghdad Railway, in an effort to extend German influence in Asia.

German infiltration into Russian aviation dwindled by the mid-1920s. The Moscow — Baku route was taken over by **Ukrvozdukhput** (see next page). But Junkers aircraft were put to good use all over the Soviet Union (see also pages 20 and 24).

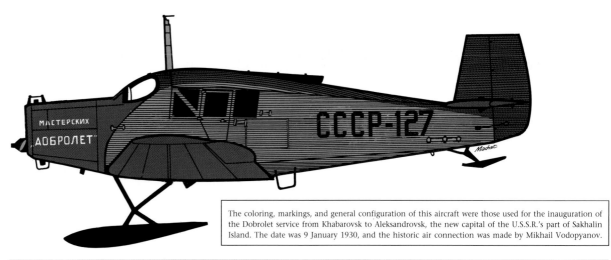

The coloring, markings, and general configuration of this aircraft were those used for the inauguration of the Dobrolet service from Khabarovsk to Aleksandrovsk, the new capital of the U.S.S.R.'s part of Sakhalin Island. The date was 9 January 1930, and the historic air connection was made by Mikhail Vodopyanov.

Junkers-L5 (1 x 280hp) ■ MTOW 2,500kg (5,500lb) ■ Normal Range 640km (400mi)

JUNKERS-JU 13 IN SOVIET SERVICE

Regn.	MSN	Remarks	Regn.	MSN	Remarks	Regn.	MSN	Remarks
D 226	638	(Deruluft, URSS-226)	R-RDAC			R-RECL	651	*Bremse* (Junkers Luftverkehr)
D 230	641	(Deruluft)	R-RDAD	655	*Hornisse* (Dobrolet)	R-RECJ	643	*Wachtel*
D 261	653	*Drohne* (Dobrolet)	R-RDAE	656	*Hummel, Prombank* (Dobrolet)	R-RECK	659	*Albatross* (Junkers Luftverkehr)
D 269	657	*Libelle* (Dobrolet)	R-RDAG	659	*Moskito* (Dobrolet)	R-RODB		
D 270	658	*Matte* (Dobrolet)	R-RDAM		*Sibrevkom* (Dobrolet)	R-RUAZ		
D 307	670	(Deruluft)	R-RDAO		*Krasnya Kamvol`shcik* (Dobrolet)	URSS-301	765	*Königsfischer*
D 308	671	(Deruluft)	R-RDAS		also RR-DAS (Dobrolet)	URSS-307	723	*Eismöwe*
D 424	702	*Emmerling* (Deruluft)	R-RDAU		(Dobrolet)	URSS-308	720	*Königsadler*
D 558	752	*Mauersegler* (Deruluft)	R-RECA	569	*Albatros* (RR-ECA)	URSS-320		*Sokol*
RR 38	2017	(Deruluft)	R-RECB		(Junkers Luftverkehr)	SSSR-L85		
RR 40	650	*Eisvogel* (Deruluft)	R-RECD	572	*Lerche* (RR-ECD)	SSSR-127		*Masterskih*
RR 41	757	*Steinschmetzer* (Deruluft)	R-RECE	614	*Papagei* (Junkers Luftverkehr)	SSSR-M752		
R-RDAA		*Mossoviet* (Dobrolet)	R-RECG	693				
R-RDAB	654	*Fliege, Samolet* (Dobrolet)	R-RECH	636	*Piepmatz*			

Note: Some known names of otherwise-unidentified Ju 13s include: Prezidium VSNCh, Tjervonets, Turkrespublike, Kirgizii, Sibiri, Dalili gu Vostoku, Mossoviet 2, Nauka, Tsckebu, Krasnyj Pisjtjek, Prombank 2-j, & Krasnyj Ural.

JUNKERS-W 33 IN SOVIET SERVICE

Regn.	MSN	Remarks
R-RDAH	2528	Dobrolet
R-RDAJ	2529	Dobrolet
R-RDAO		Dobrolet
R-RDAU		Dobrolet
SSSR-144		
SSSR-145		} based at Verkne Udinsk
SSSR-146		} (Ulan Ude) for Urga
SSSR-147		} (Ulan Bator) route, 1929-
SSSR-175		
SSSR-176		} based at Irkusk for
SSSR-177		} Yakutsk route, 1929-
SSSR-182		
SSSR-441		deld 2/30
SSSR-442		deld 2/30
SSSR-443		deld 3/30
SSSR-444		deld 4/30
SSSR-445		deld 3/30

Ukrvozdukhput and Zakavia

An Airline for the Ukraine

In the Ukraine, the spirit of republican independence manifested itself by the formation of an airline. On 1 June 1923, less than three months after the formation of Dobrolet, **Ukrainskoe Obschestvo Vozduzhnyk Shoobshcheniy (The Ukrainian Airline Company)** (abbreviated to **Ukrvozdukhput**) was founded. Headquarters were at Kharkov, a potential hub for air services throughout the European part of the U.S.S.R.

Dornier Establishes a Presence

Ukrvozdukhput opened for business on 15 April 1925, when it started to operate from Kharkov to Odessa and Kiev. Two months later, on 15 June, routes to Moscow and Rostov-on-Don completed a commendable spoke network centered on Kharkov. The Kalinin aircraft factory was in that city, and a cooperative arrangement was forged with the Dornier company. This latter had connections with the German Lloyd transport group which, in turn, was a partner in Deruluft. Ukrvozdukhput's first fleet consisted of four-passenger **Dornier Komet IIs**, and a half a dozen six-seat **Dornier Komet IIIs**.

Recognition of the Soviet Union (see page 15) had given Germany a doorway for trade, and effective control of the airlines provided a pathway through that door. Aside from being a strong influence on the airline operation, Dornier's methods of construction could clearly be detected on the first Kharkov-based Kalinin aircraft, the K-1, K-2, K-3, and K-4. None went into service with Ukrvozdukhput, but were later to see service with Dobrolet.

Zakavia

A small airline was also established, on 10 May 1923, at Tiflis (Tbilisi) in Georgia. Its name

This small building was the hub of Ukrvozdukhput at Kharkov during the 1920s.

was **Zakavia**, derived from Zakavkazie, or Trans-Caucasus, and there were also plans to form an airline called Kakavia, but this never happened. Zakavia operated one route, to Baku, Azerbaijan, probably with a Junkers Ju 13. Late in the year, it was associated with **Azerbajdzhanskogo dobrovol'nogo vozdushnogo flota**, or **Azdobrolet**, which existed for a few months. Beset by political upheaval, civil wars, and surrounded by high mountains, Zakavia had the odds stacked against it from the start, and after about two years of frustrated effort, it combined with Ukrvozdukhput.

Independence Lost

The Ukrainian airline took over the Junkers operation (see page 15) which, with the Zakavia franchise, gave it almost the whole of the southern part of the European U.S.S.R. as its traffic catchment area. Uzkrvozdukhput carried 3,050 passengers in 1928.

But its very success perhaps fell foul of government policy centered in Moscow. One of the items contained in the first Soviet Five-Year Plan was to create an all-Soviet airline which, in 1930, not only inherited the Russian Dobrolet, but engulfed Ukrvozdukhput as well.

Aircraft operated by Ukrvozdukhput included Dornier Komet IIs RRUAA, RRUAC, RRUAD, RRUAE, RRUAF; Komet IIIs RRUAG, RRUAL, RRUAN; Kalinin K-4s RRUAB, RRUAX; and Kalinin K-2 RRUAT.

Deruluft Progress

Top Deruluft aircraft at Moscow-Khodinka during the 1920s. Four of the airline's fleet of the Fokker F.IIIs can be seen, including RR2, RR9, and RR10. (photo: Lufthansa)

During the mid-1920s, the Soviet aircraft manufacturing industry was slowly getting on its feet. Not until the Kalinin K-5 was introduced in 1929, and the ANT-9 in 1931, did the U.S.S.R. have anything to match the products of western Europe. Meanwhile, however, the joint Soviet-German airline, Deruluft, had the advantage of a steady source of supply from Germany (see page 13).

The early **Fokker F.IIIs** were replaced by **Dornier Merkurs**, transferred from Deutsche Luft Hansa (D.L.H.) from 1929 onwards. Bearing in mind the pioneering element of the operating environment at the time, during a period when commercial air transport was still feeling its way everywhere, Deruluft's standards were high, and, as the illustrations show, this was evident on the ground as well as in the air.

Deruluft had handsome service vehicles, even in the embryo years. (photo: Lufthansa)

These vehicles did credit to Deruluft's ground service department. Each has the Mercedes emblem on its radiator. (photo: Lufthansa)

Dornier Merkurs of Deruluft. The lower picture is of the airfield at Königsberg, the western terminus of the line until 1927. (photos: Lufthansa)

DERULUFT FLEET 1927-1937

Regn.	MSN	Remarks
Dornier Komet III		
RR 16		
RR 17		
RR 18		
Dornier Merkur		
D 1102	87	Edelmander
RR 27	89	to D 427
RR 28	94	to D 1078 *Iltis*
RR 29	97	to D 1082
RR 30	130	to D 1451
RR 33	126	to D 1465, *Hermelin*
D 1079	127	to D 1079, *Blaufuchs*
D 1080	128	to D 1080, *Wiessfuchs*
D 1081	129	to D 1081, *Kreuzfuchs*
RR 34	173	to D 1605, *Kreuzfuchs*
RR 35	174	to D 1595
RR 36	175	to D 1629, *Blaufuchs*
D 1445	176	to D 1445, *Nerz*
D 1455	177	to D 1455, *Wiessfol*
D 1458	178	to D 1458, *Hermelin*
D 1076	121	*Silberlöwe*
URSS-304	122	to D 1077, *Wiesel*
URSS-305	130	to D 1451
RR 30, D 1081, & D 1076 to Aeroflot		
Rohrbach Ro VIII Roland I		
D 1280	35	*Feldbei*
Rohrbach Ro VIII Roland II		
D 1712	45	*Schönburg*
D 1735	48	*Marksburg*
D 1729	43	*Drachenfels*
Tupolev ANT-9		
URSS-D308	143	*Chaika*
URSS-D309	145	to D 2831
URSS-D310	135	*Orel*
URSS-D311	160	*Yastreb*
URSS-D312	112	*Korshun*
URSS-D313	Golub	
Junkers-Ju 52/3m ge		
D-AREN	4051	Crashed 31 Jan 35
D-AHUS	4049	*Milan*
D-AGIS	4048	*Kormoran*
D-AXES	4052	*Kondor*
D-ADAL	4046	*Almenröder/Flamingo*

Note: Deruluft's Junkers Ju 13s are included in the table on page 15.

Dobrolet's First Steps

An Infant Aircraft Industry

Vladimir Lenin did not live to see the outcome of some of the policies that he had instigated. He died on 21 January 1924, and only a few days later, on 1 February, the British Government recognized Soviet Russia, the first foreign power to do so, excluding Germany, which had done so earlier. Simultaneously with the easing of tension overseas, the Russian industry, which had been laying dormant during the political upheaval and economic disruption caused by the Revolution, began to revive.

The aircraft manufacturing plants stirred into life. At Fili, in Moscow, the German Junkers company started a small production line of the sturdy metal-built F 13, (known as the Ju 13 in Russia) and deliveries began to Dobrolet in 1924. At least 24 aircraft are believed to have been completed. For several years, reports of Ju 13s performing various services all across the Soviet Union included, in addition to inaugurating new routes, demonstrations of the benefits of air travel to the amazed citizenry of remote lands, and joyrides for workers who had shown special talents in exceeding their assigned quotas.

Also, the TsAGI (see page 12), under the direction of V.L. Alexandrov and V.V. Kalinin, completed, on 8 March 1924, the first test flight of the first successful transport aircraft to be designed and built entirely in the Soviet Union (also see page 12). The **AK-1** (AK for Alexandrov-Kalinin) could carry three passengers and attained 146km/h (90mph). It was a start, and on 15 June 1924, the AK-1 was assigned to Dobrolet's Moscow-Nizhne Novgorod-Kazan route.

Reference has already been made (page 16) to the activity of **K.A. Kalinin**, the designer working in conjunction with Dornier in Kiev. On 20 April 1925, a series of government-supervised experimental flights was completed with the **K-1**, Kalinin's first design. Back at **TsAGI**, **A.N. Tupolev** had become head of the organization which had an experimental laboratory, and was building engines and aircraft, including the all-metal **ANT-2**, able to carry two passengers.

Then on 20 August 1925, an improved version, the **ANT-3**, was flown. Tupolev was proceeding cautiously. This aircraft weighed only 2,100kg (960lb) but it flew at 201km/h (125mph), and was considered a worthy enough product to carry the Soviet flag overseas (see opposite page). Tupolev was on a roll. On 26 November 1925, the **ANT-4** took to the air; and more designs were to come.

In Central Asia

On 1 May 1924 — possibly to coincide with the May Day celebrations, and also as a practical measure to demonstrate the benefits of rule from Moscow, **Dobrolet** began to operate scheduled services in the area formerly under the Tsarist governor-generalship of Turkestan. The Soviet Government had replaced this, by setting up several Peoples' Republics in 1921 to supplant the khanates of Khiva and Bukhara; and by 1925 the new republics of Uzbekistan, Turkmenistan, Tadjikistan, and Kirghizia were formally incorporated into the U.S.S.R.

Most probably with Junkers Ju 13s, Dobrolet opened a route from Khiva to Dushanbe, via Bukhara. While hardly operating with clockwork regularity and punctuality, it was reasonably successful, as the alternative land transport was by horse or camel. There were also boats on the Amu Darya river, but these were often left stranded when the river shifted course.

ANT-3 RR-SOV Aviakhim S.S.S.R. Proletarii at Königsberg during Mikhail Gromov's circuit of Europe in 1926. (photo: Lufthansa)

At the end of their epic flight from the U.S.S.R. to the U.S.A. in 1929 the Soviet crew was welcomed by the Mayor of Oakland. Left to right: the helmeted Sterligov, Shestakov, the Mayor, Bolatov, and Fufayev. (photo: Eugene Altunin)

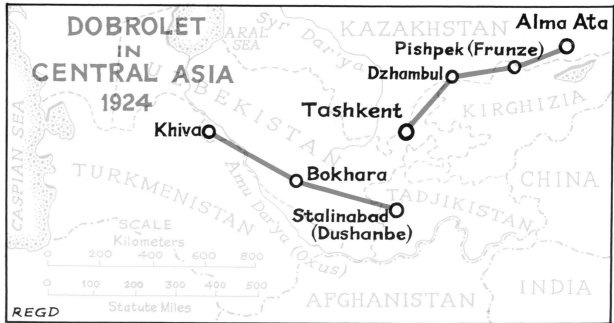

DOBROLET IN CENTRAL ASIA 1924

SCALE
Kilometers
0   200   400   600   800

0   100   200   300   400   500
Statute Miles

REGD

Alma Ata
Pishpek (Frunze)
Dzhambul
Tashkent
Khiva
Bokhara
Stalinabad (Dushanbe)

Showing The Flag

Feeling Its Way

Following the exhausting civil war, Russian aviation had struggled to pick up the pieces of a shattered industry. Carefully, almost methodically, it had begun to rebuild. Between 1918 and 1922, several exploratory flights were made with foreign-made aircraft, Farmans, L.V.G.s, and British types, not only from Moscow but in other parts of Russia and Central Asia. From 16 to 20 September 1922, B.K. Bellint made a round-trip in a Russian-built Junkers Ju 13 from Moscow to the Crimea, and from 20 May to 1 June 1923 flew another Ju 13 to Tashkent, as a prelude to Dobrolet's pioneering activities there (see page 18).

From 10 to 22 July, 1924, piloting an **AK-1** — the first successful all-Soviet transport design — A.N. Tomashevskya flew from Moscow to Kazan; and from 29 September to 1 October of the same year, P.Kh.Mezheraup, in a **Polikarpov R-1**, flew to Kabul, Afghanistan. From 2 February to 8 April the next year, V. Ch. Kopilov, in a **Junkers Ju 13**, made a 10,400km (6,500mi) round-trip circuit in the northeastern and eastern regions of European Russia. And this kind of activity increased in intensity throughout the year, culminating on 10 June 1925 when six aircraft (two R-1s, two Ju 13s, an R-2, and an AK-1) took off from Moscow to Peking (Beijing), China. Piloted by **Mikhail M. Gromov** (R-1), N.E. Nadenov (Ju 13), M.A. Volkovoynov (R-1), A.N. Ekatov (R-2), E.K. Polyakov (Ju 13), and A.E. Tomashevsky (AK-1), all six aircraft covered the 6,476km (4,025mi) in a little more than a month, arriving on 17 July. Gromov capped the performance by flying on to Tokyo, via Manchuria and Korea, from 30 August to 2 September.

(Left) Mikhail Gromov
(Right) S.A. Shestakov, pilot of the ANT-4 Strana Sovyetov *(Land of Soviets) and his flight engineer, D.V. Fufaev. (photo: Eugene Altunin)*

Circuit of Europe

As if to emphasize that the products of TsAGI amounted to more than drawings and announcements, the Russians began to show their metal in western Europe where, because of the dearth of information emanating from Moscow, foreign politicians, press, and public alike were understandably skeptical about reports of aircraft construction in the brave new world of the Soviet Union. On 31 August 1926, **Mikhail M. Gromov** made a courageous demonstration which was quite literally a proving flight, as it proved to the skeptics that the Russians did have flying hardware.

Gromov took his **ANT-3** from Moscow to Königsberg, Berlin, Paris, Rome, Prague, Vienna, Warsaw, and then back to Moscow. The *Proletarii (Proletariat)* completed this European circuit on 2 September, having covered the 7,150km (4,444mi) in 34hr 15min of flying time, at an average speed of 209km/h (130mph) (see map, p. 23).

Across the World

The following year, the ANT-3 made another important flight that must have given encouragement to the design team at TsAGI. On 20 August 1927, **S.A. Shestakov** flew an ANT-3 (RR-INT *Osoaviakhim SSSR Nash Otvet (Our Answer)* from Moscow to Tokyo, arriving there on 1 September. The 22,000km (13,670mi) round-trip was completed in 153 flying hours, at a leisurely speed of 144km/h (89mph) and both the pilot and his mechanic, D.V. Fufaev, were awarded the Order of the Red Banner.

Two years later, with gaining confidence, Shestakov made a more ambitious flight, this time with an **ANT-4** (URSS-300 *Strana Sovyetov (Land of Soviets)*. Between 23 August and 2 November 1929, he made an historic flight from the U.S.S.R. to the U.S.A., via the Pacific northern rim. As with most long-distance flights, high speed was not the objective. The 21,200km (13,200mi, about the same as the Moscow — Tokyo round-trip) were covered in 137 flying hours, at an average speed of 155km/h (96mph). The twin-engined aircraft was fitted with floats at Khabarovsk for the occasion, and the arrival in the U.S. was on Lake Washington, Seattle.

Note: The characteristics of the ANT-3 and ANT-4 aircraft featured on this page are in the table on page 23.

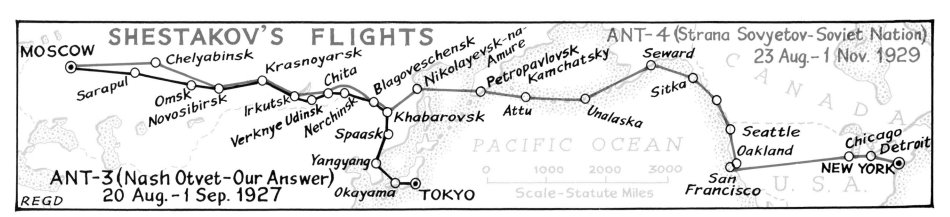

SHESTAKOV'S FLIGHTS

ANT-4 (Strana Sovyetov-Soviet Nation)
23 Aug. – 1 Nov. 1929

MOSCOW · Chelyabinsk · Krasnoyarsk · Chita · Blagoveschensk · Nikolayevsk-na-Amure · Petropavlovsk Kamchatsky · Seward · Sitka

Sarapul · Omsk · Novosibirsk · Irkutsk · Verknye Udinsk · Nerchinsk · Khabarovsk · Attu · Unalaska

Spaask · Yangyang

ANT-3 (Nash Otvet-Our Answer)
20 Aug. – 1 Sep. 1927

REGD · Okayama · TOKYO

PACIFIC OCEAN

0 1000 2000 3000
Scale-Statute Miles

CANADA

Seattle · Oakland · Chicago · Detroit · NEW YORK · San Francisco · U.S.A.

Dobrolet Spreads Its Wings

Putting Aviation to Work

The first crop-dusting experiment in Russia — and perhaps the world — took place in 1922 (see page 14). Aircraft started to use chemical spraying on 8 May 1929 to control forest vermin in infected tracts in Siberia's Kyltykstom district. Other ways of putting airplanes to good use had already been tried. On 21 August 1924, one was delivered by ship to the Matochkin Shar Polar Station, from which point — further north than Alaska — B.G. Chukhnovsky made the first sortie to aid ships navigating the polar ice. In September 1925, an aviation photography agency was established. On 4 March 1926, for the first time, an aircraft located schools of whales. The opportunities for putting aircraft to work seemed endless for a country the size of the Soviet Union.

Dobrolet's function during the mid-1920s seemed to be to provide air service only where the government required it, in 1925, for example, to connect the goldfields on the Siberian Aldan River, a tributary of the Lena, with the Trans-Siberian Railway. Normal communication by packhorse along forest paths took about 35 days.

International Service

For several years, Russia and Great Britain had sparred for political control of Afghanistan. The Soviet Government won a round by securing an agreement to begin direct communications and to advise the king in forming an Afghan Air Force. Dobrolet helped by opening, on 14 September 1926, an air route from Tashkent to Kabul, via Samarkand and Termez. In Mongolia, in lieu of a railway yet to be built (Ulan Ude — Ulan Bator, in September 1926). **Dobrolet** started service on 20 July 1926, flown by V.L. Galishev in a Junkers Ju 13.

Air Service to Yakutsk

One important Siberian city, Yakutsk, traditional center for trading and commerce and potential hub for extensive mining prospecting and operation, was far removed from the Trans-Siberian rail artery. The `road' to Yakutsk had originally been forged by Cossack conquerors in 1689, for mail; and even in the 20th century, the 2,860km (1,780mi) journey to Irkutsk; by the Lena-Angara River route, took 18 days by horse in winter, 15 days by boat (as far as Ust-Kut) and road in summer. On 1 October 1925, the first aircraft, a Sopwith 1½ Strutter, piloted by Piotr Faddayev, arrived at Yakutsk. **Dobrolet** started in 1928, when Aleksander Dyemchenko piloted a Junkers-Ju 13 from Irkutsk to Yakutsk (see map). He left on 21 August, arrived on 27 August, and returned two days later.

In 1929, seven **Junkers-W 33s** were brought to Irkutsk by the Trans-Siberian Raiway and assembled there. Four were landplanes, to be based at Verkne Udinsk (Ulan Ude), and three were float-planes, for the service to Yakutsk. These sturdy aircraft maintained this pioneering route until the mid-1930s, when **Dornier Wals**, together with two **Douglas Dolphins** (four were imported by the Soviet Union) arrived. One crashed in 1941 in a heavy landing; the other operated until 1947.

Breaking the Inertia

On 21 September 1926, **Dobrolet** was reorganized, following a decree issued by the Council of Peoples' Commissars, from a purely Russian to an all-Soviet company. A year later, on 27 July 1927, the Council for Labor and Defense transferred responsibility for technical supervision of civil aviation from the Air Force to the Inspectorate for the Civil Aviation Fleet. Routes in Central Asia were extended, so that all five central Asian republics, including four of the capitals, now had air service.

On 15 May 1929, at last, regular air service began, for mail only, on the arterial Moscow — Irkutsk route, cutting the journey time of several days by rail to 35 hours. The aircraft is believed to have been the **Kalinin K-4**, and was the first route to be flown at night. Passenger service began on 1 May 1931. The K-4 had also started service from Moscow to Tashkent, via Orenburg, on 27 June 1929.

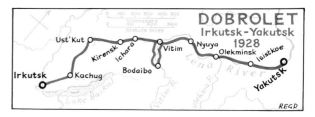

A Dobrolet Junkers-W 33 (SSSR-175) at the landing stage on the Lena River at Yakutsk. (photo: Vladimir Pesterev)

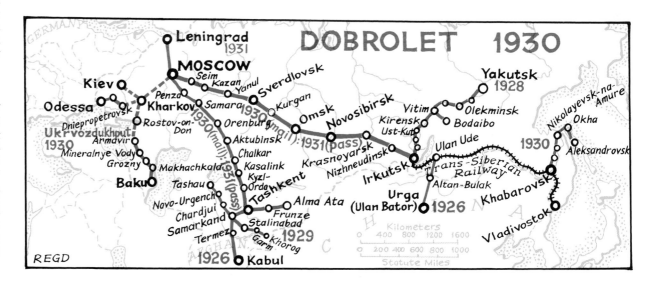

Kalinin K-5

8 SEATS ■ 155km/h (100mph)

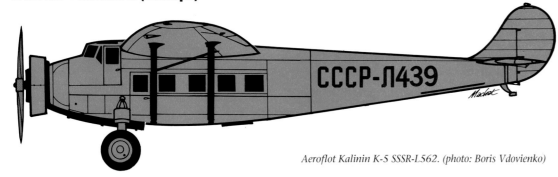

Aeroflot Kalinin K-5 SSSR-L562. (photo: Boris Vdovienko)

M-22 (1 x 480hp) ■ MTOW 3,600kg (7,900lb) ■ Normal Range 820km (500mi) ■ Length 16m (52ft) ■ Span 20m (66ft)

The Elliptical Wing

Some Kalinin aircraft pictures strongly suggest Dornier ancestry, and clearly the designer drew some inspiration from the German company, which was closely associated with Ukrvozdukhput, the Ukrainian airline which was based at Kharkov, and used Dornier Komets, some of which were assembled in its workshops. Kalinin shared floor space in these shops.

But in one important respect, the Kalinin aircraft differed. Whereas both the leading and the trailing edge of the Dornier and Merkur aircraft were parallel, a plan view of the Kalinin wing showed an almost perfect ellipse.

Early work

Konstantin Alekseyevich Kalinin was born in December 1889 at Valuki, near Kharkov. In 1905 he was arrested for suspected revolutionary activities, but by 1912 he had entered the Military School at Odessa. After serving in the Russian Army in the Great War, he entered the Air Training School at Gatchina, near Petrograd, in 1916. When the 1917 Revolution broke out, he was with the 26th Corps Aviation Squadron on the Romanian front. Emerging from the civil war, he studied aviation, first at the Red Army's Aviation Institute, then at the prestigious Zhukovskiy Academy.

After many a brush with bureaucratic interference, Kalinin was finally able to design his first aircraft, aided by some like-minded friends at Kiev. The **K-1** made its first flight on 26 July 1925, was flown to Moscow on 11 April 1926, and used by Dobrolet for crop-spraying, aerial photography, and as an air ambulance. Kalinin then transferred his base to Kharkov, and successive designs followed (see table), using all-metal construction, rather than welded steel framework, with wood and fabric.

The Kalinin K-4

During the summer of 1928, Kalinin demonstrated the moderately successful **K-4**, which was not used for passengers until the summer of 1929.

But on 27 June 1929, the K-4 inaugurated service on the important route from Moscow to Tashkent; and in August, the *Chervona Ukraina (Heart of Ukraine)*, piloted by **M.A. Chyegirev**, demonstrated its performance and reliability by flying round-trip from Kharkov to Irkutsk, via

KALININ TYPES USED IN SERVICE

Type	First Flight Date	Dimensions (m)		Pass. Seats	Engines			MTOW kg	Cruise Speed km/hr	No. Built	First Airline
		Length	Span		No.	Type	h.p.				
K-1	26 Jul 25	10.72	16.76	4	1	Salmson	180	1,972	130	1	Dobrolet
K-2	May 26	11.17	16.70	4[1]	1	BMW IV	240	2,236	140	1	Ukrvozdukhput
K-3	22 Oct 27	11.25	16.70	4[1]	1	BMW IV	240	2,300	140		See note 3
K-4	Summer 28	11.35	16.75	4	1	Ju L5	310	2,350	145	22	Ukrvozdukhput
K-5	7 Nov 29	15.70	20.50	8	1	M-22 (Jupiter)	480	3,600	157	260[2]	Dobrolet
K-6	9 Aug 30	15.00	20.00	(mail)	1	M-15 (Jupiter)	420	2,820	170	1	Dobrolet

Notes : [1] Ambulance layout [2] Includes versions with M-15 Jupiter and 715hp M-17f engines [3] Used in ambulance version by Red Air Fleet

Moscow, a distance of 10,800km (6,700mi). Twenty-two K-4s were built and used extensively on Dobrolet's routes until the early 1930s.

The Kalinin K-5 and the End of the Line

Kalinin's finest aircraft was the **K-5**, first flown by Chyegirev on 7 November 1929. It had various engines, the Russian 450hp M-15 (for the prototype), the Pratt & Whitney Hornet, the 480hp M-22 radial based on the Bristol Jupiter, and the 730hp M17F water-cooled in-line, which gave the K-5 a cruising speed of 170km/h (105mph). Of welded construction, it had dual controls, a toilet, and baggage compartment. It could fly across the Caucasus, reducing the Moscow-Tblisi distance by several hundred miles. Two hundred and sixty aircraft were built, retiring only at the beginning of the Great Patriotic War in 1941.

As shown in the table, Kalinin built other types after the K-5, but none went beyond the prototype stage. Of special mention is the **K-7**, a seven-engined twin-boom monster, designed to carry 120 passengers. Chyegirev first flew it on 11 August 1933, made a few test flights, then crashed on its ninth flight on 21 November, killing him and 14 of the total of 20 on board. Seven years later, Kalinin himself was to die on 24 April 1940, a victim of Stalin's purges.

Dobrolet Becomes Aeroflot

Growth of an Aircraft Industry

The **Polikarpov U-2** (or the **Po-2** after the death of Polikarpov in 1944) made its first flight on 8 January 1928. A two-seat biplane, it was to become a maid-of-all-work, and particularly an elementary trainer. Thousands of them were built, used even for bombing in the Great Patriotic War, and **Nikolai Nikolayevich Polikarpov's** design was an essential factor in the development of Soviet aviation, akin to the role played by Britain's Tiger Moth and America's Piper Cub. Production of the PO-2 continued until 1944, and was built in Poland from 1948 until 1953. Produced for 35 years, it was the most popular light aircraft in the Soviet Union.

Of aircraft in the transport category, the **ANT** (**Andrei Nikolayevich Tupolev**) series, prefaced by the Models 3 and 4 (see page 19) led to the **ANT-9**, which first flew on 1 May 1929, and is more fully reviewed on the page opposite. The **Kalinin** series, already described on page 21, was establishing itself, especially the Model **K-5**. On 22 December 1930, Andrei Tupolev watched the first flight of his four-engined bomber, the **ANT-6**, which was put to good use as a transport airplane in 1937 in support of the Polar expeditions (see pages 30-31). Often overlooked, or even ignored by western observers, this was a big aircraft, and no freak, in its time.

Then in 1931, the little **Shavrov Sh-2** amphibian and the **Stal'2**, designed by A.I. Putilov, made their appearance. Of steel construction (Stal is Russian for steel) it could carry four passengers. It first flew on 11 October 1931 from Frunze airfield (Khodinka) in Moscow.

Reorganization

On 29 October 1930, as a feature of the First Five Year Plan of 1928, Dobrolet was replaced by as an all-state airline, a joint-stock company, **Grazdansiy Vozduzhniy Flot (G.V.F.)**. It acquired Ukrvozdukhput (page 16) and developed a domestic hub at Moscow, with passenger services to all important cities, as far east as Irkutsk.

Air Pravda

On 3 June 1930, the first experimental delivery was made of type matrices of the official *Pravda* newspaper, and on 4 June 1931, it appeared in Kharkov only eleven hours after being type-set in Moscow. On 16 June, a special aviation section was created to ensure matrix delivery to Leningrad, Kharkov, Sevastopol, Pyatagorsk, Grozny, Odessa, Kazan, Rostov-on-Don, Tiflis, and Sverdlovsk.

A five-engined airliner, the **ANT-14**, first flew on 14 August 1931. With 36 seats, it was too large for the traffic on airline routes but was used extensively by Pravda for sightseeing and propaganda flights, mainly around Moscow. Only one was built, and its only long-distance foray was to Bucharest; but it carried 40,000 passengers during its ten-year service life, quite an achievement for the time.

Maturity of an Airline

During the 17th Congress of the All-Soviet Communist Party, held in Moscow from 30 January to 4 February 1932, a resolution was passed that ``air travel should expand in all directions, as it is one of the important communication links with remote rural regions, and with major industrial centers.'' On 25 February, Grazdansiy Vozduzhniy Flot (G.V.F.) was reorganized as the Main Directorate of the Civil Aviation Fleet. On 26 March 1932 it was given the trading name of **Aeroflot.**

Aeroflot continued the good work of its predecessors. On 15 December 1933, the final link to the east was completed, by an extension from Irkutsk to Vladivostok (see page 24). Moving up the learning curve, an Aeroflot PS-9 (version of the ANT-9) opened up the first all-Soviet westward route on 31 August 1935, to Prague, Czechoslovakia. The joint Soviet-German airline **Deruluft** was wound up on 31 March 1937, and in the same year Aeroflot service began from Leningrad to Stockholm, Sweden, in cooperation with A.B.A. The expansion of the Soviet airline was gathering momentum.

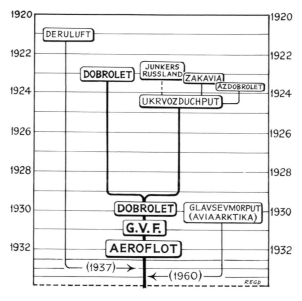

AEROFLOT SERVICE AIRCRAFT 1929-35
ORIGIN OF MANUFACTURE

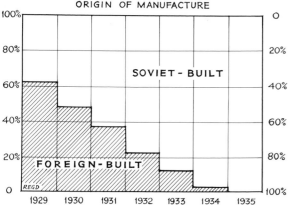

The twin-engined PS-9 was the main production version of the ANT-9. (photo: Boris Vdovienko)

The only example of the ANT-14, and one of the few five-engined aircraft ever built. (photo: Boris Vdovienko)

ANT-9

9 SEATS 170km/h (105mph)

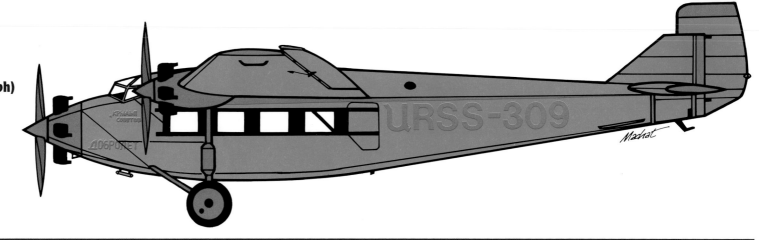

Wright J6 Whirlwind (3 x 300hp) ■ **MTOW 6,000kg (13,200lb)** ■ **Normal Range 1,000km (620mi)** ■ **Length 17m (56ft)** ■ **Span 24m (79ft)**

Tupolev Makes His Mark

Andrei Tupolev produced his first multi-engined type, the **ANT-9** nine-seat passenger transport, which first flew on 7 May 1929, and was publicly presented in Red Square. It had a metal corrugated fuselage and wing, fixed landing gear, and air-cooled engines, initially Gnome-Rhône Titans. Compared with previous Tupolev designs, it not only looked more elegant and aerodynamically efficient, its performance matched its looks.

Wings of the Soviets

On 10 July 1929, the same day when a common flag was adopted for the civil aviation fleet of the U.S.S.R., **Mikhail Gromov** took off in the prototype ANT-9, named *Krylya Sovyetov (Soviet Wings)*, on a tour of Europe that included five foreign capital cities. He returned in triumph on 8 August. For the first time, the Soviet Union had an airliner that was possibly the best in Europe. Indeed, there is a report that, calling as it did twice in Berlin, it influenced the Junkers firm to convert the Ju 52 from a single-engined aircraft into a tri-motor. The ANT-9 went into service with **Deruluft** and **Dobrolet** early in 1931, initially as a tri-motor with M-26, later U.S. engines. Production of the ANT-9 totaled 75, of which 60 were M-17-powered twins, known as **PS-9s**, and the type remained in the fleet of **Aeroflot** until the end of the Second World War.

EARLY TUPOLEV TRANSPORT AIRCRAFT

Type	First Flight Date	Dimensions (m)		Pass. Seats	Engines			MTOW kg	Cruise Speed km/hr	Range (mi)	No. Built
		Length	Span		No.	Type	h.p.				
ANT-3 [1]	Aug 1925	9.4	13.2	see note 3	1	Liberty	400	2,085	150	880	
ANT-4 (G-1) [2]	26 Nov 1925	18.0	28.7	see note3	2	M-17	680	7,500	156	950	
ANT-6 (G-2)	22 Dec 1930	24.4	39.5	see note3	4	M-17F	715	22,000	150	1,350	60?
ANT-7 (P-6)	11 Sep 1929	15.0	23.2	see note3	2	M-17	680	5,990	150	1,480	
ANT-9 [4]	1 May 1929	17.0	23.8	9	2/3	M-17	680	5,040	180	700	75
ANT-14	14 Aug 1931	26.5	40.4	36	5	GR9-AKX (Gnome-RhôneJupiter)	480	17,530	195	900	1

Notes: [1]*Prolaterii, flown by Mikhail Gromov on European demonstration flight in 1926 (see page 19)* [2] *Strana Sovyetov, flown by C.A. Shestakov from U.S.S.R. to U.S.A. in 1929 (see also page 19)* [3] *Bomber types, some of which were used for special flights, notably the ANT-6 and ANT-7 on Polar expeditions (see pages 26-27)* [4] *Used by Gromov in his Wings of the Soviets European circuit (see map).*

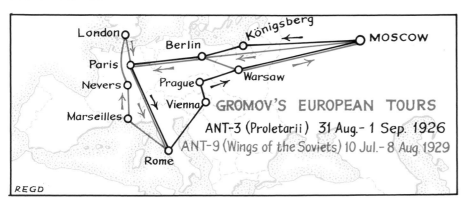

The tri-motor ANT-9 prototype URSS-309 Krylya Sovyetov (Soviet Wings) at Berlin's Tempelhof Airport in July 1929, during Mikhail Gromov's second European tour. Note the three waiters in the foreground preparing champagne for the dignitaries. (photo: Lufthansa)

To The End of the Line

Island Outposts

While the Soviet Union was, geographically, one vast land area, there were a few offshore islands. Those in the Arctic Ocean were of little commercial importance, although they had some strategic value; but those in the far east were very important strategically, and contained some natural resources. If only because of a latent suspicion of Japanese ambitions in the area, Moscow had to ensure close ties to the extremes of its empire. The island of Sakhalin, though only a few kilometers from the Asian land mass at one point, was difficult to reach; while the peninsula of Kamchatka, separated from the rest of Russia by the Sea of Okhotsk, might as well have been a distant island.

A plan to build a railway from Khabarovsk to Nikolayevsk-na-Amure was postponed because of the difficulties of building a line through the Amur swamplands. Instead, **Dobrolet** was given the task of building an air route.

Pioneer Route

During 1929, Comrade Nijnakovsky blazed a trail by dog-sled from Khabarovsk to Nikolayevsk. He laid down supplies of fuel, food, shelter, and medical supplies (and not forgetting waterproofed packets of matches), ready for any emergency en route. Then, on an historic day, 9 January 1930, **Mikhail Vodopyanov** left Khabarovsk in a **Junkers Ju 13** floatplane (illustrated on page 15), and flew to Aleksandrovsk-Sakhalinskiy, the chief city of Sakhalin, which in those days

was divided between the U.S.S.R. in the north and Japan in the south. The first flight took eleven days, but as time went on, the journey was normally flown in two or three, and occasionally, in the summer, in a single long day. It was a true pioneering effort.

The Ju 13s were supplemented by the diminutive **Shavrov Sh**-2 amphibians, which also deputized for the S.55s in later years. First built in 1928, they were used extensively along the great river routes throughout Siberia.

U.S.S.R. Transcontinental

Dobrolet was gradually spreading its wings, as noted on pages 20 and 22. It had expanded the route map to include, by 1930, all the major cities of European Russia and the Caucasus, and beyond to Central Asia; and had reached Irkutsk, beyond the Ural Mountains, in Siberia. On another historic occasion, on 15 December 1933, after a new airport had been built at Khabarovsk, and by which time Dobrolet had become **Aeroflot**, the final section of the Trans-Siberian air route was completed, from Irkutsk to Vladivostok. The inaugural flight was made by a **Kalinin K-5**, an aircraft that did not possess the appeal or reputation of the ANT-9, but which nevertheless did more than its share of the work.

By this time, as narrated on the page opposite, Aeroflot had also reached Petropavlovsk-Kamchatskiy, ten time zones away, and almost halfway round the earth.

The tiny terminal building at Okha, Sakhalin, in 1933. At that time this was `the end of the line' for Aerofot. (photo: Far Eastern Regional Directorate Museum, Khabarovsk)

Pilots ready for takeoff at Aleksandrovsk, Sakhalin, in the early years when open-cockpit Junkers-F 13s were the flagships of the line. (photo: Far Eastern Regional Directorate Museum, Khabarovsk)

Giving It The Boot

Vodopyanov himself recalls how resourceful and ingenious were the ground crews who serviced the aircraft in those times at the dawn of aviation in Russia's far east. During the winter, with temperatures at 30° below zero (Celsius), the engines were most reluctant to start, even after heating the oil and other methods of coaxing them into life. He remembers that, when all else failed, the crew would place a knee-length rubber boot on the propeller, loop a rope over the foot of the boot, haul on it very sharply, whereupon, after several tries, the engine would fire, and the boot would slip off, thus saving the crew from a possible whip-lash, at the very least. Dobrolet did not recommend this process in the instruction manuals, but it worked.

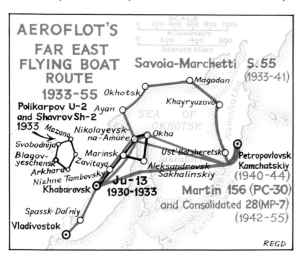

AEROFLOT'S
FAR EAST
FLYING BOAT
ROUTE
1933-55

Savoia-Marchetti S.55 (1933-41)

Polikarpov U-2 and Shavrov Sh-2 1933

Ju-13 1930-1933

Martin 156 (PC-30) and Consolidated 28 (MP-7) (1942-55)

SCALE — Kilometers 200 400 600 800 1000 — Statute Miles 200 400 600

Okhotsk · Magadan · Khayryuzovo · Ayan · Mazano · Nikolayevsk-na-Amure · Okha · Svobodnija · Marinsk · Ust Bolsheretsk · Blagov-yeschensk · Zavitaya · Aleksandrovsk Sakhalinskiy · Petropavlovsk Kamchatskiy (1940-44) · Arkhara · Nizhne Tambovsky · Khabarovsk · Spassk-Dal'niy · Vladivostok

SEA OF OKHOTSK

REGD

AEROFLOT
TRANS-SIBERIAN
ROUTE COMPLETED
1933

Kalinin K-5

REGD

Irkutsk · Verkne Udinsk · Chita · Nerchinsk · Magocha · Rukhlovo · Tigda · Khabarovsk · Tikhonkoye · Botchkarevo · Archara · Lazo · Vladivostok

Trans-Siberian Railway · Amur River

SCALE — Kilometers 100 200 300 400 500 600 — Statute Miles 100 200 300 400

Flying Boats of the Far East

MARTIN 156
50 SEATS ■ 225km/h (140mph)

Wright Cyclone GR-1820-G2 (4 x 850hp) ■ MTOW 28,100kg (62,000lb) ■ Normal Range 2,000km (1,200mi) ■ Length 28m (92ft) ■ Span 48m (157ft)

The Savoia-Marchetti S.55P

Local services began to develop in the Far East area. A circular route was established to some small communities to the north and east of Blagoveschensk, with **Polikarpov Po-2** and **Shavrov Sh-2** amphibians, and the Junkers Ju 13s were replaced with larger aircraft. Aeroflot negotiated for five **Savoia-Marchetti S.55P** twin-boom flying boats, the same type that had been used by Marshal Balbo in the famous trans-Atlantic squadron flight from Italy to Brazil in 1930. The S.55P inaugurated **Aeroflot** service to Petropavlovsk in 1933, by the circuitous route around the Sea of Okhotsk (see map opposite), the aircraft having been delivered from Italy by a circuitous route via the Black Sea, the great Russian rivers, as well as Lake Baikal.

The Russian Clipper

Flying to Sakhalin, and especially to Kamchatka, was an adventure, and the journey by S.55P to Petropavlovsk usually took about five or six days in the summer. Accordingly, Aeroflot upgraded to larger equipment, the **Martin 156**, the so-called `Russian Clipper', an improved version of the famous *China Clipper* Martin 130 delivered to Pan American Airways in 1935.

The **Far East Region of Aeroflot** needed an aircraft that could combine a good payload with a good range, enough to traverse the southern part of the Sea of Okhotsk, preferably non-stop from Khabarovsk to Petropavlovsk. The Glenn Martin (as it was always referred to in Russia) could normally carry 50 passengers, and on shorter trips, for example, Khabarovsk to Nikolayevsk-na-Amure, it could carry 70. The Martin 156 — designated **SP-30** by Aeroflot — was delivered in 1940 and operated successfully during the summer months until 1944, when it had to be retired because of the difficulty in obtaining spare parts.

The Clipper was replaced by the **Consolidated Catalina** in 1943 or 1944. Three Consolidated Model 28-1s had been imported from the U.S. in 1938 and, from 1940, license production of the type was undertaken at Taganrov, on the Sea of Azov, as the **GST** (Gidro Samolyet Transportnyi, or hydro aircraft transport) for the Soviet Navy. A few civil examples, designated **MP-7**, were delivered to **Aeroflot**. Some **Lisunov Li-2s** are believed to have been used also.

The Martin 156 `Russian Clipper'. (photo: Far Eastern Regional Directorate Museum, Khabarovsk)

A Savoia-Marchetti S.55P (msn 10528) used on the route from Khabarovsk to Petropavlovsk-Kamchatsky in the mid-1930s. (photo: Far Eastern Regional Directorate Museum, Khabarovsk)

Aviaarktika

First Cautious Steps

As early as 1912, **Igor Sikorsky** himself had visualized the possibility of using aircraft to survey and explore the frozen wastes of Russia's northlands. Even before the Revolution, this advice was soon followed, when, in 1914, **Jan Nagursky** a Pole, flying a Farman, helped to locate the Sedov expedition that was lost in the Arctic ice of Novaya Zembla. On 20 April 1920, barely two months after the last British troops had left Arkhangelsk, the **Northern Sea Route Committee** was formed, and this was reinforced in March 1921 by the formation of the **Floating Naval Scientific Institute**.

During 1924, **Boris Chukhnovsky** made a dozen flights in a Junkers Ju 13 to survey the Barents and the Kara Seas; while on 4 August 1925 **Otto Kalvits** reached Matochkin Shar, at a latitude of 73⁰ on Novaya Zembla. During the latter 1920s, led by **Mikhail Babushkin**, aircraft were used to aid seal hunters and to guide shipping. On 15 February 1929, **Ivan Mikheyev** made a successful ambulance mission. Soviet aviation was ready for the Arctic.

The Northern Sea Route Administration

Much in the same manner that western navigators had speculated about the Northwest Passage from the Atlantic to the Pacific, so did Russian seamen dream of linking Arkhangelsk and Murmansk with Vladivostok via the Arctic Ocean and the Bering Strait. The role of the airplane was fully recognized from the start, and in 1 September 1930, **Glavnoe upravlenie Severnogo morskogo puti**, or **Glavsevmorput (Northern Sea Route Administration)**, was formed, headed by **Dr Otto Schmidt**, known familiarly as the Ice Commissar. He had made several voyages in the Arctic, reaching Franz Josef Land, the northernmost islands of Eurasia.

Glavsevmorput's **Department of Polar Aviation**, established at Krasnoyarsk on 1 September 1930, and familiarly known as **Aviaarktika**, was headed by Schmidt's deputy and right-hand man, **Mark Shevelev**. It moved to Moscow in 1932, and survived independently from Aeroflot until 3 January 1960, when the state airline took over all its operations. Except for the wartime years and until he retired from the Air Force, Shevelev was in charge throughout.

The Administration was equipped from the start with a fleet of Junkers Ju 13 floatplanes and six Dornier Wal flying boats. By 1933, the fleet had been increased to 42, including among other types, the four-engined **ANT-6** and the twin-engined **ANT-4**. Much pioneer work was done in establishing air routes with waterborne aircraft along the great rivers of

An Aviaarktika ANT-7 (SSSR-N28) on skis. (Vdovienko)

Special container attached to the wing of the Polikarpov R-5C aircraft, to rescue survivors of the wrecked Chelyuskin *in 1934. (Vdovienko)*

Pavel Golovin (second from right) with crew members (from left) Volkov, Kyekushev, and Terentiev, in front of the ANT-7 reconnaissance aircraft on the Papanin expedition. (Vdovienko)

The terminal building at Noriilsk, in northern Siberia. (Vdovienko)

The Chelyuskin Rescue

Soviet aviators won their spurs in a remarkable rescue mission. In 1933, the good ship *Chelyuskin* left Leningrad to attempt another circumnavigation of the Soviet Union, at least as far as Vladivostok. It was almost within sight of the Bering Strait when in November it stuck in the ice. On 12 February it was crushed by an iceberg and the entire ship's company were marooned. Dr Schmidt organized a floating — and constantly moving — camp on the ice flows, and built a landing field — also constantly moving — in preparation for the rescue aircraft. A whole team of aviators won their spurs, including **Mikhail Vodopyanov**, and especially **Vasily Molokov**. In a series of flights from a coastal airstrip near the ship, they saved all 104 marooned personnel, a great testimonial to the new aviation technology.

Siberia: the Ob, with a base at Omsk, on its tributary, the Irtysh; on the Yenesei, at Krasnoyarsk; at Irkutsk, on the Angara, near Lake Baikal; and on the Lena, at Yakutsk.

Expanding the Horizons

During the mid-1930s, Glavsevmorput sent out its long tentacles throughout the sparsely populated Siberian lands that occupy more than half of the area of Russia. Its achievement could not be measured by conventional statistics — in 1933, only 180 passengers and about 15 tons of mail were carried; but Polar Aviation pilots were learning their trade. They carried vital supplies, including medicines, doctors, and teachers out-bound, and valuable furs inbound — furs that would otherwise have taken two years to reach the stores in Moscow or Leningrad. Gathering confidence, the aircraft flew further and more often, with some pilots making some notable flights, such as those of *Chelyuskin* hero Molokov, reviewed on the opposite page.

Opening Up The North

Two Soviet Worlds

As **Aeroflot** settled down to its task of providing all Soviet citizens with an air service (see page 33), it concentrated on speeding up the journey times along the traditional main arteries that had been built by the Russian railroads to connect Moscow with all the main centers of population. Routes in European Russia extended to Leningrad, the Black Sea, the Caspian Sea, to Central Asia, and — keeping strictly to the route of the Iron Road, the Trans-Siberian Railway, to the far eastern port of Vladivostok. Except for one branch line from Irkutsk to Yakutsk, along the Lena River, the Aeroflot network was an aerial reflection of the railroad map. By the mid-1930s, this had become the framework and foundation for an ever-expanding system of air routes.

In contrast, **Glavsevmorput (Aviaarktika)** fashioned its sorties into the far north of Russia by a different surface mode of travel. It had to; for in the 1930s, rail lines to the north ran only to Arkhangelsk and to Murmansk, the latter completed only during the Great War of 1914-1918. Instead, therefore, of following the railway lines like Aeroflot, Aviaarktika followed the rivers and waterways, the seas and the lakes; and in the summer used flying boats and floatplanes, while in the winter it exchanged the floats for skis. Only the largest aircraft, such as the **ANT-6**, were ever fitted with wheels.

ANT-6 SSSR-N170, the four-engined transport that led the squadron of aircraft to the North Pole in 1937. Mikhail Vodopyanov flew Ivan Pananin and his scientific team from Rudolf Island. This picture was taken in August, when it returned to Moscow.
(photo: Boris Vdovienko)

It's a Long Way to Krasnoyarsk

Vasily Molokov was one of many highly trained pilots who flew for Aviaarktika, gaining experience with every flight into the snows and the ice, the swamps and the marshlands of the northlands. He came into the public eye when, in the famous 1934 Chelyuskin rescue saga, he carried 34 people — a third of the total — to safety. The next year, on 11 February, he flew a **Polikarpov R-5** from Moscow to Krasnoyarsk, on the Yenesei River, via Yanaul, near Izhevsk, and Tayga, near Tomsk. He then made a flight to the mouth of the Yenesei, at Dickson, on the Kara Sea coast, arriving on 19 March, to prove the feasibility of an air route to link important locations of mineral wealth, such as Noril'sk, with the vital Trans-Siberian trunk rail line and the Aeroflot transcontinental airway.

Molokov then made two epic journeys that should rank with other great, and much better known, pioneer aerial explorations. In the first, flying a **Dornier Wal**, he left Krasnoyarsk on 13 July 1935, and followed various rivers to the northeast, picking up the Lena near Kirensk, thence via Yakutsk to a point near Magaden, on the Sea of Okhotsk, then to the most easterly point of Russia, at Uelen (see map), and returning along most of the north Siberian coastline, to arrive at Dudinka on 12 September. He had covered a distance of 21,000km (13,000mi).

The following year, Molokov did even better. Leaving Krasnoyarsk on 22 July 1936, he followed the same route around Siberia, surveyed the Severna Zemlya islands to the far north, and flew westwards via Arkhangelsk to arrive in triumph in Moscow on 19 September. In both flights, he had followed as much as possible the courses of the great rivers and their tributaries, but east of Yakutsk, he had had to cross a formidable mountain range, between the Aldan tributary of the Lena, and the Sea of Okhotsk. From Moscow after the 1936 flight, he returned to base at Krasnoyarsk from 30 September to 5 October. The circumnavigation of Russia during the three-month odyssey covered a distance of 31,000km (16,400mi) in 200 flying hours. It was a pioneering performance of immense trailblazing significance.

The North Pole

The Preparations

Aviaarktika had already reached ever northwards during the late 1920s and had spread its wings far and wide across the expanses of the Soviet Union, in those areas where Aeroflot had no reason to go, for lack of people to carry in a vast mainly frigid region that was almost completely unpopulated, except for isolated villages and outposts. Rather like expeditions on the ground, such as those to the South Pole, **Otto Schmidt**, assisted by his deputy, **Mark Shevelev**, pushed further beyond the limits, very methodically.

The northernmost landfall in the Soviet Union is the tiny Rudolf Island, an icy speck on the fringes of the island group known as Franz Josef Land (named after an Austrian explorer). At a latitude of 82° North, Rudolf is only about 1,300km (800mi) from the Pole and a good location for a base camp and launching site. Access to Franz Josef Land, while hazardous because of the severe climate and terrain, is feasible as the twin-island territory of Novaya Zemlya accounts for about 800km (500mi) of the distance from the Nenets region.

On 29 March 1936, **Mikhail Vodopyanov** set off with Akkuratov in a two-plane reconnaissance of the possible air route to Rudolf Island (see map). Flying blind for much of the time, and having to contend with inconveniences such as boiling six pails of water before starting the engines with compressed air, they reached their destination, and reported that the conditions, while not ideal, were not impossible. On his return to Moscow on 21 May, Schmidt was sufficiently satisfied to make plans. He arranged for the ice-breaking ship *Rusanov* to carry supplies to Rudolf, appointed **Ivan Papanin** to lead the assault on the Pole, and selected a combination of four **ANT-6 (G-2)** four-engined bomber transports, and one **ANT-7 (G-1)** twin-engined aircraft for the task. Vodopyanov was to be the chief pilot.

The Assault

The working party sent to Rudolf did their work well. In addition to setting up a base camp and a small airstrip on the shoreline, they rolled out a longer runway, with a slight slope to assist take-off, on a dome-shaped plateau about 300m (1,000ft) above the base camp. The squadron of aircraft flew up from Moscow, leaving on 18 March 1937. Reaching Rudolf, they began final preparations. The ANT-6s were estimated to need 7,300 liters (1,600USg) of fuel for the 18-hour round-trip to the Pole, and 35 drums were needed for each aircraft. Ten tons of supplies of all kinds were to be taken, and elaborate steps were taken to design light-weight and multi-purpose equipment.

There were frustrating delays, as they waited anxiously for Boris Dzerzeyevsky, the resident weather-man, to report favorable conditions, and for Pavel Golovin, pilot of the ANT-7 reconnaissance aircraft, to confirm Dzerzeyevsky's forecasts, and to test the accuracy of the radio beacons. On one flight, Golovin was stranded for three days when he had to make a forced landing on the ice. But eventually, the expedition received the all-clear.

Flying an ANT-6 (registered SSSR-N170), Mikhail Vodopyanov, with co-pilot M. Babushkin, navigator I. Spirin and three mechanics landed at a point a few kilometers beyond the North Pole (just to make sure) on 21 May 1937, at 11.35 a.m. Moscow time. Ivan Papanin, with scientists Yvgeny Federov and Piotr Shirsov, together with radio operator Ernst Krenkel, immediately established the first scientific Polar Station (PS-1) on the polar ice, on which they eventually drifted on their private ice-floe in a southwesterly direction until they were picked up off the coast of Greenland by a rescue ship on 19 February 1938.

Dr Otto Schmidt (center) rests in front of an ANT-6 on 25 March 1937, en route to Rudolf Island and thence to the North Pole. On his left is his pilot Mikhail Vodopyanov and to the right of the picture is M.S. Babushkin, his co-pilot. (photo: Boris Vdovienko)

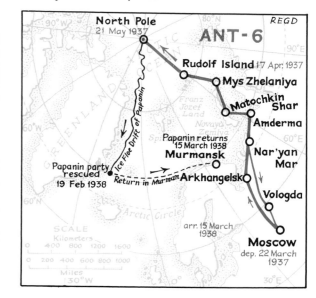

The Arctic Experience

Well-Earned Fame

After the various great flights made by Soviet aircraft, the pilots and crew were lavishly decorated, receiving many medals and testimonials in the Soviet tradition. Moscow witnessed receptions that were as impressive, if not quite so lavish, as those bestowed in New York on Lindbergh, Earhart, or Hughes. And they were well earned. **Mikhail Vodopyanov**, for example, had built up hundreds of hours of flying in remote parts of Russia, including the opening of the Dobrolet route to Sakhalin (page 24). He had pioneered the route to Rudolf Island, and had campaigned for aircraft landings on the North Polar ice, in opposition to other views that the Papanin party should be dropped by parachute. His crew members **Mikhail Babushkin** and **Ivan Spirin** had both flown big airplanes as early as 1921, in the Il'ya Murometsy, no less. **Vasily Molokov** had been one of the heroes of the Chelyuskin rescue, and his radio operator had been with him on the long Siberian circuit (page 27). **Anatoly Alexeyev** had flown on a relief party to the Severnaya Zemlya islands in 1934; while **Ilya Mazuruk** and **Pavel Golovin** already had outstanding records. When the Soviet Union decided to Go For The Pole, it had the best cadre of trained and experienced pilots in the world to face the daunting challenge.

FLIGHT TO THE NORTH POLE, 1937

Director of Operations	Dr Otto Shmidt	
Deputy Director of Operations	Mark Shevelev	
Meteorologist at Rudolf Island	Boris Dzerdzeyevsky	
ANT-6	**N-170**	**Total on board** (inc. Papanin party, below), 11
Pilot, M.V. Vodopyanov • Co-pilot, M.S. Babushkin • Navigator, I.T.Spirin Radio Op., S.A. Ivanov • Air Mechanics, F. Bassein, Morozov, Petenin		
ANT-6	**N-171**	**Total on board, 11**
Pilot, V.S. Molokov • Radio Operator, Stromilov • Navigator, Ritsland		
ANT-6	**N-172**	**Total on board, 11**
Pilot, A.D.Alexeyev • Navigator, Zhukov, Moshkovsky		
ANT-6	**N-169**	**Total on board, 5**
Pilot, I.P. Mazuruk • Rozlov, Akkuratov		
ANT-7	**N-166**	**Crew only, scout aircraft)**
Pilot, P.G. Golovin • Navigator, Volkov, Terentyev • Mechanics, Shekurov, Timofeyev		
Polar Party	**(with N-170)**	**Remained at the North Pole**
Leader, I.D. Papanin • Navigator, Y.K. Fedorov • Radio Operator, E.T. Krenkel, P.P. Shirshov		
Total weight of supplies carried to the North Pole		**9 tons**

The Papanin Expedition team (left to right) E.T. Krenkel, radio operator; I.D. Papanin (expedition leader); Y.K. Fedorov, navigator; and P.P. Shirshov. (all photos: Boris Vdovienko)

Dr Otto Schmidt, Director of the Northern Sea Route Administration.

Mikhail Vodopyanov, Chief Pilot of the fleet that carried Papanin to the Pole.

Il'ya Mazuruk, one of the veteran Arctic pilots who launched the attack on the North Pole.

Life Support for A Polar Station

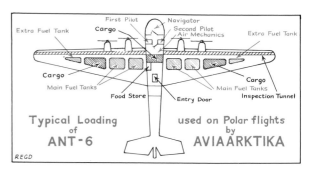

Weight Watchers

To equip the **Papanin Expedition**, every ingenious precaution was taken to avoid superfluous weight. Tents were of light-weight silk and aluminum. Utensils were of plastics or aluminum. The aircraft ladders were convertible into sleds. Special equipment such as the sounding line and the bathymeter were re-designed to save weight. Both the aircraft crews and the members of the expedition were eternally grateful for the innumerable contributions made by the `back-room boys' in Leningrad, Moscow, and other sources of equipment supply.

How Much Extra

To carry even this finely tuned total weight of nine tons, divided between the four ANT-6 load-carrying aircraft, extra fuel also had to be taken, in addition to the provisions listed in the tables on this page. Almost two tons extra had to be carried by each aircraft. But the dome-shaped airfield on the plateau at Rudolf Island offered shallow slopes, down which the departing aircraft could gain speed and lift; and every item of nonessential equipment was stripped from the interior, and every non-essential item of personal effects was left behind.

Test Bombing

Landing a 24-ton aircraft on an ice-floe, no matter how big, was a speculative proposition. It was determined that the minimum ice thickness required was 70cm (2ft); engineers then devised a 9.5kg (21lb) `bomb'. It was shaped like a pear and fastened at its rear or trailing end was a 6-8m (20ft) line with flags attached. If the ice was less than 70cm, the `bomb' went straight through. If more, it stuck, and the flags, draped on the ice, indicated that landing was possible. This method was first utilized on the Papanin expedition.

Their Tiny Hands Were Frozen

During the final flight from Rudolf Island to the North Pole, **Mikhail Vodopyanov** realized that one of the ANT-6's engines was leaking water from its radiator, with its precious anti-freeze liquid disappearing into thin air. Vodopyanov's trusted chief air mechanic, **Flegont Bassein**, together with co-mechanics **Morozov** and **Petenin**, crawled along the tunnel in the wing (see opposite and diagram below) and tried to stop the flow. They came up with an ingenious solution, by placing cloths over the leak, soaking up the outflow, squeezing them out into a container, and pouring the liquid back into the radiator. The engine kept going.

The mechanics did too, but barely. To reach the leak, they had had to force an opening in the leading edge of the wing, radiators obviously being exposed to the airflow. It was an act of fortitude that nearly cost them their hands.

PAPANIN EXPEDITION
TOTAL FUEL, FOOD, AND EQUIPMENT

Food, Fuel, and Equipment	Tons
Food for 2,800 man-days (i.e. 700 days for a party of 4 men)	3.5
Fuel for Primus Stoves, Lamps, Engines	2.5
Various Scientific Instruments	0.7
Radio Receiver-Transmitters	0.5
Power Apparatus	0.5
Clothing, Tents, Boats, Maps, Domestic Needs	1.3
Total	9.0

FOOD TAKEN ON PAPANIN EXPEDITION

(Weights in Grams 1gram = 0.035 ounce)

1470	Fish Roe/Caviar	2500	Sugar	1000	Powdered Milk
1430	Milk	300	Salt	1000	Powdered Eggs
150	Tomatoes	5000	Pemmican	1250	Chicken Pate
2500	Sweet Butter	2500	Rye Biscuits	1250	Chocolate
2500	Lard	300	Bread Crumbs	600	Fruit Jelly
1250	Smoked Fish	120	Dried Onions	125	Tea
1250	Hunter's Sausage	700	Bean Soup	500	Cocoa
1000	Cream Cheese	240	Barley Soup	250	Coffee
1250	Rice	360	Borsch	120	Fruit Drinks
500	Green Peas	360	Fresh Necks	30	Pepper
500	White Flour	1250	Meat Cutlets	2	Bay Leave
93	Potato Flour	1250	Chicken Cutlets	300	Vitamin C Candy
100	Noodles	950	Chicken Stock	125	Dried Strawberries
800	Stewed Fruit	1500	Beef Stock	5	Lemon Extract
500	Dried Potatoes	300	Beef Jerky		

PAPANIN EXPEDITION
CLOTHES/PERSONAL ITEMS PER TEAM MEMBER

No.	Item	Pairs	Item
2	Sleeping Bag	18	Socks/Stocking (Wool)
1	Cookware Set	4	Socks (Fur)
1	Shirt and Pants (cloth)	3	Sock-boots (Reindeer)
3	Shirt (cloth)	1	" " (Seal)
2	Combinations (cloth)	2	Boots (Felt) (Mukluks)
1	Fur Trousers (Reindeer)	1	Boots (`Russian')
1	" " (Seal)	6	Gloves (Wool)
1	Fur Coat (Reindeer)	1	" " (Fur)
3	Sweaters	12	" " (Canvas)

One of the North Pole aircraft at Arkhangelsk, on the way back.

Two ANT-6s of Aviaarktika (SSSR-N211 and N212), warming up to go to search for Levanevsky in October 1937.

An ANT-7 in a typical Arctic scene. (all photos: Boris Vdovienko)

ANT-6

12 SEATS ■ 180km/h (112mph)

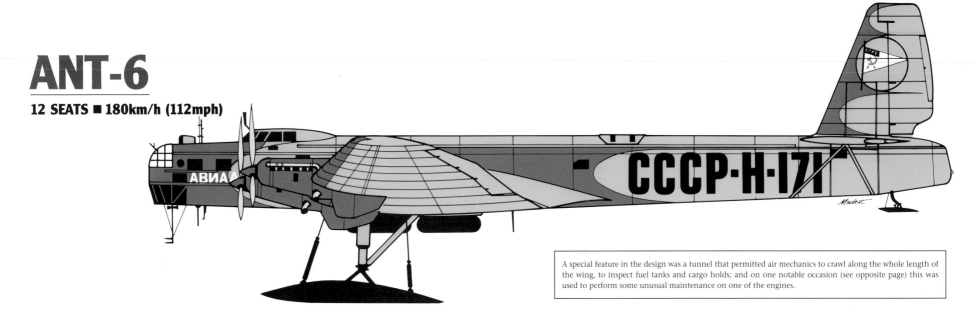

A special feature in the design was a tunnel that permitted air mechanics to crawl along the whole length of the wing, to inspect fuel tanks and cargo holds; and on one notable occasion (see opposite page) this was used to perform some unusual maintenance on one of the engines.

AM-34RN (4 x 970hp) ■ MTOW 22,600kg (49,820lb) ■ Normal Range 1,350km (840mi)

A Great Airplane

Bill Gunston, renowned technical aviation authority and compiler of encyclopedic volumes about aircraft, including a masterpiece on Soviet types, says this about the Tupolev-designed **ANT-6**, also known as the **TB-3** or the **G-2**: ``This heavy bomber was the first Soviet aircraft to be ahead of the rest of the world, and one of the greatest achievements in aviation history'' and that, ``the design was sensibly planned to meet operational requirement and was highly competitive aerodynamically, structurally, and in detail engineering.'' This was in 1930.

A Big Airplane — and Plenty of Them

Give or take a ton or two, depending on the version, the ANT-6 weighed, fully equipped for take-off, about 22 tons. Most G-2s weighed 22,050kg (48,500lb). By comparison, the contemporary German Junkers-G 38 weighed 24 tons, but only two were built, compared with no less

A rear view of ANT-6 SSSR-N-170 in which Vodopyanov took Papanin to the North Pole. This picture well illustrates the excellent basic 1930 design of the world's first heavy transport that went into series production. (photo: Boris Vdovienko)

Comparison with Il-86
LENGTH 25m (82ft) SPAN 40m (131ft)

than 818 ANT-6s. Of these, the vast majority were for the Soviet Air Force, painted dark green, with sky blue undersides; about ten or twelve ANT-6s were allocated to Mark Shevelev's Polar Aviation (Aviaarktika), and painted in the orange-red and blue colors. The four special versions prepared for the Papanin expedition, according to Tupolev historians, were in bare metal, probably to save precious weight. The British and French industries had nothing in the same league, and the U.S.A. had not yet thought of the B-17.

A Versatile Airplane Too

Designed primarily as a bomber, the type was adapted for other purposes. Design started way back in May 1926, wind tunnel testing was completed in March 1929, and **Mikhail Gromov** made the first test flight on 22 December 1930. Throughout its lifespan (production ceased early in 1937) it underwent many improvements, culminating in the **ANT-6A**, specially modified for Dr Otto Schmidt's **Aviaarktika's** assault on the North Pole; and it was also used during the 1930s by **Aeroflot**, reportedly carrying as many as 20 passengers.

BREAKDOWN OF ANT-6 WEIGHT

Item	Kilograms
Empty Weight on Skis	13,084
Radio and Navigation Equipment	297
Spare Parts and Special Expedition Equipment	262
Crew of 8 (120kg each)	960
Provisions for crew (20kg each)	160
Gasoline	7,200
Oil	640
Total	22,603

(excluding cargo carried for ice station)

The Great Polar Flights

The Meeting

On 3 August 1935, the latest product of the **TsAGI** design organization, the **ANT-25**, designed by **Andrei Tupolev**, was on a proving flight over the Barents Sea, north of Murmansk. The crew consisted of **Sigismund Levanevskiy**, then considered to be the Soviet Union's leading pilot, Georgy F. Baidukov, and Victor Levchenko. The aircraft had fuel system problems and, nearing the point of no return, Lavanevskiy turned back, landing near Novgorod, instead of the Moscow base.

In mid-September, a meeting was held in **Josef Stalin's** office in the Kremlin. It was attended by the three crew members, faced across the table by Molotov, Voroshilov, and Andrei Tupolev. At the head of the table, Stalin conducted an enquiry, aided by his pipe, whose smoke drifted over the room. He asked Levanevskiy about his plans, whereupon the pilot said he did not trust the ANT-25, and Tupolev left the room in disgust. Stalin suggested that, for the next flight into the Arctic, American assistance should be sought; but Baidukov felt that the aircraft's problem could be rectified. Answering Levanevskiy's allegation that a single-engined aircraft (the ANT-25) had a 100 percent chance of disaster if an engine failed, Chkalov responded with the remark ``With four engines, you have a 400 percent chance!'' He won the day.

The Flight to Udd

Although Stalin had originally wished to make a prestige-seeking flight across the Pole to the U.S.A., he decided, early in 1936, that, for political reasons, a flight to the U.S.S.R.'s Far East would be preferable. Later, he was reported to have said that the successful flight had been ``worth two armies.'' By this time, Baidukov had begun to work with **Valery P. Chkalov**, a pilot with a reputation for taking risks, but a master of his trade. The ANT-25's fuel problems were corrected.

On 20 July 1936, Chkalov, Baidukov, and navigator Aleksander V. Belyakov flew the aircraft from Moscow, by a route that took them first due north from Moscow and then by a near-Great Circle course over eastern Siberia, aiming for Petropavlovsk-Kamchatskiy, which, however, was blanketed by impenetrable weather. Turning west, they made landfall across the Sea of Okhotsk, on the tiny island of Udd, near the mouth of the Amur River. On this island, now renamed Chkalov (along with neighboring islands Baidukov and Belyakov), a dignified

monument commemorates this notable flight of 9,374km (5,825mi) in 56hr 20min. The ANT-25 had made its case.

The First Trans-Polar Flight

The following year, from 18 to 20 June 1937, they made the historic flight that ranks as one of the greatest trail-blazing conquests of the air, and one of the most dramatic. Flying at first due north to the Pole and then continuing due south, they made their way to Portland, Oregon, landing, however, at the military Pearson Field at Vancouver, Washington State. The ANT-25 had covered a distance of about 10,000km (6,200mi), officially recorded as a Great Circle distance of 8,504km (5,285mi) in 63hr 25min. The flight captured the imagination of the whole world and Chkalov was hailed as the Russian Lindbergh.

The Second Trans-Polar Flight

As if to trump Chkalov's ace — and perhaps to remind everyone in the U.S.S.R. that he was once the premier Soviet pilot — **Mikhail Gromov**, with Andrei B. Yumashyev and Sergei A. Danilin, made a second trans-Polar flight only a month after Chkalov. On 12-14 July, also in an ANT-25, with its bright red wings making a dramatic impact, this crew flew from Moscow to a grass meadow near San Jacinto, in southern California. This time the Great Circle distance of 10,148km (6,306mi), flown in an even shorter time (62hr 17min) than Chkalov's, because of more favorable winds and conditions, beat the world's distance record held by the Frenchmen Codos and Rossi.

Tragic Postscript

One month later still, it was Levanevskiy's turn. Convinced that a multi-engined aircraft was the best suited for long-distance flying (and who could argue this point today?) he set off from Moscow on 12 August 1937, in a **DB-A** (URSS-N209). Designed by Viktor Bolkovitinov, this was a mid-winged and much-developed version of the veteran but well-trusted **ANT-6**, the very same type that so successfully had made the flights to the North Pole earlier in the year (see page 30). Levanevskiy had a crew of five: Nikolai Kasteneyev (co-pilot), Viktor Levchenko (navigator), Grigory Pobezhimov (mechanic), Nikolai Godovikov (mechanic), and Nikolai Galkovsky (radio operator). After 17hr 35min, the radio station at Cape Schmidt, in the far northeast of Siberia, heard a brief message, reporting severe trouble. The DBA and its crew were never heard of again, although repeated searches have been made.

This dignified monument on an island near the shore of the Sea of Okhotsk, commemorates the flight by Chkalov, Baidukov, and Belyakov from Moscow to Udd Island in 1936. (photo: R.E.G. Davies)

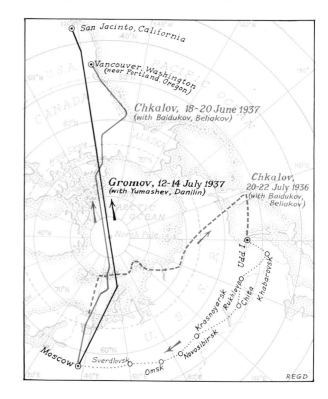

ANT-25

Going For the Distance

For propaganda and prestige reasons alone, the goal of beating world records, especially in a technological field such as aviation, was attractive to the Soviet Union during the early 1930s. **Andrei Tupolev** realized that the existing long distance record was within its grasp, and obtained authorization from the Revolutionary War Council on 7 December 1931 to proceed with a new design, the **ANT-25 RD** (Rekord Dal'nost, or record distance). It was a carefully-fashioned product. The corrugated wing had an aspect ration of no less than 13-0, with fuel tankage distributed along the whole length, to relieve bending stress (later the corrugations were smoothed over with fabric, and the drag coefficient was reduced by 36 percent.) The fuel load was eventually increased to 6.1 tons, more than half the total gross weight of the airplane. Instrumentation included the first Soviet gyro-compass, a 500 W, 12 V generator, MF and HF radios, and a sextant in a hinged room station.

Mikhail Gromov made the first flight on 22 June 1933. After the modifications, a series of closed circuit flights in 1934 culminated in Gromov, with A.I. Filin and I.T. Spirin, setting a new world's record on 10 September, at 12,411km (7,713mi) in a multi-lap triangular flight lasting 75hr 2min. Then, as preparations were made for a spectacular demonstration — trans-Polar flight — Gromov fell ill. In August 1935, the reputable **Sigismund Levanevskiy** flew towards the North Pole, but had to turn back (see opposite page); and that led to the critical meeting with Stalin. As

the table below shows, the ANT-25 was in a great tradition of long-range specialist aircraft. And the honor of matching words with deeds fell to **Valery Chkalov**. About 16 ANT-25s were built. No more record-breaking flights were attempted, but the aircraft were used for experimental test flying.

This aerial view of ANT-25 URSS-N025 clearly emphasizes the large wing area and the high aspect ratio.

SPECIALIST LONG-RANGE AIRCRAFT COMPARED

Aircraft Type	Year of Long Range Flight	MTOW (kg)	Dimensions (m) Length	Span	Fuel Capacity (litres)	Range Achieved Distance (km)	Route
Dewoitine 33	1931	9,200	14.4	28.0	8,000	10,367*	Paris-Siberia (crashed)
Fairey Long-Range Monoplane II	1933	7,940	14.8	25.0	5,214	8,705	Cranwell, England-Walvis Bay, S.W. Africa
ANT-25	1933	11,524	13.1	34.0	8,189	10,146	Moscow-San Jacinto, Cal.
Vickers Wellesley	1938	8,364	12.0	22.7	5,863	11,517	Ismailia, Egypt-Darwin, Australia

*Notes: All single-engined monoplanes, high aspect ratio wing *Previously-achieved close circuit. Attempt to break distance record thwarted by engine failure.*

In an amiable mood, the designer of the ANT-25, Andrei Tupolev, and Chkalov's co-pilot, Georgy Baidukov, meet at Moscow airport in 1975. With them is General Bykov, Deputy Minister of Aviation. (photos: Boris Vdovienko)

Valery Chkalov, pilot of the first trans-Polar flight of 1937.

Sigismund Levanevskiy, pilot of the third, and tragic attempt to fly across the North Pole in 1937.

Georgy Baidukov (front), pictured here with Gromov, was Chkalov's co-pilot.

The ANT-25 crew that flew from Moscow to California in 1937 (left to right) Danilin, Gromov, and Yumarshov.

A Nationwide Airline

Aeroflot Consolidates

While all the headlines were being captured by Aviaarktika, with its brilliant support of the Papanin Expedition; by Chkalov's and Gromov's trans-Polar flights, and by Levanevskiy's tragic disappearance; **Aeroflot** was building an air network, not so much by adding more routes (to those shown on the map on page 27) but by introducing better aircraft and more frequencies on the trunk lines and by adding small feeder services and bush routes to connect with the main arteries.

On 15 May 1937, for example, improved service from Moscow to Tashkent was announced, to augment the flights first started by Dobrolet in 1929, but which carried mainly mail and Pravda matrices. Rather as in the formative years of air transport in the United States in the 1920s, the passengers, mainly government officials, had lower priority. But from 1937 onwards, there was a distinct upgrading of service standards.

International Probing

The Prague route had opened, with PS-9 (modified ANT-9) service, on 31 August 1936, and following the demise of Deruluft on 31 March 1937, Berlin was added to the Aeroflot map. Service also started from Leningrad to Stockholm in 1937, but this was superseded — handsomely — on 11 November 1940, by a direct service from Stockholm to Moscow, via Riga and Velikie Luki. Operated jointly with the Swedish Airline A.B.A., both airlines used the Douglas DC-3; the Soviets, however, also flying the license-built Lisunov Li-2 version, production of which had begun in 1938, a contract having been made between Douglas and AMTORG (American Trading Organization) in August 1935 (see page 37). In an interesting preview of future events, the two airlines offered service from Stockholm (neutral during World War II) and Tokyo, via the Trans-Siberian Railway (interestingly, not by Aeroflot); while an even more ambitious connection was offered, from Scandinavia to San Francisco in 30 days, by Japanese ship from Kobe. This, of course, did not last very long.

Other indications of Aeroflot's following the flag during this confused period of uncertain world politics were the opening of lines to Bucharest and Cluj, Romania, in 1938, and to Sofia, Bulgaria, in 1939. In that year also, a joint Soviet-Chinese air link was forged, from Alma Ata to Hami, in northwest China, the two points giving a name to the airline: Hamiata. But all hopes of further international expansion were dashed when Hitler's Germany invaded the Soviet Union with *Operation Barbarossa* on 22 June 1941.

Gaining Stature

By 1940, the unduplicated mileage of Aeroflot's route system was close to 100,000, and in that year it carried 350,000 passengers. The productivity, measured in passenger-miles flown, was 160 million. Aeroflot was now bigger than Deutsche Lufthansa, Europe's biggest, and it was now the third biggest airline in the world.

The Lisunov Li-2, license-built version of the Douglas DC-3, superseded the old generation, at Moscow-Khodinka. (Boris Vdovienko)

The ANT-9 and the Junkers-Ju 52/3m, both flying for Deruluft just before it stopped service, were representative of the generation of airliners that depended on corrugated metal for longitudinal stiffness. This picture was taken at Königsberg. (photo: Lufthansa)

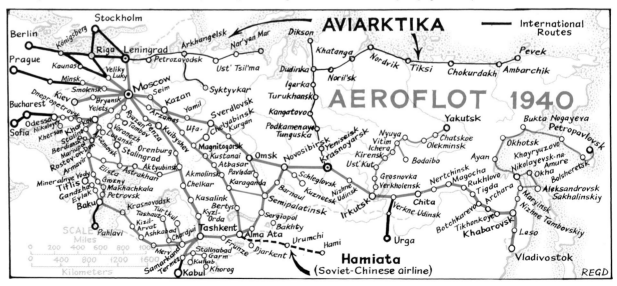

Flights Long and Short

The Lights Go Out Again

Europe was an unsettled part of the world in 1938 and 1939. The seizure of Austria and the Sudentenland by Nazi troops had put every country on a war-alert footing. Old-style diplomacy had been replaced by a policy of might-is-right, and war seemed inevitable as Adolf Hitler pursued his insatiable desire for power. While some countries took defensive measures — France built its Maginot Line and Britain belatedly modernized its Royal Air Force — the U.S.S.R, disenchanted with trying to come to terms with the western democracies, signed a non-aggression pact with Germany — the infamous Molotov-Ribbentrop Pact — in August 1939. On 3 September, Germany invaded Poland, and the Second World War began. Echoing a famous phrase by British statesman Edward Grey in 1914, the lights went out in Europe once again.

Flight of the Moscow

Against the far-reaching political events, the world of commerce and culture, as always, carried on until the guns and torpedoes were actually fired. In the United States, New York was planning a spectacular World's Fair, and rather surprisingly, the Soviet Union decided to mark the occasion by what was intended to be a spectacular airplane flight. Although the Chkalov and Gromov trans-Polar flights had been impressive, the disappearance of Levanevskiy had tarnished the image; and his death had further emphasized the severe dangers of

challenging the Arctic wastes.

Accordingly, a shorter route was chosen, the Great Circle route westward from Moscow via Iceland and Greenland. The pilot was **Brig Gen Vladimir Kokkinaki**, flying an Ilyushin TsKB-30 (DB-3B) twin-engined bomber aircraft, the *Moskva* (*Moscow*), the same one in which he had made a non-stop flight to the Far East in June 1938. Accompanied by Major Mikhail Kh. Gordiyenko, he took off from Moscow on 28 April 1939, and then proceeded to face filthy weather, temperatures down to 54°C below zero, and, approaching the North American continent, dense fog. They lost their way and, with a certain amount of luck, managed to make a wheels-up forced landing in an ice-covered marsh on the little island of Miscou, New Brunswick, 6,250km (3,900mi) and 22hr 56min after leaving Moscow. They had actually flown farther, while they were lost, and made their landing with empty tanks.

Vladimir Kokkinaki

(photos: Boris Vdovienko)

Departure of the flight to Novaya Zemlya on 29 March 1936. Vodopyanov's first segment, however, was only a few kilometers.

Polikarpov R-5 (SSSR-N127), one of only two built, and in which Mikhail Vodopyanov made a flight to Novaya Zemlya in 1936.

Vodopyanov's Shortest Hop

When the famous pilot **Mikhail Vodopyanov** set off on his epic survey flight of 29 March 1936, to determine if a route to the North Pole was feasible via selected locations in Novaya Zemlya and Franz Jozef Land (see page 28), he was given an enthusiastic send-off by a crowd of well-wishers at Moscow. He took off in a **Polikarpov R-5 (SSSR-N128)**, ostensibly en route to the Frozen North.

Little did the crowd know of a certain hesitancy in the hero Mikhail's demeanour. For the day was a Sunday, and he was superstitious about flying on a Sunday. The first leg of his arduous route to the dreaded Franz Jozef Land was as short as he could make it — just over the rooftops and hedges to the nearest landing strip; and out of sight of the adoring fans.

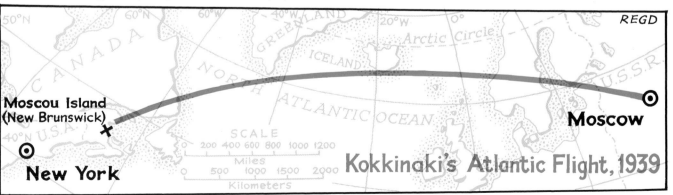

Kokkinaki's Atlantic Flight, 1939

The Great Patriotic War

Mobilization

With shattering force, and with the element of surprise, Hitler's Germany launched *Operation Barbarossa* and invaded the Soviet Union on 22 June 1941. Within two or three days, at least half of the Soviet Air Force had been destroyed before the aircraft could take to the air. All **Aeroflot** services to the west were immediately suspended — including the one to Berlin! — but those to the east continued for a while, as did some of the routes of **Aviaarktika**. On 25 June, Grazdansij Vozduzhnij Flot (Aeroflot) effectively became a unit of the Soviet Air Force. **Vasily S. Molokov**, hero of the *Chelyuskin* rescue, and veteran of Polar aviation, was appointed head of the military transport organization, with the rank of Major-General.

The Battle of Moscow

In October 1941, the Germans made a concentrated effort to capture Moscow. The Soviet forces desperately defended their capital. On 16 October, the Government transferred to Kuibyshev (Samara), although Stalin himself (in an uncharacteristic reflection of a similar decision by King George VI) stayed in Moscow. Aeroflot was directly involved in the defense of Moscow. The published statistics were impressive: 32,730 flights (845 behind enemy lines); 49,822 troops carried; and 1,365 tons of supplies, arms, and medicines carried.

Organization

Late in 1942, two special groups were formed: the **First Transport Aviation Group** (renamed in 1944 as the 10th

A Soviet Navy GST (license-built Consolidated 28 Catalina) at Khabarovsk in the early 1940s. The military GST was also used for passenger transport along with a few civil versions (designated MP-7) built for Aeroflot. The pilot on the right is Mikhail Vodopyanov. (photo: Far Eastern Regional Directorate Museum, Khabarovsk)

Guards Aviation Division); and the **Special Communications Aviation Group** (later to become the 3rd Communications Aviation Division). The fleets were composed of the former aircraft of Aeroflot, plus a number of obsolete types no longer useful as military equipment, such as the **TB-3 (ANT-6)** four-engined bomber, designed back in 1930, but still useful as a load-carrier. Additionally, 15 **Detached Aviation Regiments** were formed in 1943. Equipped with **Polikarpov U-2/Po-2s**, these units were highly mobile, providing close support to individual regiments at the front line, with ambulance, reconnaissance, and communications missions.

Reinforcements

With their backs to the wall in 1942 and the early part of 1943, the Soviet armed forces gladly accepted any help they could get, from whatever source. Paramount among such efforts was the American Lend-Lease program, and among the thousands of aircraft ferried from the east (see opposite) were hundreds of **Douglas C--47s**, which were promptly delivered to the First Detached Aviation Division, for operations on the Central Front, where they were joined by their matching twins **Lisunov Li-2s**, manufactured at Tashkent under a DC-3 license from Douglas, negotiated through AMTORG.

Other help to augment the meager resources of Aeroflot during the desperate conflict came from an unexpected source. Between 31 January and 2 February, the city of Stalingrad was the site of one of the greatest victories of the Great Patriotic War — or of any war. During the final days of the doomed German armies, they had been supplied by a large number of **Junkers-Ju 52/3m** transports. About 80 of

The Lisunov Li-2 was the transport workhorse for the Soviet Union during the Great Patriotic War. (photo: Boris Vdovienko)

In the Arctic, aircraft frequently stuck in the snow when icing effectively glued them to the runway. Such scenes as this were familiar in the north. The aircraft is an ANT-7. (photo: Boris Vdovienko)

these abandoned `Tante Ju's' were repaired and put into service with Aeroflot.

A Great War Record

The Great Patriotic War ended on 9 May 1945. Aeroflot's contribution to the war effort had been considerable, and was so recognized: 15,000 of its staff received medals and honors; 15 pilots were proclaimed Heroes of the Soviet Union; six of the Front-line Sections became Guards Units; and ten Sections were awarded special medals. They had been well earned. During the War, Aeroflot had carried 2,300,000 passengers and 300,000 tons of freight, including materiel and medical supplies. Of the passengers, 330,000 were wounded soldiers.

A Polikarpov U-2 (Po-2), diminutive maid-of-all-work, was to be seen everywhere during the War. This Aeroflot U-2 (SSSR-L3373) pictured at Tobolsk in 1941 has a sliding canopy enclosed cockpit for the pilot, and three passenger windows in the fuselage and containers underneath the wings. (photo: Boris Vdovienko)

Aeroflot Turns to Douglas

Technical Slowdown

Although the ANT-9 of the late 1920s had been on a par with the commercial aircraft of other countries; and the ANT-6 had been an adequate heavy lifter, Soviet designers lost momentum during the 1930s. Kalinin was executed. Tupolev himself spent much of his time under house arrest, and escaped being shot only by the intervention of, of all people, Beria, head of the secret police.

Buying the Best

In August 1935, AMTORG (American Trading Organization) in New York, took delivery of the first DC-2 (NC14949, msn 1413) and Boris Lisunov was sent to California to prepare for the licensed production of the Douglas twin. The Soviet-built Douglases were first designated PS-84s (Pashazhyrski Samolyet, or passenger aircraft), and from 17 September 1942, Lisunov Li-2s. These were standard DC-3s, with a right-side entry door. By the end of World War II, 2,258 had been built. The type remained in production until 1954, by which time a total of 6,157 had been built at Tashkent, Uzbekistan.

Lend-Leases

After the Nazi invasion of the summer of 1941, much of western Russia and the Ukraine had been devastated or pillaged. In a mighty display of determination and improvised organization, all the aircraft production lines in Europe were moved eastwards to cities beyond the Ural Mountains. This massive logistics task took many months, and meanwhile the Air Force had to be reinforced.

At an Allied conference in Moscow on 31 July 1941, Harry Hopkins, President Roosevelt's special envoy, laid the foundations of what was to become the Lend-Lease Program. Slow to get under way at first — few aircraft arrived in time for the Battle of Moscow, and these were from Britain, via Murmansk — the unprecedented machinery of the historic airlift began on 29 September 1942, when the first Bell P-39 Airacobra left Fairbanks, Alaska, and arrived in time to go into action early in October.

Of the 18,700 aircraft supplied under the Allied Lend-Lease program, 14,750 were flown along this route, by U.S. pilots to Fairbanks, where Soviet flyers took over. Of these, over 4,900 were P-39 Airacobras, 2,400 P-63 Kingcobras, 2,900 Douglas DB-7/A-20 Havocs, and 860 North American B-25 Mitchells. About 640 were lost in transit. The Lend-Lease aircraft accounted for 12% of the 136,800 of all types used by the Soviet Air Force in the Great Patriotic War.

Of the several other types, other than those mentioned above, 700 were **Douglas C-47s**, the most widely used of the military variants of the DC-3 workhorse transport airplane. They were used everywhere. The Soviet pilots liked them as much as did the U.S.A.A.F. 'Gooney Bird' and the R.A.F. Dakota flyers. And they were to make a solid contribution to Aeroflot's recovery after the conflict came to an end. On 1 March 1946, for instance, the 14th Cargo Aircraft Group of Aeroflot was formed at Yakutsk. Fifteen C-47s were transferred from the Soviet air fleet, together with, remarkably, three Junkers-Ju 52/3m's that had been captured on the eastern front.

COMPARISON OF DOUGLAS DC-3 AND LISUNOV LI-2

Type	First Flight Date	Dimensions- m(ft)		Seats	Engines				MTOW kg (lb)	Speed km/h (mph)	Range km (mi)	No. Built
		Length	Span		No.	Type	h.p.					
DC-3	17 Dec 1935	19.66 (64,6)	28.96 (95,0)	21-28	2	Wright Cyclone P & W Double Wasp	860 1,200		11,430 (25,200)	290 (180)	2,000 (1,250)	11,413*
Li-2	1940	19.66 (64,6)	28.96 (95,0)	18-28	2	Shvetsov M-62	900		11,280 (24,900)	225 (140)	1,600 (1,000)	6,157

*Notes: * This figure includes 10,493 military versions, mainly C-47s, built in the U.S.; 487 built in Japan; but only 433 commercial DC-3s built specifically for airlines. Li-2 figure also includes production for military.*

The old Yakutsk terminal building, in traditional Russian wood construction, first erected for the Lend-Lease program, is still there, as this photo, taken in 1992, shows. Just down the street is the original building which housed the offices of the Lend-Lease program during the vital years, 1942-1945. (R.E.G. Davies)

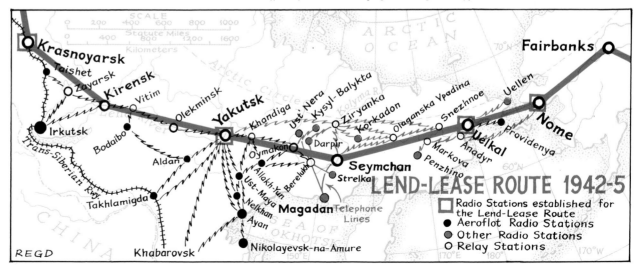

Post-War Struggle

Resumption of European Services

The Soviet Union emerged from World War II (The Great Patriotic War) weakened by its sustained and intensive efforts to beat the Nazi war machine into the ground. **Aeroflot** had to re-group as the national flag carrier, as Moscow began to isolate itself from its allies in the west, at the same time trying to dominate the countries on its borders, simultaneously spreading the creed of communism and fashioning a *cordon sanitaire* to guard against a repetition of the events of 1920.

In 1944, the U.S.S.R. had declined an invitation to attend the historic Chicago Conference, at which most of the world's nations hammered out the basis for what was to become the International Civil Aviation Organization (ICAO). The Five Freedoms of the Air were not wholly accepted in Moscow, where, nevertheless, plans were quickly made to spread Aeroflot's wings westwards. By the end of 1945, services had been reinstated, or started anew, to most of the capitals of eastern and central Europe, and also to Teheran. At home, the trans-Siberian and other main arterial routes were revived, and the social work in the Arctic, which had continued even during the war, was maintained.

Like the British, French, and nations other than the exceptionally well-equipped United States, the U.S.S.R. had to make the best with what it had: the trusty **Lisunov Li-2s** and the ex-Lend-Lease **Douglas C-47s**.

Baidukov Has Problems

The Fourth Five-Year Plan had provided for ambitious Aeroflot expansion, with a target of 175,000km (110,000mi) of routes

The Ilyushin 18, first flown on 30 July 1947, was a 60-seat four-engined airliner which never went into production. It was too large for the traffic of the day and demanded ground support which would not be available for years. (photo: Ilyushin Design Bureau)

throughout the Soviet Union. Yet to service this great plan, Aeroflot had little more than a large fleet of Li-2s for the main routes, and hundreds of little **Polikarpov Po-2s**.

This was the situation confronting **Georgy Baidukov**, veteran crew member of the Chkalov trans-Polar flight of 1937, and Stalin's personal envoy to the United States during the war years, when he was put in charge of Aeroflot in 1947. The equipment upgrading prospects were gloomy. **Sergei Ilyushin** had made preliminary drawings for what was to become the **Ilyushin Il-12** as early as 1943, and this unpressurized tricycle-geared twin made its first public appearance on 18 August 1946. But this was no `DC-3 Replacement'.

On the ground, airports were totally inadequate, with poor runways, bad passenger buildings, and maintenance, as often as not, in the open. Baidukov effectively made his point by taking a party of officials, including Mikoyan, on a proving flight from Moscow to Khabarovsk. The shortcomings were only too obvious, and this inspection trip no doubt had some effect on subsequent actions taken with the next Five Year Plan.

The First Ilyushins

Making the best of a sub-standard inventory, Baidukov introduced the Il-12, on a few selected routes, on 22 August 1947, and more widely in the following year when the summer schedules started on 23 May. Some relief was expected from the 60-seat four-engined **Ilyushin Il-18** (the piston-engined one, not the later turboprop) but although it made its first flight on 30 July 1947, and went into service — again on selected trunk routes — at the end of 1948; it was too big and complicated for the traffic and ground infrastructure of the day, and very few were built. They were withdrawn from service by 1950.

Baidukov fought off official skepticism and introduced flight attendants on the more important routes; and he witnessed the introduction of the amazing 12-seat **Antonov An-2** biplane, which made its first flight in March 1948.

Widening Responsibilities

After two and a half years, during which the Politburo often accused him of poor management, Baidukov resigned — without incidentally apologizing for anything, a procedure that was the expected protocol in those times. He had been sorely tried. For apart from the problems of inadequate aircraft, airfields, ground services and engineering staff, pilots who were apt to take on too much vodka and not enough fuel, and a meager budget, he had been given additional responsibilities.

This picture was taken in 1959 but is representative of the Ilyushin design team that produced the series of post-war airliners. Sergei Ilyushin stands in the middle; his successor, Genrich Novozhilov, is second from the left; and Vladimir Kokkinaki, technical advisor, is on Ilyushin's immediate left. (photo: Boris Vdovienko)

Back in 1932, Aeroflot had taken on the task of **agricultural support** in crop-dusting and crop-spraying, an activity in which the U.S.S.R. had been a pioneer. In 1937, it had added **ambulance and medical supply** flights to supplement its other work, with a `flying doctor' service. Now, on 23 September 1948, it added **forestry patrol**, ice reconnaissance and water-bombing; and on 30 November 1949, it was given the additional task of supporting **fishing fleets** by surveying the seas to locate shoals of fish.

Yet in spite of all the difficulties, Aeroflot must have been doing something right. In 1950, it carried 3.8 million passengers, and flew over a network of 75,600km (47,000mi).

Lisunov Li-2

18 SEATS ■ 225km/h (140mph)

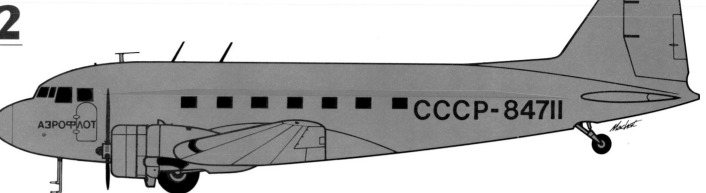

Li-2s differed from DC-3s in having an extra window aft of the cockpit, modified engine nacelles and cowlings, and a right-hand passenger door. This Li-2 did not have de-icer boots.

Shvetsov M-62 (2 x 900hp) ■ MTOW 11,280kg (24,900lb) ■ Normal Range 1,600km (1,000mi) ■ Length 20m (65ft) ■ Span 29m (95ft)

Joint Ventures

The term 'joint venture' has become part of the language of international commerce during the past few years,. But such a device was common in airline associations back in the early 1940s when, for example, Pan American Airways set up such partnerships in Latin America. In exchange for certain privileges, such as exclusive mail contracts, Pan Am would provide the technical and administrative expertise, and supply aircraft at bargain rates, to set up local airlines, ostensibly as national carriers, but in reality Pan Am subsidiaries.

During the latter 1940s, as Europe rearranged itself into two halves of political persuasion, the U.S.S.R. took a leaf out of Pan Am's book, and set up similar airlines in eastern Europe, with **Aeroflot** as Big Brother. Ironically, the ubiquitous Douglas DC-3, in its **Lisunov Li-2** disguise, was invariably the basis of the small post-war communist-directed airline fleets, just as with Pan American on the other side of the world.

The First Exports

Interestingly, therefore, a California-designed aircraft, license-built in the U.S.S.R., was the key factor in this particular channel of political influence. The Lisunovs were the only aircraft in adequate supply in 1945 and 1946; but they were to be the basis for a secure Soviet foothold in what was later to become known as the Six-Pool group of eastern European airlines. This foothold was to prevail for the next half-century.

JOINT VENTURE AIRLINES IN POST-WAR SOVIET SATELLITE COUNTRIES

Country	Airline	Date Founded	Date of First Service	Initial Aircraft Fleet	Date Terminated	Remarks
Poland	LOT*	6 Mar 1945	Dec 1945	Li-2 Po-2	(still operating)	Rejuvenated pre-war airline. Most of post-war fleet was Soviet-built.
Czechoslovakià	CSA*	14 Sep 1945	4 Mar 1945	DC-3 Ju 52/3m	(still operating)	Rejuvenated pre-war airline. Used Soviet equipment exclusively after coup of 1968.
Hungary	Maszovlet*	29 Mar 1946	15 Oct 1946	Li-2 Po-2	Late 1954	50% Soviet shareholding in new airline to succeed MALERT. Succeeded in turn by MALEV, which used only Soviet aircraft.
Romania	TARS*	1945	1947	Li-2 Ju 52/3m	Late 1954	50% Soviet shareholding in new airline to succeed LARES. Succeeded in turn by TAROM which used mainly Soviet aircraft.
Yugoslavia	JUSTA	Late 1946	Apr 1947	Li-2	1948	50% Soviet shareholding in new airline to succeed Aeroput. Terminated when Tito severed relations with Soviet Union.
Bulgaria	B.V.S.	Early 1947	29 Jun 1947	Li-2 Ju 52/3m	1954	50% Soviet shareholding in new airline. Succeeded by TABSO* which used Soviet-. built aircraft
North Korea	SOKAO	1950	1950	Il-14	1954	50% Soviet shareholding in new airline. Succeeded by CAAK, which operated only Soviet aircraft.
East Germany	Deutsche Luft Hansa	1 Jul 1955	4 Feb 1956	Il-14	1991	Name changed to Interflug* 13 Sep 1958. Liquidated with German reunification.
Mongolia	Air Mongol	1956	7 Jul 1956	Li-2 Po-2, Il-12	(still operating)	Currently operates as Mongolian Airlines (MIAT-Mongolyn Irgeniy Agaaryn Teever).

*Members of Six-Pool, formed 15 February 1956

This Lisunov Li-2 is pictured at Mirnyy, the center of the diamond industry in the Yakut autonomous republic of eastern Siberia in 1961. The 'Russian DC-3' performed sterling work for over a quarter of a century, and the Yakuts held it in such high esteem that they have preserved one on a pedestal at Chersky, near the delta of the Kolyma River, on the East Siberian Sea of the Arctic Ocean, 240km (150mi) north of the Arctic Circle. (Y. Ryumkin, courtesy John Stroud)

Piston-Engined Twilight

Ilyushin Il-14 of Polar Aviation at the Soviet scientific station SP-10 in 1962. (photo: Boris Vdovienko)

The Kukuruzhnik

Reference has been made (page 38) to the widening responsibilities of Aeroflot. In 1948 and 1949, forestry patrol and fisheries support, respectively, were added to the normal air transport work. Crop-spraying had already been taken on in 1932 and ambulance flying—an early flying doctor service — in 1937. Now, in 1953, aerial photography and mapping rounded off the list of Aeroflot's responsibilities that were all-embracing.

Much of the supplementary work, other than airline scheduling, was performed by the **Polikarpov U-2**, which, after the death of the designer in 1944, became known as the **Po-2**. During the Great Patriotic War, it had performed magnificently, far beyond the ab initio training role for which thousands of Soviet pilots affectionately remember it.

During that period of desperate defense, from July 1941 to November 1942, the diminutive Polikarpovs made upwards of 450,000 flights over enemy territory, and rescued 580,000 people, including 150,000 wounded soldiers. They carried almost 50,000 tons of supplies and materiel, and their versatility extended to rescuing survivors of Lend-Lease convoy ships lost on the supply route to Murmansk. Many of them would fly quietly during the night, penetrating enemy lines, and dropping saboteurs for aiding the partisans. The supreme accolade was perhaps awarded by the Germans themselves: the reward of 2,000 marks paid for downing a Po-2 was twice that paid for a fighter aircraft.

After the war, in a close analogy to the `swords into ploughshares' metaphor, when squadrons of Polikarpovs were deployed from battlefields to arable fields, they were to be seen everywhere, crop-spraying and crop-dusting; and they became such an essential part of the agricultural scene that they were called **Kukuruzhniks**. Freely translated, this

U-2S Sanitarnyi Samolyet, or ambulance aeroplane (msn 6350).

Soviet designers, A.S. Yakovlev (left) and N.N. Polikarpov (right) compare notes.

might be `Little Cornhuskers' and was a mark of their continuing usefulness other than as a basic trainer, in which Aeroflot pilots first won their wings.

The Ilyushin Il-12

While the first Soviet commercial aircraft (other than the short-lived Ilyushin Il-18) to go into postwar airline service had its problems (see page 38) the **Ilyushin Il-12's** contribution was important, if only because, in the transformation from war-time military production, the manufacturing industry cut its teeth, as it were, and learned some hard lessons of what had to be done to produce a successful airliner. Even though the improved Il-14 (see opposite) made its first flight in 1953, its earlier relative was able to supplement the Lisunov Li-2s. The Ilyushin 12, in fact, was on hand to inaugurate the first sorties into western Europe in 1954, when Aeroflot broke out of the Iron Curtain with services to Stockholm and Paris, and in 1955, with services to Beijing (on 1 January), to Tirana (a month later) from Kiev, and to Vienna (on 10 September).

An Ilyushin Il-12B at Helsinki-Malmi in 1951. (John Stroud)

Ilyushin Il-14

32 SEATS ■ 350km/h (217mph)

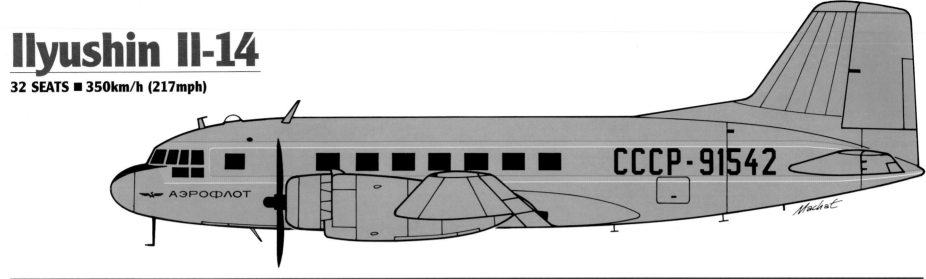

CCCP-91542

ДЭРОФЛОТ

Machat

Shvetsov ASh-82T (2 x 1,900hp) ■ MTOW 17,500kg (38,580lb) ■ Normal Range 1,500km (930mi)

The improved version of the Ilyushin Il-12, the **Ilyushin Il-14**, went into service on 30 November 1954. Although modified, the fuselage was substantially the same as its predecessor's and passenger accommodation was unchanged because of its inability to carry a theoretical load of 40 passengers. In any case, the traffic demand in the postwar U.S.S.R., consisting mostly of bureaucrats serving the vast territory and military men visiting their regiments, was still dissipated over hundreds of sparsely-patronized routes. Only a few inter-city and summer vacation services required more than the 18 seats with which the initial **Il-14P** was fitted. Outwardly, the main changes made to the Il-12 were to fit a new wing, clean up the engine cowlings, exhausts, and nacelles, and to re-design the fin and rudder.

Once into production, the **Il-14M** (Modifikatsiya) was introduced with a 1m (3.2ft) longer fuselage to seat 24, eventually 32 passengers. The Il-14 was also built at Dresden, East Germany **(VEB Il-14P)**, and in Czechoslovakia (as the **Avia 14**). About 80 of the former and about 200 of the latter were produced, adding to 1,502 Il-12s and Il-14s built at Tashkent. Although

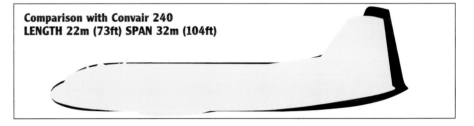

**Comparison with Convair 240
LENGTH 22m (73ft) SPAN 32m (104ft)**

eclipsed by the advent of the Tupolev jet in 1956, the aircraft continued to give good service on all the secondary routes within the U.S.S.R. and comprised the fleets of many of the communist countries for several years. It proved to be a sturdy foot-soldier of the Aeroflot fleet, in its freighter role **(Il-14G)** especially, and quite remarkably in its applications to Polar conditions it became an essential component of the inventory. As will be shown later in this book, it is one of the few aircraft that have seen regular service within the frigid zones north and south of the Arctic and Antarctic Circles.

In striking contrast to the rigors of Arctic conditions, this Aeroflot Il-14P (SSSR-61719) sits in the warmth of Makhachkala, on the shores of the Caspian Sea (at the same latitude as Barcelona). (photo: Boris Vdovienko)

COMPARISON OF IL-12, IL-14, AND CONVAIR 240

Type	First Flight Date	Dimensions (m)		Pass. Seats	Engines			MTOW kg lb	Speed km/h (mph)	Range km (mi)	No. Built
		Length	Span		No.	Type	h.p.				
Il-12	1945[1]	21 (70)	32 (104)	18	2	Ash-82FN	1,775	17,250 (38,030)	350 (217)	1,250 (750)	200+
Il-14	1953	22 (73)	32 (104)	32	2	ASh-82T	1,900	17,500 (38,580)	350 (217)	800 (500)	1,582*
240	16 Mar 1947	23 (75)	28 (92)	40	2	P&W R-2800	2,400	19,300 (42,500)	400 (250)	1,600 (1,000)	566

*Total Soviet Il-12/14 production 1,502 of which 839 were Il-14Ps, plus 3 prototypes. In addition, approx. 200 Avia 14s and 80 VEB Il-14Ps were built under license. Note:[1] First flown with diesel engines.

Versatile Biplane

The Dark Horse

While the Soviet aircraft industry was pursuing the understandable goal of producing a main line aircraft to succeed the Lisunov Li-2 (DC-3), first with the Ilyushin piston-engined twins, the Il-12 and-14 series; and then with the twin-jet Tupolev Tu-104; another little aircraft was put into production in the late 1940s that at first passed almost unnoticed. Because it was a biplane, a design formula considered to be obsolete except for sporting aircraft, the aviation world as a whole dismissed it at the time as a serious contender for either technical or economic acclaim. Yet few observers today would quarrel with veteran aviation historian John Stroud's judgment, made back in the early 1960s, that it was ``absolutely unique and must be regarded as one of the world's truly great biplanes.'' The unique aircraft was the **Antonov An-2**, initially, in prototype form, designated Skh-1 (Rural Economy 1).

Its first flight on 31 August 1947 did not attract headlines, but its appearance coincided with the expansion of Aeroflot's responsibilities to include forestry patrol, fisheries survey and support, and aerial mapping and photography. These were added to the airline's air transport role during the years following the introduction of the **Kolkhoznik (Collective Farmer)**, as the An-2 was at first known. It was a partner of the **Kukuruzhnik (Cornhusker)** Polikarpov Po-2, whose many roles the larger Antonov was progressively to complement, later to replace, and, in some areas, to adopt the nickname.

The Ubiquitous An-2

The An-2 was originally built to meet a specification of the Soviet Ministry of Agriculture and Forestry, a bureaucratic agency that would seem to have been an unlikely source of aeronautic inspiration. Yet in getting it just right, it excelled the combined efforts of designers, engineers, and technicians the world over. And Antonov's ability to fulfill the Ministry's requirements produced a world-beater of which many variants were built. The An-2P (passenger version) had 12 seats, and was put into service by **Aeroflot** in increasing numbers, first a few here and a few there; then a dozen or so allocated to different areas where the superb field performances — and `field' was exactly appropriate, as any cow pasture was good enough for the versatile Kolkoznik; and finally hundreds of them deployed all over the Soviet Union.

The Antonov An-2, in many different versions, was built in thousands, not only in Kiev, home of Antonov, but in substantial numbers in China and, from 1960, in Poland, which took over complete production, and developed the turbine-engined version, the An-3. It has been exported to dozens of countries, mainly in the Soviet-oriented European east bloc, and countries of Asia, Africa, and South America. Total production perhaps has exceeded 20,000 (5,450 at Kiev, the remainder mostly by Pezetel, at Mielec, Poland, as well as in China), placing it ahead of the DC-3 and its variants as the most produced commercial aircraft of all time.

Other aircraft, the sleek jets, the sturdy turboprop transports, and the remarkable helicopters, have entered service, operated in the front line for periods varying from five to perhaps 25 years, and then been superseded by other types. The Antonov An-2, like the more famous DC-3, has been in operation for about 45 years, and shows no sign of flagging in the tough roles assigned to it. Some of these are more fully described in other sections of this book (pages 73 and 83). The age of the biplane is not yet over.

Supreme Accolade

In 1991, Aeroflot was estimated to be operating about 2,500 Antonov An-2s, in every one of its 32 regional sub-divisions, especially those in the northern tundra and the taiga of Siberia and the far eastern areas. For millions of mainly Russian citizens, the An-2 has been their only form of public transport, providing the channels for communications, education, and health services, apart from its other duties in forestry and agriculture. In the annals of air transport history, if ever a commercial aircraft deserved the supreme accolade, it is the unlikely but nevertheless worthy Antonov An-2.

An An-2 (SSSR-92968) loading freight at Nikolayevsk-na-Amure in 1990. (photo: R.E.G. Davies)

ANTONOV AN-2 VARIANTS

Date	Variants	Application	Description
1947	SKh-1	Prototypes	First flew 31 Aug 1947
1948	An-2T	Transport	Initial version, Transportny
	An-2SKh	Agriculture	Crop-dusting (see also An-2M, below)
	An-2ZA	Meteorological	First known as An-6
1949	An-2TP	Aeroflot	Standard scheduled service version, 12 seats
	An-2P	Aeroflot	Passarzhirski: 14 lightweight seats
	An-2S	Ambulance	Capacity for 6 stretchers
	An-2TD	Parachute	Capacity for 12 trainee parachutists
	An-2V	Floatplane	Also known as An-4. Twin floats
	An-2L	Water-Bomber	Used for fire fighting
1955	An-2F	Military	Fedya, also known as An-2NRK/An-2K
1961	An-2PP	Forest Patrol	Floatplane. Water scooped up, carried, and sprayed from floats
1964	An-2M	Agricultural	Modified version of An-2S
1965	An-2R	Utility	WSK-PZL-Mielec version
1982	An-3	Transport	Turboprop version

An An-2 fitted with skis, pictured at Nikolayevsk-na-Amure in 1990. The normal Aeroflot blue paint scheme is replaced by a red one, for better visibility in snow and ice conditions. (R.E.G. Davies)

An-2V floatplane versions of the Antonov maid-of-all-work.

Antonov An-2

12 SEATS ■ 190km/h (117mph)

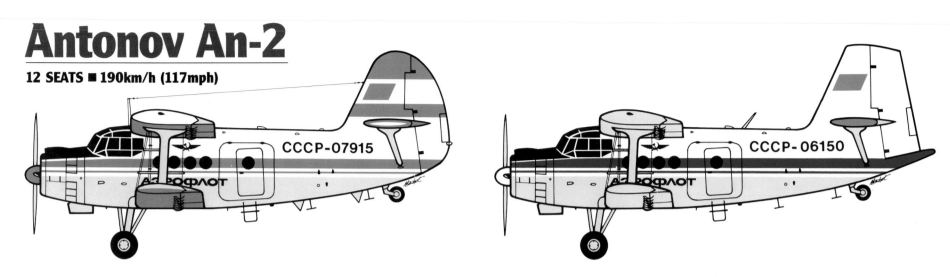

CCCP-07915

CCCP-06150

Shvetsov ASh-621R (1 x 1,000hp) ■ MTOW 5,500kg (12,125lb) ■ Normal Range 845km (520mi)

This picture encapsulates the role of the Antonov An-2 in providing the rural bus service to hundreds, perhaps thousands of small communities, such as this one in northern Kamchatka. (photo: Boris Vdovienko)

AN-2 REGISTRATION NUMBER BLOCKS

(all prefixed SSSR-)
01xxx-09xxx
13xxx
15xxx-17xxx
19xxx
23xxx
25xxx-26xxx
28xxx-33xxx
35xxx
40xxx-49xxx
50xxx
52xxx
54xxx-58xxx
62xxx
65xxx
68xxx
70xxx-72xxx
74xxx
79xxx
81xxx-82xxx
84xxx-85xxx
87xxx-88xxx
91xxx-94xxx
96xxx-98xxx

Aeroflot currently has some 2,500 An-2s in service.

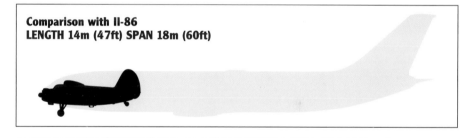

Comparison with Il-86
LENGTH 14m (47ft) SPAN 18m (60ft)

Unexplained Incident

The versatility of the An-2 'Annushka' became legendary. But on one occasion, it met its match. The story goes that, at a small community far from direct authority, a pilot had to stop over at a weekend, having arrived with the mail and other contents on the Friday. The local populace, fishermen all, persuaded him to make an unscheduled flight to a local river which was reputed to be gushing fish. Fourteen good men and true piled on to the 12-seat aircraft, together with complete fishing gear, and enough provisions to last a week.

The augmented load was too much for even such a willing horse as the An-2. It managed to get off the ground, but only just. The pilot, realizing that he was not going to make it, switched off the engine, to avoid a fire, if it crash-landed. And crash-land it did, ignominiously, distributing pieces of aircraft around the field. The assembled company fled.

Came the dawn the next day, and the local constabulary investigated the tangled remains. Strangely, nobody in the whole community had the slightest knowledge of the incident, and the official report, in essence, decided that this was an unsolved mystery. Some dastardly vandals from foreign parts, perhaps.

The World's First Sustained Jet Service

Surprise, Surprise

Under Stalin's rule, aviation progress seemed always to be heavily censored. In air transport, by the 1950s, when western aircraft manufacturers were making great strides in turboprop and jet airliner development, the Soviet airline's flagship was still, at the beginning of 1955, the twin-engined Ilyushin Il-14, whose equivalent American counterpart, the Convair-Liner, was faster and more efficient.

When, therefore, on 22 March 1956, the prototype **Tupolev Tu-104** (SSSR-L5400) made a special flight to London, it caught the aviation world completely by surprise, and the authorities at London's Heathrow Airport had problems keeping the journalists under control. While the Tu-104 was clearly based on the Tu-16 (Tu-88) twin-jet bomber, the conversion was certainly not a make-shift job.

A Place in History

The Tupolev Tu-104 entered service on the Moscow — Omsk — Irkutsk route on 15 September 1956. The seven-hour journey time superseded the 17hr 50min of the Ilyushin Il-12s and Il-14s that it replaced, a remarkable improvement, cutting the time by almost two-thirds. At first, the seating capacity was only 50, but this was later increased. By western standards, the interiors appeared rather old-fashioned, with anti-macassars on the seat headrests; but interestingly, today, all

Tupolev Tu-104 SSSR-L5415 prepares for the world's first sustained jet airline service, Moscow-Irkutsk, on 13 September 1956. (photo: Boris Vdovienko)

the best airliners regard these as a necessary amenity.

Andrei Tupolev's airliner quickly extended jet service throughout the Soviet Union (see map below) and was the standard-bearer of a new range of commercial aircraft that pulled the Soviet Union and Aeroflot up from the technological cellar to the upper floors of achievement, placing both country and airline on a par with the West. Its true place in history is illustrated in the accompanying table.

Oops!

All aircraft have teething troubles, and some have more than their share of introductory snags. On one occasion, at Vnukovo Airport, Moscow, in 1961, a Tu-104 was taking off when, right at the intersection with a taxiway, another aircraft, in tow by a ground service vehicle, moved leisurely across its path. Not yet at take-off speed, the pilot nevertheless hauled back on the stick and, miraculously, the Tu-104 'hopped' over the obstruction, carried on and took off. The pilot received the Soviet equivalent of a gold watch.

THE WORLD'S FIRST TEN JET AIRLINES

Airline	Date	Aircraft	Seats	Route	Remarks
1. B.O.A.C	2 May 52	De Havilland Comet 1	36	London-Johannesburg	
2. U.T.A.	19 Feb 53	De Havilland Comet 1	40	Paris-Dakar-Casablanca	All services terminated after two crashes in 1954
3. Air France	26 Aug 53	De Havilland Comet 1A	44	Paris-Beirut	
4. South African Airways	4 Oct 53	De Havilland Comet 1A (B.O.A.C. lease)	36	Johannesburg-London	
5. Aeroflot	15 Sep 56	Tupolev Tu-104	50	Moscow-Omsk-Irkutsk,	First sustained jet services
6. C.S.A.	9 Dec 57	Tupolev Tu-104A	70	Prague-Moscow	Second sustained jet
(B.O.A.C.)	4 Oct 58	Comet 4	72	London-New York	First trans-Atlantic jet
7. Pan Am	26 Oct 58	Boeing 707-100	160	New York-Paris	First 'Big Jet'
8. National Airlines	10 Dec 58	Boeing 707-100 (Pan Am lease)	160	New York-Miami	First U.S. domestic jet
9. American Airlines	25 Jan 59	Boeing 707-100	160	Los Angeles-New York	First U.S. domestic jet (own aircraft)
10. T.W.A.	20 Mar 59	Boeing 707-100	160	San Francisco-New York	

TU-104 REGISTRATION BLOCKS (ALL PREFIXED SSSR-)

L5400-L5460	(some Tu-104A)	42399-42450	(Tu-104B)
42313-42398	(most Tu-104A)	42451-42456	(Tu-104A)
		42457-42512	(Tu-104B)

Some aircraft in the L54xx block are believed to have been re-registered in the 423xx series. Not all registrations within blocks have been confirmed.

Tupolev Tu-104 routes 1956-62

London 16 May 59
Amsterdam 2 June 58
Copenhagen 7 Dec. 57
Leningrad 15 Apr. 59
Sverdlovsk 21 May 59
Moscow
Omsk 15 Sep. 56
Novosibirsk
Irkutsk 15 Sep. 56
Petropavlovsk 24 Oct. 57
Jan. 57 Khabarovsk
Vladivostok 21 May 59
Bruss.
Prague 12 Oct. 56
Paris 1 Aug. 58
Kiev July 59
Budapest
Tirana 5 Dec. 58
Tiflis
Tashkent 14 Aug. 58
Alma Ata
Peking Dec. 56
Pyong-yang 3 Mar. 59
Cairo 5 Dec. 58
Delhi 14 Aug 58
To Rangoon and Jakarta 31 Jan 62

Dates of first Tu-104 services shown in red

The last Tu-104 retired in 1981

SCALE
Miles 500 1000 1500
800 1600 2400
Kilometers

REGD

Tupolev Tu-104

50 SEATS ■ 770km/h (480mph)

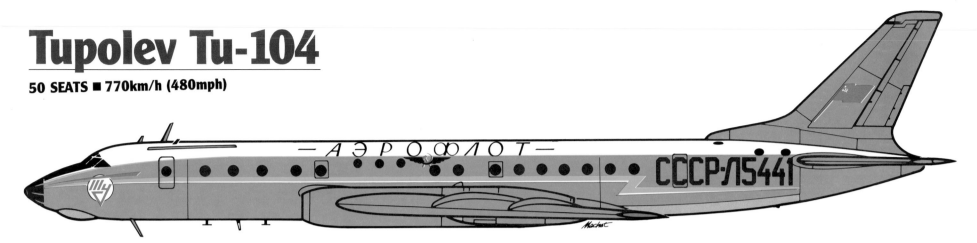

Mikulin AM-3M (2 x 8,700kg st, 14,890lb st) ■ MTOW 76,000kg (167,500lb) ■ Normal Range 2,650km (1,650mi)

The Break-Out

Six months after the Ilyushin Il-14 had entered service with Aeroflot on 30 November 1954, a silver lining appeared behind the dampening clouds of modest piston-engined performance. On 17 June 1955, the **Tupolev Tu-104** jet airliner made its first flight. A conversion from a bomber design, it was nevertheless commercially acceptable. Unusually for the Soviet manufacturing industry, normally conservative in its approach to launching new airliners, the Tu-104 took the world by storm (see opposite page) and soon entered service with Aeroflot on 15 September 1956.

Not before time. Ominously, the British had gone back to the drawing boards and were producing a new line of Comets, which had previously done their own world-storming in 1952, but had met with tragedy two years later. More ominously, the Boeing Company of Seattle, U.S.A., had, on 15 July 1954, demonstrated the Model 367-80 as a prototype for a future airliner, the 707, which was to conquer all before it. Curiously, the famous Boeing `Big Jet' was also developed from a bomber design, the B-47.

Andrei N. Tupolev.
(photo: Boris Vdovienko)

Comparison with Il-86
LENGTH 39m (127ft) SPAN 34m (113ft)

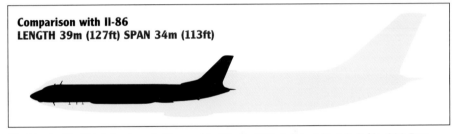

The Tupolev Tu-104 design team (with a model of the Tu-124). Left to right: A.R. Bokin, S.M. Eger, A.N. Tupolev, A.A. Arkhangelski, B.M. Kondozski, and I.F. Nezval. (photo: courtesy Vasily Karpy)

Technical Transformation

Tupolev Sets The Pace

Because of the debut of the Tupolev Tu-104, 1956 was a watershed year. But the years that followed were no less significant in Soviet commercial aviation. The **Ilyushin Il-18 Moskva** four-engined turboprop airliner, reliable workhorse for Aeroflot (and other airlines) in the years to come, made its first flight on 4 July 1957. At about the same time, Tupolev developed the **Tu-104A**, which proceeded to break a number of official load-carrying and speed records for turbojets.

Then, to cap everything, the impressive Tupolev Tu-114 made its first flight on 3 November 1957. But this important news of the world's largest airliner at the time (see pages 52-53) was eclipsed on the following day, when, to the astonishment and admiration of the world (and to the chagrin of complacent defense agencies in Washington, D.C.) the U.S.S.R. carved its name indelibly in the annals of world history by launching, with complete success, the world's first man-made satellite, *Sputnik*.

Consolidation

During 1958, Aeroflot concentrated on expanding its Tu-104 services (see page 44) and opened its first scheduled helicopter routes in the Crimea and on the Black Sea coast. Then, in 1959, the 100-seat **Tupolev Tu-104B** went into service on the busy Moscow-Leningrad route on 15 April. Five days later, the **Ilyushin Il-18B** also started service, on the equally busy vacation route from Moscow to Adler (with helicopter connection to Sochi). Not yet ready for scheduled service, the Tu-114 demonstrated its range with a non-stop flight from

Tu-104 No. 29 operated the first service of the type to Vladivostok on 19 January 1958. This was after a ceremonial circling of the city and being `talked down' by photographer Boris Vdovienko.

Moscow to Khabarovsk on 21 May. The 90-seat **Antonov An-10 Ukraina** turbo-prop, which had first flown on 7 March 1957, went into service on 22 July 1959.

In the Front Pack

Within three years, with Aeroflot carrying the banner, the Soviet Union had rocketed from being an also-ran right into the front pack of runners in the highly-competitive technological race. In almost every category of airliner, the design bureaux of Tupolev, Ilyushin, and Antonov were producing aircraft comparable in performance, if not in economics, with equivalent airliners in the West.

Tupolev Tu-104B SSSR-42431 at Moscow's Vnukovo Airport. (photo: Aeroflot)

The galley of a Tupolev Tu-104B. (photo: Boris Vdovienko)

The passenger cabin of a Tupolev Tu-124.

THE WORLD'S FIRST JET AIRLINERS

First Service Date	Aircraft Type	Dimensions-m(ft)		Speed km/h (mph)	Mixed Class Seating	MTOW kg (lb)	Normal Range km (stm)	First Airline	No. Built
		Length	Span						
Initial version, before development									
2 May 1952	De Havilland Comet 1	28 (93)	35 (115)	800 (500	36[1]	52,300 (115,000)	2,400 (1,500)	B.O.A.C.	21
15 Sep 1956	Tupolev Tu-104	39 (127)	34 (113)	770 (480	50	76,000 (168,000)	2,650 (1,650)	Aeroflot	110[2]
26 Oct 1958	Boeing 707-100	44 (145)	40 (131)	960 (600)	132	112,000 (247,000)	4,800 (3000)	Pan American	141
Representative developed versions									
4 Oct 1958	De Havilland Comet 4	34 (112)	35 (115) 810	(505)	72	73,600 (162,000)	4,800 (3,000)	B.O.A.C.	75
15 Apr 1959	Tupolev Tu-104B	40 (131)	34 (113)	770 (480)	100	76,000 (168,000)	2,650 (1,650)	Aeroflot	100
26 Aug 1959	Boeing 707-300	47 (153)	45 (146)	960 (600)	144	153,000 (336,000)	6,400 (4,000)	Pan American	580

Notes: [1] The Comet 1's seating was all first-class   [2] Includes Tu-104A

Tupolev Tu-124

Momentum Maintained

With a variety of airliners coming off the production lines (see opposite) Aeroflot entered the 1960s with prospects of expansion and upgrading of equipment in all directions. On 3 January 1960, it took over **Polar Aviation (Aviaarktika)** and directed attention to the northern routes, to new settlements on the Arctic Sea, and a new route to the Far East. On 24 April, a **Tupolev Tu-114** non-stop Moscow-Khabarovsk schedule inauguration immeasurably extended the range potential. On 15 December 1961, a specially-equipped **Ilyushin Il-18** became the first airliner to fly to **Antarctica**, and this aircraft opened up new routes to several African countries during the next few years. The **Tupolev Tu-104**, too short in range for use on trans-ocean routes, was nevertheless able to carry Aeroflot's flag to south-east Asia, with a service, opened on 31 January 1962, to Jakarta, via Tashkent, Delhi, and Rangoon. By this time, Aeroflot was carrying more than 20 million passengers each year (with fares at railroad levels) with a total fleet of about 2,000 aircraft.

Junior Jet

The short-haul routes were not neglected. While the U.S.S.R. was a country of vast distances, much of the western parts embraced an area characterized by dozens of cities only an hour's flight from Moscow. Many of these were of medium size, not large enough to justify 100-seat aircraft such as the Tu-104 or the Il-18. To meet this need, the Tupolev design bureau produced a scaled-down version of the Tu-104, the 44- seat, later 56-seat **Tupolev Tu-124**, which entered service on the Moscow — Tallinn (Estonia) route on 2 October 1962. Trailing the French Caravelle by over three years, and a derivative, rather than an original design, it was, however, ahead of British and American short-haul jets by a similar margin.

TU-124 REGISTRATION NUMBER BLOCKS

(all prefixed SSSR-)	
45000-45095	
45135	45173
45146	45199
45158	64452

Not all registrations in the 45xxx block have been confirmed as allocated to Tu-124s.

Tupolev Tu-124 SSSR-45028 shares the ramp at Vilnius, Lithuania, on Christmas Day, 1962, with two Li-2s. (photo: Boris Vdovienko)

Tupolev Tu-124 SSSR-45013 in flight. (photo: Boris Vdovienko)

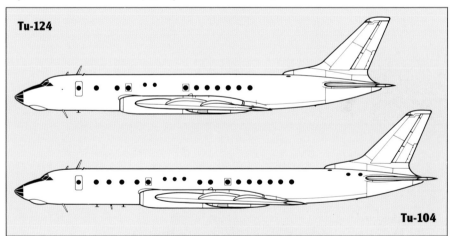

Tu-124

Tu-104

FIRST GENERATION SHORT-HAUL JETS

First Service Date	Aircraft Type	Dimensions-m(ft)		Speed km/h (mph)	Mixed Class Seating	MTOW kg (lb)	Normal Range km (mi)	First Airline	No. Built
		Length	Span						
6 May 1959	Sud SE 210 Caravelle	32 (105)	34 (113)	700 (435)	70	43,600 (95,900)	1,250 (780)	Air France	282
2 Oct 1962	Tupolev Tu-124	31 (100)	26 (84)	770 (480)	50	37,500 (82,700)	1,250 (780)	Aeroflot	112

Turboprop Workhorse

Ilyushin Keeps Pace

Believing that the turbopropeller solution to turbine-engined power was a good alternative to that of the pure jet, the British and American manufacturers had persevered with different designs. Following the successful four-engined (but only medium-range) Vickers Viscount of 1952, the Bristol company in England had developed the Britannia, a long-range four-engined airliner that, but for slow production and unforeseen engine problems, would have gone into service in 1956. Even so, by 1957, the Britannias were making their mark around the world. In the United States, Lockheed produced the Model 188 Electra, a smaller but efficient aircraft designed primarily for U.S. domestic inter-city routes, but not with full transcontinental range. Quickly brought into service early in 1959 — too quickly perhaps — the Electra had severe problems with the engine installation, and came close to being grounded because of fatal accidents soon after entering service.

Coinciding with the announcement of the Sixth Five-Year Plan, which once again emphasized the need to increase air travel on all fronts, **Sergei Ilyushin** and his team produced a Soviet four-engined turboprop which, as the table on the opposite page shows, fell in between the Britannia and the

Two great aircraft designers, Andrei Tupolev (left) and Sergei Ilyushin (right) photographed informally in 1963. (Vdovienko)

Electra in performance and size. In outward appearance, all three aircraft looked somewhat similar.

Solid Performance

The Ilyushin Il-18 — at first called the **Moskva** — went into **Aeroflot** service on 20 April 1959, on the Moscow-Adler route, to provide needed extra capacity for Muskovite vacationers seeking the sun. Simultaneously, it started a non-stop route from Moscow to Alma Ata, the fast-growing capital of Kazakhstan. A direct Leningrad-Adler service, begun on 23 May, helped the citizens of Russia's former capital to enjoy

the sun too; and on 20 June, the Il-18 reached Alma Ata by a circuitous route via Baku and Tashkent, the capitals of oil-rich Azerbaijan and Uzbekistan, respectively.

The Polar Mainliner

Reference has already been made to the expansion of Aeroflot's horizons in 1960 by its taking over **Aviaarktika** (page 47), so that it could now study the potential for route expansion on a broad front north of the Trans-Siberian Railway. While Ilyushin had a set-back on 17 August of that year, when an Il-18 crashed near Kiev, another Il-18 made a proving flight on a new trans-Siberian route, by the great circle itinerary (as did also an Antonov An-10) and on 10 January 1961, opened regular service to Magadan, via the Arctic Sea port of Tiksi. Nine months later, another branch brought Anadyr, in remote Chukotka, within only eleven hours journey time of Moscow, eleven time zones away.

The Ilyushin Il-18 quickly established a reputation as a reliable, if not record-breaking airliner. It seemed to be at home in frigid climates of the northlands, and soon it was to experience an even more formidable challenge. For on 15 December 1961, it was selected to make the first flight by a commercial airliner to the Last Continent, Antarctica. For such a journey, extra tankage was provided, but later on, with growing maturity, a long-range version of the turboprop, the **Ilyushin Il-18D**, became almost standard equipment.

This dramatic picture of an Ilyushin Il-18 was taken at Tiksi, on the Arctic coast of northern Siberia, in 1960, during the long polar night, as it was being serviced. (photo: Boris Vdovienko)

Mark Shevelev, the head of Polar Aviation, responsible for the pioneering development by air of vast areas of northern Russia, greets Sergei Ilyushin (right), one of the aircraft designers who made his work possible. (photo: Boris Vdovienko)

Ilyushin Il-18

100 SEATS ■ 625km/h (390mph)

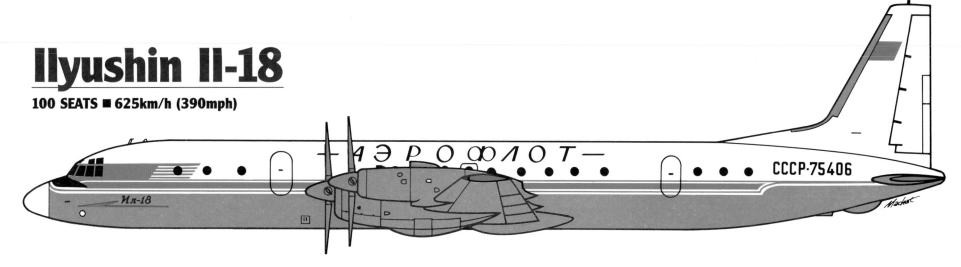

Ivchenko AI-20M (4 x 4, 250ehp) ■ MTOW 61,200kg (135,00lb) ■ Normal Range 4,425km (2,750mi)

THREE LARGE FOUR-ENGINED TURBOPROPS COMPARED

First Service Date	Aircraft Type	Dimensions-m(ft)		Speed km/h (mph)	Mixed Class Seating	MTOW kg (lb)	Normal Range km (mi)	First Airline	No. Built
		Length	Span						
19 Dec 1957[1]	Bristol Britannia 310	38 (124)	43 (142)	620 (385)	110 (185,000)	84,090 (3,750)	6,000	B.O.A.C.	85[3]
12 Jan 1959	Lockheed 188 Electra	32 (105)	30 (99)	650 (405)	85 (116,000)	52,700 (2,500)	4,000	Eastern Airlines	170
20 Apr 1959	Ilyushin Il-18	36 (118)	37 (123)	640 (400)	100 (135,000)	61,200[2] (2,750)	4,425[2]	Aeroflot	565

Notes: [1]The medium-range Britannia 102 entered service on 1 Feb 1957. [2]The long-range Ilyushin Il-18D had a MTOW of 64,000kg (141,000lb) and a range of 6,500km (4,000mi). [3]All Britannias including 100 Series.

Comparison with Il-86
LENGTH 53m (174ft) SPAN 43m (142ft)

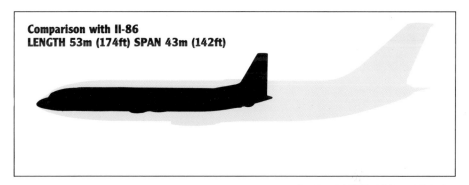

Sergei Ilyushin.

Il-18s still serve in a variety of roles today. This modified aircraft (SSSR-75449) surveys the extent of the polar ice pack from its Moscow-Sheremetyevo base. (photo: Patrick Vinot-Préfontaine)

IL-18 REGISTRATION BLOCKS

(all prefixed SSSR-)	
L5811	prototype
L5818-L5821	
04330	Polar division
04350	Polar division
04770	Polar division
33569	
74250-74255	
74256-74270	Il-18D
74288-74299	
75400-75480	Il-18D
75481-75499	
75500-75580	Il-18V
75581	Il-18D prototype
75582-75595	Il-18V
75597-75598	Il-18D
75601-75714	
75715-75903	Il-18V

(Not all registrations within blocks confirmed)

A Mainliner from Kiev

The Antonov An-8

Oleg Antonov's post-war **Antonov An-2**, whose versatility as a small maid-of-all-work for feeder and bush operations gave it a longevity which keeps it in production even today (pages 42-43), was the harbinger of greater things to come. For in 1956, the Soviet industry sprang another of its surprises and put on display a new military aircraft that had first flown a year earlier.

Though little known, and rarely seen outside its native land, the twin-engined **Antonov An-8** deserves recognition as one of the design trend-setters in aircraft construction development history. Its main purpose was to carry troops, military vehicles, and equipment into small unprepared fields for front-line support, and as such, design aspects were directed without compromise to this objective. The An-8's wing was on top of the fuselage and the landing gear housed in fuselage fairings so that loading through its wide rear ramp/door did not require special ground equipment. The high tail permitted the rear-loading ramp plenty of space for ancillary loading ground equipment. The twin tandem main wheels, four on each side, distributed the load to aid the rough field performance requirements. Antonov perfected the design for specialized freighter aircraft (pages 68-69).

The Ukraina

While the An-8 was strictly a military aircraft (although it appeared in Aeroflot markings), a larger variant, the four-engined, pressurized **Antonov An-10**, at first called the **Ukraina**, started to come off the production line in 1959. The general aerodynamic lines were cleaned up, the outer sections of the wing were anhedral — a pronounced feature of later developments of the breed — and behold, a new 90-seat airliner was ready for **Aeroflot**.

An-10A SSSR-11219 displays the definitive configuration with two vertical fins and no endplate tailplane fins. (Courtesy John Stroud)

The military Antonov An-8, progenitor of subsequent all-purpose commercial aircraft with the same basic design criteria. Although Aeroflot never operated An-8s, aircraft appeared with the airline's titles. (photo: Paul Duffy)

An-10 SSSR-11158 in original configuration with single vertical fin and endplate fins on the tailplane. (Courtesy John Stroud)

Consolidation of Domestic Routes

As noted on the page opposite, the developed **Antonov 10A**, the most successful of the basic type, was quickly brought into service, on 10 February 1960, on the routes from Moscow and Leningrad to the south. Production of modern aircraft was now in full swing at the Antonov, Ilyushin, and Tupolev factories and assembly plants scattered throughout the U.S.S.R., and Aeroflot seemed to have come of age at last. The fleet strength at this time was reported to be 1,900 aircraft, of which about 120 were Tupolev Tu-104s, 60 Ilyushin Il-18s, 30 Antonov An-10s. A Tu-104 flew to Toronto for an aviation Expo on 6 September 1959, and an An-10 flew to the U.S.A. on 24 December. The Il-18 began service to London, and in April 1960 started non-stop flights to Cairo. The Moscow-Leningrad intercity service was upgraded to a frequency of 15 daily flight on 1 June 1960, and Aeroflot was now carrying more than 20 million passengers a year.

Aeroflot to the Arctic

Coinciding with this widespread traffic upsurge, Aeroflot expanded its route network. On 3 February 1960, all the operations of **Polar Aviation** (see pages 26-27) were transferred to the state airline. An-10s were deployed to the northern wastelands, cargo flights starting on 5 April 1960. Then in August, an An-10 had the honor of pioneering the great circle route from Moscow to Khabarovsk, via Syktyvkar, Noril'sk), and Yakutsk. By June 1961, it had become the standard aircraft for the polar air routes, replacing the Lisunov Li-2 and the Ilyushin Il-14.

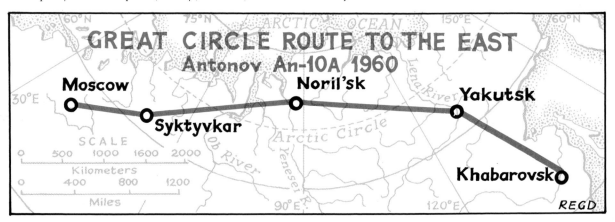

Antonov An-10A

100 SEATS ■ 680km/h (423mph)

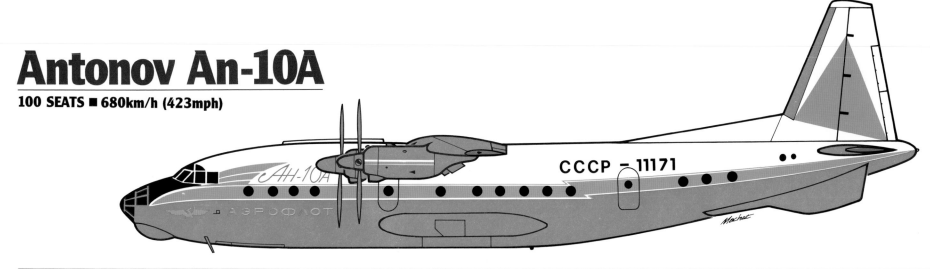

CCCP - 11171

Ivchenko AI-20K (4 x 4,000ehp) ■ MTOW 55,200kg (121,500lb) ■ Normal Range 1,200km (745mi)

The Antonov An-10

The commercial version of the An-8, the **Antonov An-10**, piloted by Ya. I. Vernikov and V. P. Vazin, made its first flight on 7 March 1957 from Kiev, less than two years after the initiation of the basic design. Following Soviet custom, the aircraft underwent thorough testing and proving before it was allowed to venture into commercial service, and even then, during summer 1959, the first An-10s were freighters, which quickly established a good reputation in the northern frontiers of the Soviet Union along the fringes of the Arctic Ocean, not only for Aeroflot, but also for **Polar Aviation**, which had not yet been assimilated by the national airline.

The 90-seat passenger version of the An-10 went into service on the Moscow-Simferopol route on 22 July 1959, adding much-needed capacity to the popular holiday vacation movement between the Russian capital and the sunny south of the Crimea.

The Antonov An-10A

The Design Bureau must have realized that it had a winner, for it quickly moved on to stretch the fuselage by 2m (6.4ft), so as to add two more seat rows and to provide seating for 100 passengers. The resultant **An-10A's** seating capacity was thus the same as the Ilyushin Il-18's. Because it was not designed for long-range operations, it was not normally deployed on international routes, as was the Il-18; but it was used extensively throughout the Aeroflot domestic system, especially in the Ukraine, the land of its birth.

Comparison with Il-86
LENGTH 34m (112ft) SPAN 38m (125ft)

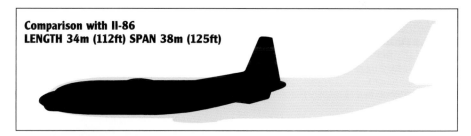

THE FIRST ANTONOV AIRLINER FAMILY

First Service Date	Aircraft Type	Dimensions-m(ft)		Speed km/h (mph)	Mixed Class Seating	MTOW kg (lb)	Normal Range km (mi)	No. Built
		Length	Span					
1956[1]	An-8	31 (101)	37 (121)	600 (373)	Cargo	38,000 (83,770)	2,500 (1,600)	100
22 Jul 1959	An-10	32 (105)	38 (125)	680 (423)	85	54,100 (119,050)	1,200 (745)	300
10 Feb 1960	An-10A	34 (112)	38 (125)	680 (423)	100	55,200 (121,500)	1,200 (745)	300
1965[2]	An-12	37 (121)	38 (125)	670 (416)	Cargo	61,000 (134,000)	3,600 (2,000)	250[3]

Notes: [1]Military transport only. [2]Military type produced simultaneously with An-10, but not fully modified for commercial use until 1965. [3]Civil production only

AN-10 REGISTRATION BLOCKS

(all prefixed SSSR-)	
11134-11144	
11146-11147	
11148	An-10A
11149-11169	
11170-11172	An-10A
11173	
11174-11175	An-10A
11179-11182	
11184-11185	An-10A
11188	
11191-11195	An-10A
11196	
11202-11203	An-10A
11205-11217	
11219-11220	An-10A
11221-11229	

Not all aircraft within blocks have been confirmed.

Oleg Antonov. (*Vasily Karpy*)

51

Long-Range Turboprop

The Bigger The Better

The Soviets have always been in the forefront in building large aircraft. The tradition started in 1913 with Igor Sikorsky's Il'ya Muromets, the world's first transport aircraft, and is maintained today with the giant Antonov load-carriers from Ukraine. Only one five-engined ANT-14 was built in 1931, and only one eight-engined ANT-20 *Maxim Gorky* ever flew, in 1934. Neither went into commercial airline service with Aeroflot. The six-engined ANT-20*bis*, as the PS-124, saw limited service between 1939 and 1941. Twelve years after the end of the Second World War, however, Andrei Tupolev produced the **Tupolev Tu-114**, that, for more than a decade, was the largest airliner in the world.

The Tupolev Tu-114D

The Tupolev Tu-114 was a direct development of the Tu-20 (Tu-95) long-range turboprop bomber, itself a formidable piece of military hardware. Although the commercial Tu-114 made its first flight on 3 November 1957, and was proudly named the **Rossiya** (Russia), thoughts had already been directed to a conversion, for civil use, of the bomber fuselage. This **Tu-116** first flew late in 1956 and was accepted by **Aeroflot** and designated **Tu-114D** (Dalnyi, or long-range). In 1958, the Tu-114D made several proving flights, including a remarkable three-stop circumnavigation of the entire Soviet Union, each stage designed not only to test the long-range capability, but also to 'show the flag' over all the capital cities of the 15 republics of the Union. But the Tu-114D was too narrow, permitting only 30 seats in its pressurized rear fuselage section; only one was built.

The Tupolev Tu-114

The re-designed fuselage, some 4m (12.8ft) in diameter, was wide enough for a comfortable six-abreast layout, and for high density, even eight-abreast was possible, permitting a maximum of 220 seats, though this version is unlikely to have been used extensively. For the first time in any airliner, the galley was located 'downstairs' in the lower deck, and food and drinks were served by electric elevators. Seen in elevation, the Tu-114 was of orthodox outline, but the similarity with other large turbo-prop airliners of its day ended there, except in the size. In particular, the wings were swept back — unusually for a turbo-prop — and had pronounced anhedral. Mounted on the wings were four powerful Kuznetsov engines, which drove eight-bladed contrarotating propellers. In addition to the large four-wheel landing gears units, there was not only a twin-wheel nose gear, but also a small twin tail-wheel installation for protection of the fuselage on take-off. The Tupolev Tu-114 could cruise at 770km/h (480mph) at an altitude of 8,000m (25,500ft) over distances of up to 8,950km (5,560mi).

Tu-114 (SSSR-76470) after take-off. (photo: Boris Vdovienko)

One shortcoming was the height of its landing gear. The main deck was 5m (16ft) off the ground, requiring no little stamina for boarding — the equivalent of climbing two full flights of stairs. Nevertheless, the Tupolev Tu-114 was a truly remarkable airliner. There was none other like it in the world, and it raised a few technical and political eyebrows every time it landed on foreign shores.

Aeroflot Spreads Its Wings

The Soviet national airline took the Tupolev Tu-114 to its heart, realizing that this aircraft could reach the furthestmost points of the U.S.S.R. territory without intermediate stops; and could fly to Havana, capital of its trans-Atlantic communist ally, Cuba. On 21 May 1959, the Tu-114 flew non-stop from Moscow to Khabarovsk, carrying 170 passengers over the 6,800km (4,200mi) distance. The following month, on 28 June, it flew into the U.S.A., making the Moscow to New York flight in 11hr 6min. The Tu-114 did not, however, operate on schedule to the United States, this landmark being set by the Ilyushin Il-62.

Aeroflot began scheduled Tu-114 service to Khabarovsk, on 24 April 1961. The speed of the turboprop enabled it to match the 960km/h (600mph) speed of the Tupolev Tu-104 jet, because the latter's shorter range forced it to make at least two stops. Scheduled service began to Havana on 7 February 1963. Normally carrying only 60 passengers on this very long segment, the Tu-114 was routed via Murmansk, where it made a technical stop, because it was not allowed, for political reasons connected with NATO defense, to overfly Scandinavia. Also, the Murmansk-Havana distance of 8,575km (5,328mi) was shorter by 971km (618mi) than that to Moscow. Later negotiations, completed in 1968, enabled Aeroflot to fly direct to Havana, as S.A.S. and other western airlines were permitted to overfly the Soviet Union.

Tu-144 registrations were SSSR-L5411 (prototype) plus SSSR-76458 through -76461 and 76463 through 76490 (total 33). SSSR-76462 was the Tu-114D

The prototype Tupolev Tu-114 SSSR-L5611 at Idlewild, New York, in July 1959 (photo: Harry Sievers)

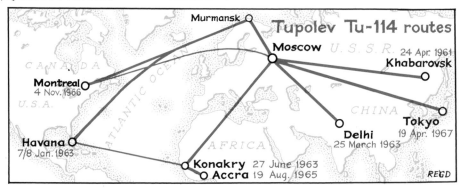

Tupolev Tu-114 routes

Murmansk
4 Nov. 1966 (Montreal)
Moscow — U.S.S.R. 24 Apr. 1961
Khabarovsk
Montreal 4 Nov. 1966
CANADA
U.S.A.
CHINA
Tokyo 19 Apr. 1967
Delhi 25 March 1963
Havana 7/8 Jan. 1963
AFRICA
Konakry 27 June 1963
Accra 19 Aug. 1965
REGD

Tupolev Tu-114

170 SEATS ■ 770km/h (478mph)

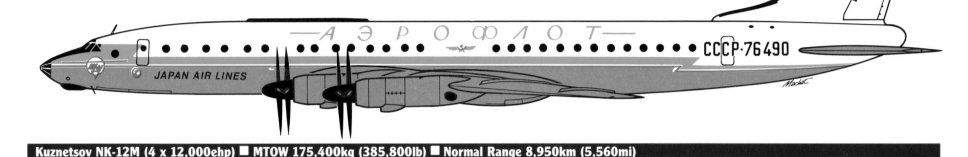

Kuznetsov NK-12M (4 x 12,000ehp) ■ MTOW 175,400kg (385,800lb) ■ Normal Range 8,950km (5,560mi)

New Lands To Conquer

On 25 March 1963, the Tupolev Tu-114 took over the direct Moscow-Delhi service from the Tu-104 and the Il-18; and on 27 June of that year started service to Conakry, Guinea, with flights extending to Havana, as an alternate route to that via Murmansk. On 19 April 1965, the Conakry service was extended to Accra, Ghana. These were friendly countries, economically dependent on the U.S.S.R., but the following year the Tu-114 made its mark in the capitalist world.

On 4 November 1966, scheduled service began to Montreal, Canada, via Murmansk. The journey time from Moscow was 11½ hours for the 7,350km (4,568mi) at an average speed of about 640km/h (400mph). Then, on 19 April 1967, after delicate negotiations and demonstration flights, a joint service opened non-stop from Moscow to Tokyo, a distance of 7,488km (4,563mi). This was a remarkable achievement for both Aeroflot and for the Tupolev Design Bureau. For the first time, a Soviet-built aircraft appeared in the markings of a non-communist airline of world stature: **Japan Air Lines**. The aircraft was flown by the crews of both airlines, and cabin service was provided immaculately by the Japanese carrier.

Comparison with Il-86
LENGTH 54m (178ft) SPAN 51m (168ft)

The Tupolev Tu-114 was deployed on other routes, such as Moscow-Paris and Moscow-Tashkent, but was superseded when the faster and more airport-compatible **Ilyushin Il-62** came into domestic service in 1967, and on intercontinental routes in 1968 (see pages 54-55). Every dog, it is said, has his day; and the Tupolev Tu-114, the largest aircraft in the world until the advent of the Boeing 747, was truly a mastiff. Its only fatal accident was at Moscow, on take-off, on 17 February 1966, and this was on a non-scheduled flight.

LONG-RANGE AIRLINERS OF THE LATE 1950s

First Service Date	Aircraft Type	Dimensions-m(ft)		Speed km/h (mph)	Mixed Class Seating	MTOW kg (lb)	Normal Range km (mi)	First Airline	No. Built
		Length	Span						
19 Dec 1957	Bristol Britannia 310	38 (124)	43 (142)	620 (385)	110	84,090 (185,000)	6,000 (3,750)	B.O.A.C.	85[1]
3 Nov 1957	Tupolev Tu-114	54 (178)	51 (168)	770 (478)[3]	150[3]	175,400 (385,800)	8,950 (5,560)	Aeroflot	33
26 Oct 1958	Boeing 707-100	44 (145)	40 (131)	950 (600)	120	112,700 (248,000)	4,800 (3,000)	Pan American	141
26 Aug 1959	Boeing 707-300	47 (153)	45 (146)	960 (600)	140	152,700 (336,000)	6,450 (4,000)	Pan American	580[2]

Notes: [1]All Britannia Series. [2]All Boeing 707-300 Series. [3]Intercontinental routes. The domestic Moscow-Khabarovsk route was scheduled at 800 km/h (500 mph) with 170 seats

Andrei Tupolev (right), seen here with Eugene Loginov in front of a Tu-124, at Vnukovo Airport in Moscow in 1962. Loginov was the head of all civil aviation affairs in the Soviet Union at that time. (photo: Boris Vdovienko)

Long-Range Jet

Catching Up

The Soviet Union had had the honor of starting the world's first sustained jet airline service, with the **Tupolev Tu-104** in 1956 (see pages 44-45) but this success had to be qualified with the reservation that such service was only short-haul. When the British **Comet 4** and the American **Boeing 707** launched the North Atlantic jet services in 1958, this marked the true beginning of the global jet age, and almost a decade was to pass before Aeroflot was able to start jet service across the ocean.

Casting its eyes around for inspiration, the Soviet industry undoubtedly reviewed it options, and selected the British Vickers VC10, possibly the best of all the narrow-bodied long-range jets of the west; although its specific operating costs — less important in the Soviet-style economic environment — were marginally worse than those of the Boeing 707s and DC-8s. Much has been said about the apparent Soviet custom of copying western designs; but there was no point in trying to re-invent the wheel. Critics on this design aspect often choose to forget the similarity to the Caravelle of the DC-9 and the BAC One-Eleven, or between the Boeing 727 and the Trident. The **Ilyushin Il-62**, the so-called copy of the VC10, had its problems, but far more have been built, and it has lasted far longer in front-line service than has its British look-alike.

The Ilyushin Il-62

It first flew on 3 January 1963, yet the first recorded proving flight, from Moscow to Khabarovsk, was not made until 2 February 1966. This was apparently after problems with the

Kuznetsov turbofan engines and with the line of the leading edge of the swept-back wing had been overcome. The rear-engined configuration was apparently satisfactory. But another year passed before a regular freight service began, on the same route, on 1 March 1967. **Aeroflot** put the Ilyushin Il-62 into full passenger service, from Moscow to Khabarovsk and to Novosibirsk, on 10 March, and a third non-stop direct route was added, to Tashkent, of 14 July.

Service to the United States

The **Tupolev Tu-114** had already established trans-Atlantic service for Aeroflot, both to friendly Cuba and to fairly friendly Canada (see pages 52-53). With the Il-62, the time now seemed appropriate to start a commercial airline connection directly to the U.S.A., even though the Cold War still raged in a political atmosphere that was, if not actively hostile, clouded with deep suspicion on both sides. Moving methodically towards its goal, Aeroflot first introduced the Il-62 on the Montreal route, on a proving flight on 11 July 1967, then in full scheduled service two months later, on 15 September. The journey time of the jet airliner, 9hr 50min, compared favorably with the superseded turboprop's 12hr 5min.

Preparations were made for one of the most important inaugurals of Aeroflot's history. On 15 July 1968, the Ilyushin Il-62 began scheduled service from Moscow to New York, via Shannon, Ireland, and Gander, Newfoundland. As yet, the aircraft could not make the journey in either direction without making these two intermediate stops.

A Taste of the Sixth Freedom

During the introductory period of 1967, the Il-62 had also entered service on some of the more prestigious routes into western Europe, notably to Rome, on 9 October, and to Paris five days later, as well as replacing the Il-18 and the Tu-104 on the route to Delhi. The time-saving on these routes was not significant, but on the longer ones, to the Far East, it was enough to give Aeroflot an unprecedented opportunity to exploit the geography of its sovereign airspace, by providing a swift connection from the European capitals to Japan. Accordingly, on 29 March 1970, the Soviet airline began a through service with Il-62s from Paris to Tokyo, via Moscow, and by flying a great circle route across Siberia. This saved time, by as much as six hours, over the so-called Polar route flown by Air France, northwestwards across Greenland, and stopping at Anchorage, Alaska.

This device of circumventing the familiar Fifth Freedom traffic rights (to serve two countries by an airline foreign to both) by a convenient technical stop at an intermediate domestic point had been tried before, but had been frowned upon by international agencies such as IATA and ICAO. Possibly because the nations of Europe and elsewhere cherished the prospect of over-flying the U.S.S.R. themselves, Aeroflot's Sixth Freedom activity did not cause too much international concern. London received the Aeroflot privilege on 3 June 1970, Copenhagen on 31 March 1971, Rome on 11 June 1973, and Frankfurt on 31 July 1973.

Flight deck of an Ilyushin Il-62. This particular aircraft (SSSR-86670) is now preserved at Monino. (photo: Boris Vdovienko)

Il-62M SSSR-86521 at Khabarovsk in 1991. (photo: Vladimir Kuznetzov)

Ilyushin Il-62M

165 SEATS ■ 900km/h (560mph)

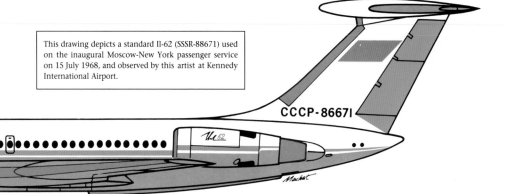

This drawing depicts a standard Il-62 (SSSR-88671) used on the inaugural Moscow-New York passenger service on 15 July 1968, and observed by this artist at Kennedy International Airport.

АЭРОФЛОТ

CCCP-86671

Soloviev D-30KU (4 x 11,000kg st, 24,250lb st) ■ MTOW 165,340kg (363,750lb) ■ Normal Range 7,200km (4,500mi)

THE ILYUSHIN IL-62 AND THE VICKERS VC10 COMPARED

First Flight Date	First Service Date	Aircraft Type	Dimensions-m(ft)		Speed km/h (mph)	Mixed Class Seating	MTOW kg (lb)	Normal Range km (mi)	First Airline	No. Built
			Length	Span						
29 Jun 1962	29 Apr 1964	VC10	48 (159)	45 (146)	930 (580)	140	141,820 (312,000)	6,400 (4,000)	B.O.A.C.	32
7 May 1964	1 Apr 1965	Super VC10	52 (172)	45 (146)	930 (580)	160	152,270 (335,000)	6,700 (4,200)	B.O.A.C.	22
3 Jan 1963	10 Mar 1967	Il-62	53 (174)	43 (142)	900 (560)	166	162,340 (357,000)	6,400 (4,00)	Aeroflot	95
1972	1974	Il-62M[1]	53 (174)	43 (142)	900 (560)	165	165,340 (363,750)	7,200 (4,500)	Aeroflot	174[2]

Notes: [1] *A later variant, the Il-62MK, came into service in about 1978, with higher MTOW, at 167,350kg (368,160lb)*
[2] *Production scheduled to continue until 1995*

The welcome of the arrival of the first Ilyushin Il-62 service to Alma Ata, Kazakhstan, on 17 October 1968, operated by SSSR-86670. (photo: Boris Vdovienko)

Comparison with Il-86
LENGTH 53m (174ft) SPAN 43m (142ft)

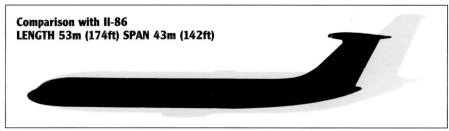

IL-62 REGISTRATION BLOCKS

(all prefixed SSSR-)

86450-86451	
86452-86542	Il-62M
86544	
86552	
86553-86555	Il-62M
86558	Il-62M
86562-86565	Il-62M (ex Interflug)
86605-86614	
86616-86617	
86618-86623	Il-62M
86624-86625	
86649-86657	
86658	Il-62M
86659	
86661-86668	
86670-86709	
86710-86712	Il-62M

Note: known prototypes were 06153/06156/06170/06176 /06300

Mixed Fortunes

The early 1970s were good for the Il-62 . On 4 November 1972, it brought the Soviet airline to a new Latin American ally, Chile, where a Marxist government under Salvador Allende assumed power. The service was routed via Rabat, Havana, and Lima; but was curtailed to the Peruvian capital when the Allende government was overthrown after only two years in office.

Of great political importance was a second route to the United States, inaugurated on 5 April 1974, with direct Ilyushin Il-62 service from capital to capital, Moscow to Washington. Still stopping at Shannon and Gander, a moderate improvement was to omit either one or the other of these technical stops with the introduction of the **Ilyushin Il-62M** (Il-62M-200), a modified variant of the original design with new engines and increased fuel capacity. For in spite of its record of carrying Aeroflot's flag throughout the world's intercontinental route network, there had been many technical problems. On 13 October 1972, on a charter flight, an Il-62 crashed at Sheremetyevo Airport in Moscow, killing 176 people. At the time, this was the greatest airline disaster on record. But the Il-62 survived all vicissitudes and remains today as Aeroflot's front-line airliner for all long-distance routes beyond the non-stop capability of the wide-bodied Ilyushin Il-86 (see page 89).

Short-Haul Turboprop

They Also Served

In the world of aviation, the headlines are always devoted to spectacular events; or to the biggest and the fastest. The smaller airliners, designed to match the traffic demand on hundreds of routes to regions of low population density, have passed almost unnoticed.

When the **Antonov An-24** entered service on 9 October 1962, it attracted little attention. This was the year when the Tupolev Tu-104 began service to southeast Asia, the Ilyushin Il-18 to West Africa, and the first Tupolev Tu-114 flights began from Moscow to Havana. The little 40-seater twin was a poor relation, compared with these.

Yet today, thirty years later, the Antonov An-24 is still to be seen everywhere, throughout the vast expanses of European Russia, Ukraine, and Siberia, dozens of them lined up at every major traffic hub, and serving countless regional route networks with regularity and reliability. While the larger and faster jets grabbed the headlines, the An-24 quietly got on with the job, serving the Soviet people in hundreds of small communities. When, by 1967, **Aeroflot** was able to claim to be the largest airline in the world, this was as much because of the efforts of the diminutive An-24 as it was of the giant Tu-114. And while the Tu-104 and the Tu-114 are now retired — honorably, it should be noted — and the Tu-134 is approaching that status, the Antonov An-24 flies on. Like its partner, the 12-seat An-2, which came out of the same design bureau at Kiev, the now 48-seater will probably still be serving Aeroflot into the next century. It has been exported to several countries in eastern Europe, Africa, and the Middle East.

Antonov An-24 SSSR-46521.

Antonov An-26 cargo aircraft at Nikolayevsk-na-Amur in 1990. (R.E.G. Davies)

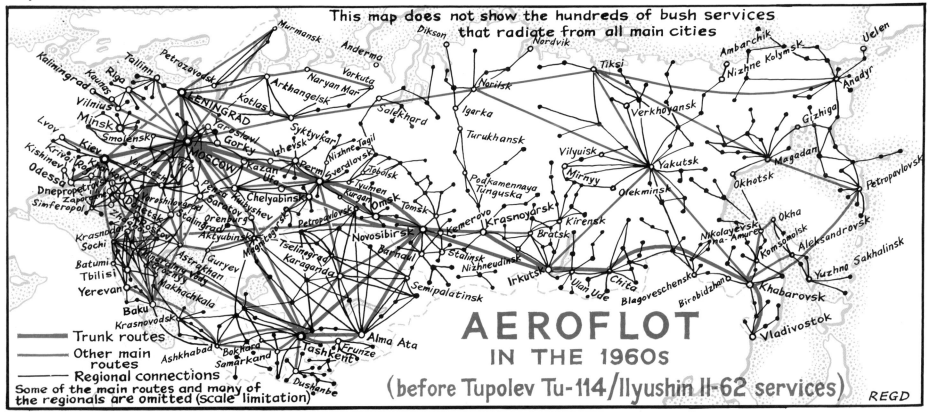

This map does not show the hundreds of bush services that radiate from all main cities

AEROFLOT

IN THE 1960s

(before Tupolev Tu-114/Ilyushin Il-62 services)

REGD

— Trunk routes
— Other main routes
— Regional connections

Some of the main routes and many of the regionals are omitted (scale limitation)

Antonov An-24

48 SEATS ■ 450km/h (280mph)

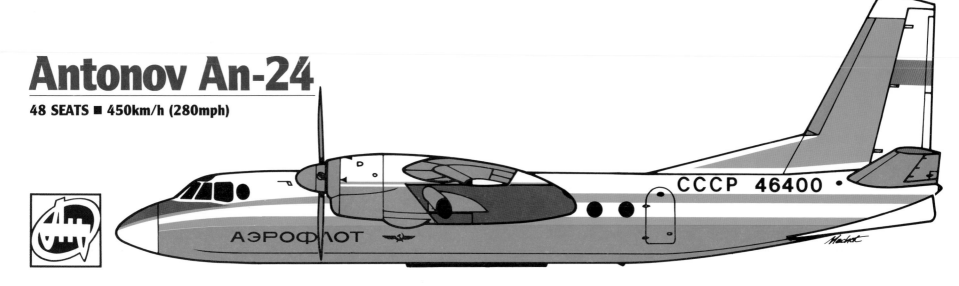

Ivchenko AI-24 (2x 2,100ehp) ■ MTOW 21,000kg (46,300lb) ■ Normal Range 600km (375mi)

THE ANTONOV TWINS

First Flight Date	First Service Date	Aircraft Type	Dimensions-m(ft)		Speed km/h (mph)	Seats	MTOW kg (lb)	Normal Range km (mi)	First Airline	No. Built
			Length	Span						
20 Dec 1959	9 Oct 1962	An-24	24 (79)	29 (95)	450 (280)	48	21,000 (46,300)	600 (375)	Aeroflot	1,100
1968	1969	An-26	24 (79)	29 (95)	440 (273)	Freight	24,000 (52,900)	960 (600)	Aeroflot	1,200+
1976	1977	An-32	24 (79)	29 (95)	470 (292)	Freight	27,000 (59,525)	860 (530)	*	50+

* Operated in Aeroflot colors by various ministries.

THE TWIN-ENGINED TURBOPROPS

First Flight Date	First Service Date	Aircraft Type	Dimensions-m(ft)		Speed km/h (mph)	Seats	MTOW kg (lb)	Normal Range km (mi)	First Airline	No. Built
			Length	Span						
24 Nov 1955	27 Sep 1958	Fokker F.27 (Fairchild F-27)	23 (76)	29 (95)	415 (258)	40	17,900 (39,400)	640 (400)	West Coast Airlines	787[1]
11 Mar 1958	17 May 1961	Handley Page Dart-Herald	23 (76)	29 (95)	430 (270)	44	19,500 (43,000)	640 (400)	Jersey Airlines	48
24 Jun 1960	1 Apr 1961	Avro/Hawker Siddeley/ BAe 748	20 (67)	30 (98)	420 (260)	40	20,225 (44,495)	700 (440)	Skyways	381
20 Dec 1959	9 Oct 1962	Antonov An-24	24 (79)	29 (95)	450 (280)	48	21,000 (46,300)	600 (375)	Aeroflot	1,100
30 Aug 1962	20 Sep 1965	NAMC YS-11	26 (86)	32 (105)	450 (280)	64	25,000 (55,000)	1050 (650)	Japan Domestic	182

Notes: [1] Includes all Dutch-built Friendships and U.S. (Fairchild) F-27s and (Fairchild-Hiller) FH-227 developments. Production continues as Fokker 50.

Comparison with Il-86
LENGTH 24m (79ft) SPAN 29m (95ft)

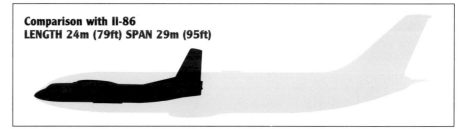

Antonov An-32 SSSR-69306 at Rshevka in July 1991. (Gary Jennings)

Short-Haul Jet

Workhorse for the Seventies

While the giant Tupolev Tu-114 was making headlines during the latter 'Sixties with its trans-Atlantic and long-haul services to east Asia, another aircraft from the same Design Bureau entered the **Aeroflot** scene rather quietly. Produced at Kharkov, the **Tupolev Tu-134** was a much-modified Tu-124, so modified, in fact, with engines moved to external nacelles at the rear and vertical stabilizer at the top of the fin, in the fashion of the BAC One-Eleven and the DC-9, that the original designation Tu-124A, was soon dropped. Rather like the Antonov An-24, its wider deployment on Soviet domestic, rather than international routes, meant that its extensive use was not at first realized by western observers. But, after entering service on 9 September 1967, the new short-haul jet quickly made its mark, as its export potential was greater than that of any previous Soviet airliner.

A Standard Airliner

Because of the sharp political barriers between east and west that prevailed during the Cold War, the Tupolev Tu-134 was not seen much in western Europe; but it quickly became a common sight at all the major airports in eastern Europe. The six countries of the `East Bloc' as well as an airline in communist Jugoslavia, all bought substantial numbers of the rear-engined short-haul jet. This success was aided by, if not inspired by, the Berlin Agreement of 27 October 1965, signed by Poland, Czechoslovakia, Hungary, Romania, Bulgaria, and east Germany, known familiarly as the `Six-Pool'. Though outnumbered by the larger Tupolev Tu-154, the smaller twin-jet was still to be seen here and there throughout the former Soviet Union well into the 1990s, a quarter of a century after its introduction.

The World's Largest Airline

The Tupolev Tu-134's debut coincided with a notable milestone in Aeroflot's history. For several years, annual announcements by the Soviet Ministers for Civil Aviation (for which Aeroflot was effectively its operating division) suggested that its statistical stature was growing to the level of parity with the largest western airlines. By 1967, the Soviet airline was able to claim that it was the largest airline in the world, whether measured in passenger journeys made, or in passenger-miles flown. As Aeroflot's presence in overseas markets was still modest, and often unobtrusive, most of this achievement was drawn from the domestic network. Fares within the

U.S.S.R., measured in terms of percentage of discretionary income, were (and still are, even in the post-Soviet era) extremely low. With state-subsidized cheap housing, public utilities, and public transport, and with cheap food, the average Soviet citizen could take an air trip to visit relatives or to take a vacation without diving too deeply into the family budget, meager though this may have appeared by a straight comparison with western income levels. The first Tu-134 service was from Moscow to Sochi, the Black Sea seaside resort, an event that was possibly symbolic of the momentum for growth that was sustained by Aeroflot during the 1970s.

The Tupolev Tu-134 was the first Soviet jet airliner to find widespread approval in eastern Europe. The one (Tu-134A SSSR-65892) was leased from Aeroflot by MALÉV. (Bob Neumeier)

An early production Tu-134 at Helsinki in 1972. (John Wegg)

Tu-134A-3 SSSR-65717. (Paul Duffy)

Eugene Loginov was the U.S.S.R. Minister of Civil Aviation during the 1960s, and effectively the head of Aeroflot. He was in charge when the Soviet airline became the largest airline in the world, measured by passenger boardings. (Boris Vdovienko)

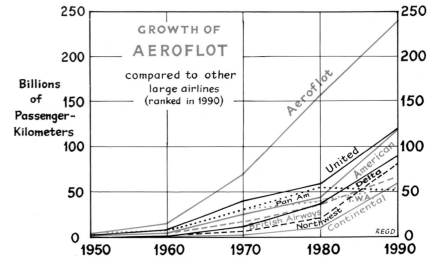

GROWTH OF AEROFLOT compared to other large airlines (ranked in 1990)

Billions of Passenger-Kilometers

Tupolev Tu-134

72 SEATS ■ 800km/h (500mph)

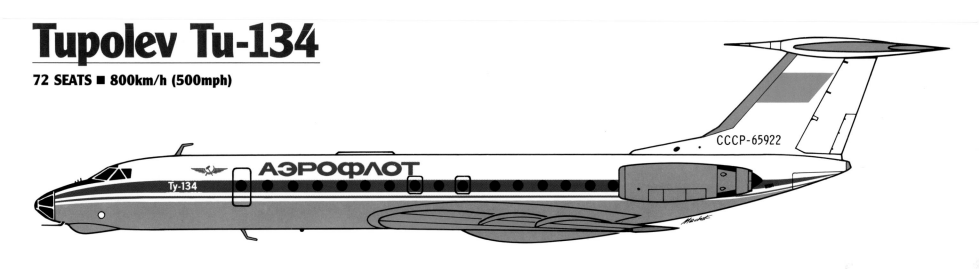

Soloviev D-30 (2 x 6,800kg st, 15,000lb st) ■ MTOW 44,000kg (97,000lb) ■ Normal Range 2,000km (1,250mi)

THE TUPOLEV TU-134s

First Flight Date	First Service Date	Aircraft Type	Dimensions-m(ft)		Speed km/h (mph)	Seats	MTOW kg (lb)	Normal Range km (mi)	First Airline	No. Built
			Length	Span						
29 Jul 1963	12 Sep 1967	Tu-134	34 (115)	29 (95)	800 (500)	72	44,000 (97,000)	2,000 (1,250)	Aeroflot	700+[1]
	1970	Tu-134A	37 (121)	29 (95)	780 (485)	76	47,000 (103,600)	1,890 (1,170)	Aeroflot	

Note:[1] Includes 80/96-seat Tu-134B without navigator's position first flown in 1980.

THE SHORT-HAUL TWIN-JETS COMPARED

First Flight Date	First Service Date	Aircraft Type	Dimensions-m(ft)		Speed km/h (mph)	Typical Seating	MTOW kg (lb)	Normal Range km (mi)	First Airline	No. Built
			Length	Span						
20 Aug 1963	9 Apr 1965	BAC One-Eleven	28 (94)	27 (89)	800 (500)	74	39,450 (87,000)	1,600 (1,000)	British United	244
25 Feb 1965	8 Dec 1965	Douglas DC-9	32 (104)	27 (89)	800 (500)	80	41,600 (91,500)	2,735 (1,700)	Delta	2,030[1]*
29 Jul 1963	9 Sep 1967	Tupolev Tu-134	35 (115)	29 (95)	800 (500)	72	47,600 (104,700)	2,000 (1,250)	Aeroflot	700+
9 Apr 1967	10 Feb 1968	Boeing 737	29 (94)	28 (93)	800 (500)	103	45,700 (100,500)	2,900 (1,800)	Lufthansa	2,350*
9 May 1967	28 Mar 1969	Fokker F.28	27 (90)	23 (77)	700 (420)	65	29,450 (65,000)	1,200 (800)	Braathens	435[2]*

*Notes: [1]Includes subsequent developments (DC-9-80 series and MD-88); [2]Includes subsequent developments (F.28-0100/Fokker 100); * production continues.*

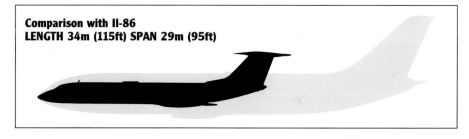

Comparison with Il-86
LENGTH 34m (115ft) SPAN 29m (95ft)

Flexible Seating

The **Tupolev Tu-134's** cabin was narrower than that of its comparable western types, with four-abreast, rather than five- abreast (and, in the case of the Boeing 737, six-abreast) seating. With this aircraft, the air traveling world in general became familiar with the standard Soviet airliner seat. Rather flimsy, and less luxurious than any western type, it was nevertheless efficient in many respects. The seat bottom could be folded upwards — a convenience for storing otherwise bulky baggage; and the seat backs could also be folded forward to a level position, a convenience which has been cheerfully put to good use by Soviet air travelers.

The Tupolev Tu-134 was designed to be able to use what are sometimes referred to as unprepared strips, with gravel or grass surfaces. Whether using these or asphalt or concrete runways, the aircraft's take-off distance was long and its landing speed high, tending to draw the comment that this was more like the performance of a military airplane. Such commentary was also directed towards the `bomb-aimer's window' in the lower part of the fuselage nose, in which the navigator took his position during flight, with the two pilots separated by the `oven-door' access. This position for the navigator is the best possible for a wide, almost 360º panoramic view; and in the Soviet Union during the 1970s, the navigator had a special responsibility for guiding his crew across the limitless and featureless taiga and tundra, with few navigational aids.

The Mini-Liners

The Smallest Jetliner

The Soviet industry had, by the late 1960s, acquired a reputation — deserved, no doubt, in some cases — of copying western aircraft designs. But one aircraft owed nothing to western influence. The **Yakovlev Yak-40** was a small jet, seating up to 32 passengers, for use on feeder routes which did not generate enough traffic to justify even the 40-48-seat Antonov An-24.

The distinguishing feature of the Yak-40 was its tri-jet engine configuration, with two in fuselage-mounted pods, and one fared into the vertical stabilizer, all at the rear, like the engines in the Trident, the Boeing 727, or the Tupolev Tu-154, but on a much smaller scale. The normal entrance was by a ventral stair. **A.S. Yakovlev**, who had produced the Yak-9 and Yak-3 fighter aircraft that did such an outstanding job in the Great Patriotic War, thus made his debut in the commercial arena with a unique formula. Not only that, but in so doing, and allowing for certain shortcomings such as a shortage of baggage space (only one overhead rack, as a rule, on the right side; and no under-floor hold), Yakovlev produced a small jet airliner for successful inter-city use; and this accomplishment has not been matched in the West.

The Yak-40 made its first flight on 21 October 1966 and entered service with **Aeroflot** on 30 September 1968. More than 1,010 were built at the Saratov production line and 130 were exported to 17 countries.

A.S. Yakovlev

Yakovlev produced a mini-airliner that has no equivalent in the west. (courtesy: Von Hardesty)

The Smallest Turboprop

Not long after the introduction of what may be described as the world's first mini-airliner, another small aircraft, designed for a similar air transport role, appeared on the scene. This was the 15-seat **Let L410** (later produced as a 19-seater), sometimes known as the Turbolet, and was produced by the **Let Narodni Podnik (Let National Corporation)** in Czechoslovakia. The pre-war Czech aircraft industry had been obliterated by the Nazi occupation, but it pulled itself together again after the War, and by the late 1960s, was ready with innovative designs. The small turboprop seemed to be just right for **Aeroflot** as a replacement for the aging Antonov An-2.In the event, it did not completely replace, but was a worthy complement to the `Annuchik' in its versatility in using grass or gravel strips.

Like the Yak-40, the L410's baggage hold is at the back, but access is through a hydraulically actuated door in the left rear fuselage. Unlike the small tri-jet, however, there are no overhead baggage racks in the three-abreast configuration. A total of 902 of the Czech mini-airliners were exported to the Soviet Union.

Line-up of more than 20 Yak-40s at Krasnoyarsk in 1992.

Let L410 SSSR-67544 at Khabarovsk.

Yakovlev Yak-40 at Nikolayevsk-na-Amure in March 1990.

Cabin of a Yak-40 in 24-seat layout. In this version, baggage racks are open and on one side only. (Photos: R.E.G. Davies)

Yakovlev Yak-40 and Let L410UVP-E

32 SEATS ■ 500km/h (290mph)

19 SEATS ■ 350km/h (220mph)

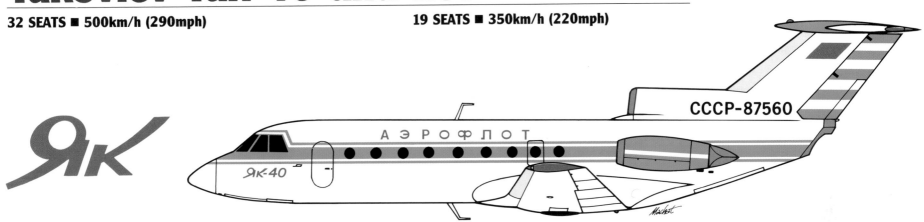

CCCP-87560

Ivchenko AI-25 (3 x1 ,500kg st,3,300lb st) ■ MTOW 13,700kg (30,200lb) ■ Normal Range 600 km (320mi)

THE MINI-AIRLINERS

First Flight Date	First Service Date	Aircraft Type	Dimensions-m(ft)		Speed km/h (mph)	Seats	MTOW kg (lb)	Normal Range km (mi)	No. Built
			Length	Span					
21 Oct 1966	30 Sep 1968	Yakovlev Yak-40	20 (67)	25 (82)	500 (290)	32	16,200 (35,710)	600 (320)	1,010
16 Apr 1969	late 1971	Let L410	14 (47)	20 (65)	350 (220)	19	6,400 (14,100)	530 (330)	1,272

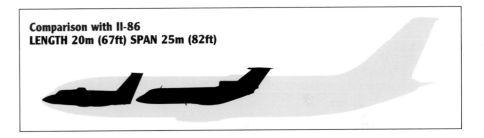

Comparison with Il-86
LENGTH 20m (67ft) SPAN 25m (82ft)

Motorlet M601E (2 x 1,750shp) ■ MTOW 6,400kg (14,110lb) ■ Normal Range 530km (330mi)

CCCP-67544

Standard Trijet

Tortoise and Hare

The **Tupolev Tu-154** and the supersonic Tupolev Tu-144 both got out of the starting gate at about the same time. The trijet made its first flight on 3 October 1968, and the Soviet SST followed only three months later, on the last day of the year (see pages 64-65). The slower aircraft went into service with **Aeroflot** on 9 February 1972, on the route from Moscow to the health resort Mineralnye Vody. But the event was almost unnoticed while the world of aviation underwent the hypnosis of supersonic aspirations.

Workhorse

Like all new civil airliners, the Tu-154 had its problems in the early years. But Tupolev and Aeroflot pressed on with what was designed to be — to quote John Stroud — ``an aircraft with the range of the Il-18, the speed of the Tu-104, and the take-off and landing performance of the An-10.'' Of these, only the Tu-104 was emulated in this specification, but the targets were substantially met. And, as the map on this page illustrates, the sometimes overworked equine metaphor can be for-

given in its application to the aircraft that produced, by the 1990s, about half of the passenger-kilometers of the entire Aeroflot fleet, or perhaps alone as much as the total output of any one of the three leading airlines of the United States.

As Ilyushin had already found (page 55), the Kuznetsov NK-8 turbofan was a thirsty one and fuel burn could be greatly improved by replacing it with the Soloviev D-30KU as had been done in the Il-62. The Tupolev design bureau was slow to accept this possibility, and it was not until 1982, ten years after the Tu-154 entered service, that a prototype **Tu-154M** with derated Soloviev D-30KU engines was produced by converting a standard production Tu-154B-2. New engine nacelles were developed from those fitted to the Il-62M, with the same type of clamshell thrust reversers, and several aerodynamic improvements were made. The first two production aircraft from the Kuybyshev factory were delivered to Aeroflot on 27 December 1984, and the type remains in production.

(Right) Flight deck of the Tupolev Tu-154. (Boris Vdovienko)

Tupolev Tu-154M SSSR-85663 taking off from Moscow-Sheremetyevo. (Paul Duffy)

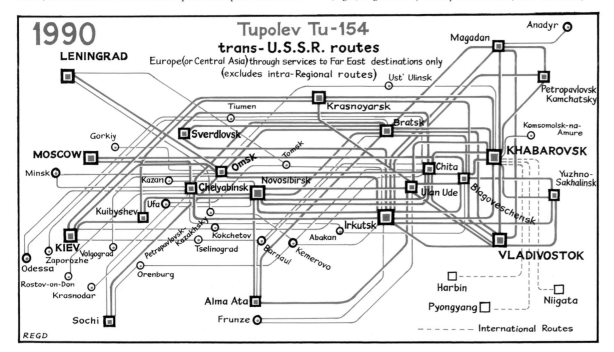

Cabin of the Tu-154. (Boris Vdovienko)

Tupolev Tu-154

164 SEATS ■ 900km/h (580mph)

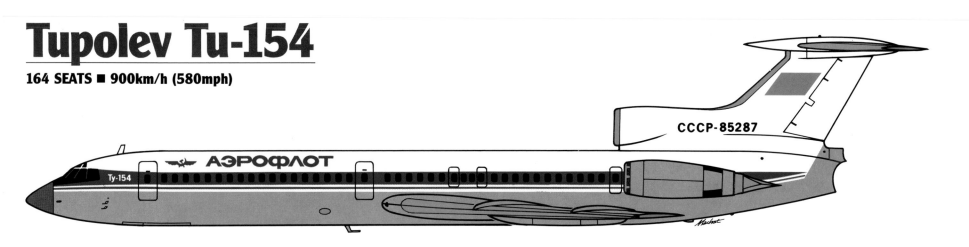

CCCP-85287

Ty-154 АЭРОФЛОТ

Kuznetzov NK-8-2 (3 x 9,500kg,20,950lb) ■ MTOW 90,000kg (198,415lb) ■ Normal Range 2,850km (1,770mi)

Unlikely Champion

For those interested in records, in terms of the greatest, the fastest, or the `mostest', the **Tupolev Tu-154** offers a fascinating exercise in statistics. The work output of the Aeroflot fleet of this type is arguably the most productive of any individual aircraft type by any individual airline in the world, measured by the standard method of calculation, based on the annual aggregate output of passenger miles.

This is not to suggest that the Tu-154 is therefore the most economical aircraft of any of its contemporary rivals. But in producing the aircraft and in operating it under the Soviet conditions of financial and operating criteria, the **Tupolev Design Bureau** and **Aeroflot** have served their country well. For offsetting the higher seat-mile costs is the excellent performance which includes the ability to take off and land at almost any reasonable airport, even those without paved runways.

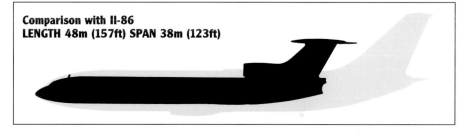

Comparison with Il-86
LENGTH 48m (157ft) SPAN 38m (123ft)

THE TRIJETS COMPARED

First Flight Date	First Service Date	Aircraft Type	Dimensions-m(ft)		Speed km/h (mph)	Seats	MTOW kg (lb)	Normal Range km (mi)	First Airline	No. Built
			Length	Span						
9 Jan 1962	11 Mar 1964	DH Trident	35 (115)	29 (95)	930 (580)	84	59,000 (130,000)	1,900 (1,200)	B.E.A.	117
9 Feb 1963	1 Feb 1964	Boeing 727-100	40 (133)	33 (108)	930 (580)	94	76,650 (169,000)	3,200 (2,000)	Eastern	572
27 Jul 1967	14 Dec 1967	Boeing 727-200	47 (153)	33 (108)	970 (605)	140	94,300 (208,000)	2,400 (1,500)	Northeast	1,260
3 Oct 1968	9 Feb 1972	Tupolev Tu-154	48 (157)	38 (123)	900 (580)	164	90,000 (198,415)	2,850 (1,770)	Aeroflot	1,000*

Notes: *Production continues.

(Right) Passengers disembark from the inaugural Tu-154 flight to Simferopol, main airport for the Crimean resort area. (Boris Vdovienko)

Supersonic Diversion

Sharing The Dream

While many in the West tended to dismiss the **Tupolev Tu-144** supersonic airliner project as being a copy of the Anglo-French Concorde, with allegations of much industrial espionage worthy of James Bond himself, the two aircraft were developed and produced simultaneously. The Tu-144, as many have surmised, was not copied, and did not follow the Concorde. In fact, it was the first to fly, and it was the first to go into service, albeit for air cargo service only, almost as a series of proving flights before the passenger service.

The Tupolev Tu-144, with its extensive use of titanium structure, and its advanced aerodynamics, gained the respect of American engineers and designers as no other Soviet aircraft had ever done before. But the Soviet supersonic program gradually lost momentum as the engineers and operator (Aeroflot) came face to face with reality; and the dream of supersonic airline schedules across the length and breadth of the U.S.S.R. faded.

Success — and Tragedy

The Tupolev Tu-144 had its moment of glory. Test pilot E.V. Yelian made the maiden flight on 31 December 1968, a date said to have been a political imperative, to be ahead of the Concorde, which first flew two months later. Both aircraft attracted world-wide publicity but then came disaster and tragedy. At the Paris Air Show, on 3 June 1973, a Tupolev Tu-144 disintegrated as it pulled out of a steep dive. At first thought to be structural failure, then pilot error, or a combination of both, later analysis has suggested that both pilot and aircraft could have been victims of enforced programming changes that jeopardized a well-disciplined demonstration routine. Whatever the reason, it was a shattering blow to the hopes and aspirations of the Soviet aircraft industry.

Curtailed Service Record

Nevertheless, production continued. At first wholly supportive of the SST, Bugayev, head of **Aeroflot**, faced formidable problems and the operation of the revolutionary aircraft

seemed impracticable. The engines could not be programmed to operate at full efficiency in alternating subsonic and supersonic speeds; high fuel consumption inhibited long range operations; the sonic boom limited the operational scope; and the cabin noise level was unacceptably high.

Ultimately, the entry of the Tupolev Tu-144 into airline service was almost a token gesture. Cargo flights began from Moscow to Alma Ata on 26 December 1975; passenger flights on the same route began on 1 November 1977; and these continued intermittently for only a few months before the service ended on 1 June 1978, after 102 flights. The dream had ended.

(Above) The Tupolev Tu-144, nose drooped, ready to take off on the inaugural passenger service from Moscow to Alma Ata on 1 November 1977. (Boris Vdovienko)

Welcoming crowd for the inaugural Tu-144 flight at Alma Ata. Behind the heads can be seen the local fleet of Antonov An-2s — piston-engined impudence against supersonic dignity.

(Below) Tu-144 SSSR-77109 at Alma Ata, with the Kungey Alatau mountains in the background. (courtesy: Von Hardesty)

TU-144 PRODUCTION

SSSR-68001/68002	Flying prototypes (2 more airframes used for static tests).
SSSR-77101/77115	Production aircraft. One painted as '77144' for display at Paris Air Show 1975. 77102 crashed at Paris, 3 June 1973. One Tu-144D crashed near Ramenskoye on 23 May 1978.

Tupolev Tu-144

60-70 SEATS ■ 2,500km/h (1,500mph)

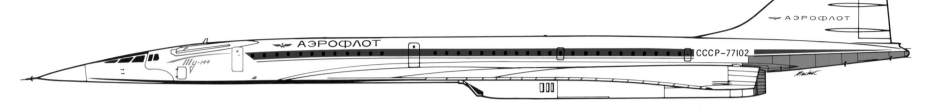

Kuznetzov NK-144 (4 x 20,000kg, 44,000lb) ■ MTOW 180,000kg (397,000lb) ■ Normal Range 3,500km (2,200mi)

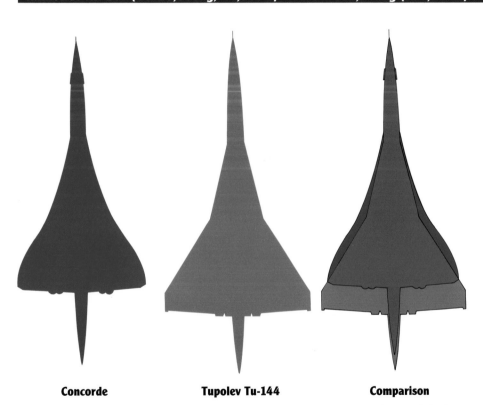

Concorde **Tupolev Tu-144** **Comparison**

Although superficially similar, the Tu-144 wing is simpler and lacks the aerodynamically complex shaping found on Concorde. Some 4m (14ft) longer than Concorde, production Tu-144s have a wing area of 438m^2 (4,715sq ft) compared to Concorde's 358m^2 (3,856sq ft). However, structural differences allow Concorde a lower empty weight and a higher maximum take-off weight.

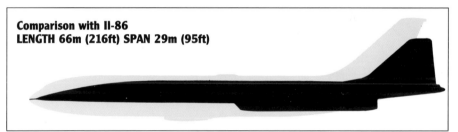

Comparison with Il-86
LENGTH 66m (216ft) SPAN 29m (95ft)

Given a specific set of performance and operational parameters, designers are usually faced with few options. Thus, at first glance, western observers tended to conclude the Tu-144 was a direct copy of the Concorde. Closer scrutiny reveals that the Tu-144 was the result of independent thinking by Andrei Tupolev's design bureau, the most noticeable external differences to Concorde being the wing planform as shown here, and the grouping of the engines underneath the fuselage. An impressive machine by any standard, despite a lengthy gestation in three considerably diverse versions, the Tu-144 was unable to achieve sustained commercial service. However, two Tu-144s are currently in use for ozone research flights from Zhukovskiy, home of the Central Aerohydrodynamics Institute (TsAGI), near Moscow.

THE TUPOLEV TU-144 AND CONCORDE COMPARED

First Flight Date	First Service Date	Aircraft Type	Dimensions-m(ft)		Speed km/h (mph)	Seats	MTOW kg (lb)	Normal Range km (mi)	First Airline	No. Built
			Length	Span						
31 Dec 1968[1]	26 Dec 1975[2] 1 Nov 1977[3]	Tupolev Tu-144	65.7 (216)	28.8 (95)	2,500 (1,500)	60-70	180,000 (397,000)	3,500 (2,200)	Aeroflot	17[4]
2 Mar 1969	21 Jan 1976	BAC-Aéro-spatiale Concorde	61.6 (202)	25.6 (84)	2,150 (1,350)	100	185,000 (408,000)	6,400 (4,000)	British Airways Air France	20[5]

Notes: 1. Prototype - six meters shorter, and generally smaller and lighter than the production version. 2. Freight only. 3. Passenger service; sustained until 1 June 1978 4. Includes two prototypes and three Tu-144D, MTOW 190,000kg (419,000kg), with greater tankage, and which flew after the Tu-144 and made only a few proving flights. 5. Includes two prototypes and two pre-production.

Air Freighter Development

The Antonov An-12

The Antonov Design Bureau at Kiev quickly realized the potential of its basic An-10 design for transporting cargo; in fact the **Antonov An-12** was developed in parallel with the passenger version and production — at Ulan Ude, Voronesh, and Tashkent — is estimated to have exceeded 800 aircraft in the military An-12BP version, in which 100 paratroopers could be carried. It first flew in 1958, went into military service in 1959, and the version for **Aeroflot**, the **Antonov An-12B**, began work in 1965.

The aircraft's main cargo hold was not pressurized; but it had some interesting features. An overhead gantry crane could move loads of up to two tons up and down the cargo hold, and, like all Soviet aircraft, the An-12 was built for rough field performance and for operations in extreme climatic conditions. The Soviet aircraft builders had been specialists in skis since the earliest days of Polar exploration by air (see page 26). Antonov was no exception. Those fitted to the An-12 for Arctic use had a braking device and were heated.

Son of Poseidon

Obviously satisfied with the success of its all-freighter design, **Oleg Antonov's** team went on to build essentially a giant version of the An-12. **The Antonov An-22** was named Antei, or **Antheus**, the giant son of the Greek god of the oceans, Poseidon. All An-22s are operated by the military, although many appeared with Aeroflot titles.

(Left) Oleg Antonov (right) presents a model of the An-12 to Aleksander Afanasiev, of Aviaarktika, at Tiksi, February 1962. (all photographs by Boris Vdovienko)

Unloading an Antonov An-12 at Ice Station 10 in August 1962, an Antonov An-12 (below) loading cargo at Tiksi in 1962, and an Antonov An-12 SSSR-04366 at Ice Station 10 in 1962.

THE FIRST ANTONOV FREIGHTERS

First Flight Date	First Service Date	Aircraft Type	Dimensions-m(ft)		Speed km/h (mph)	Cargo Capacity kg (lb)	MTOW kg (lb)	Normal Range km (mi)	No. Built
			Length	Span					
1958	18 Feb 1965*	Antonov An-12B	33 (109)	38 (125)	580 (360)	20,000 (44,090)	61,000 (134,480)	3,600 (1,940)	300 ?
27 Feb 1965	1968	Antonov An-22	58 (190)	64 (211)	600 (380)	88,000 (194,00)	250,000 (550,000)	5,000 (3,125)	55[1]

Notes: * Earlier service with VVS/VTA (Soviet Air Force/Transport Command) [1] Not including prototypes

Antonov An-22

100 tons ■ 680km/h (410mph)

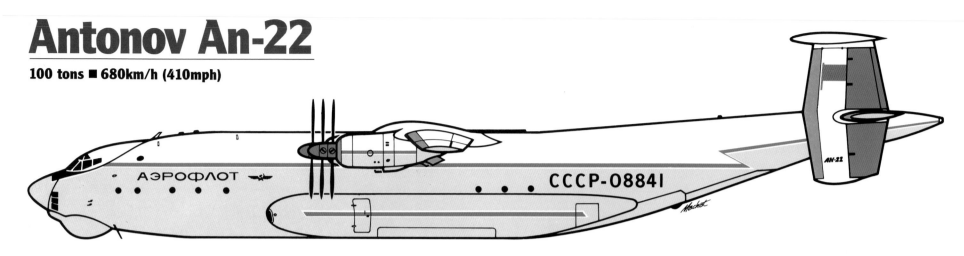

Kuznetzov NK-12MA (4 x 15,000shp) ■ MTOW 250,000kg (551,160lb) ■ Normal Range 5,000km (3,100mi)

The World's Largest

The four-engined **Antonov An-22**, complete with contra-rotating propellers, made it first flight on 27 February 1965, and four months later, on 15 June 1965, it made its international debut at the Paris Air Show, to the wonderment of the world. Habitually critical, sometimes disdainful, of the products of the Soviet aircraft industry, western observers were forced to take notice. Quite simply, this was a huge airplane.

It weighed 250 tons and had a payload of 100 tons. It could carry large battle tanks such as the T-62, the T-72, or the T-80, which did not complain against the customary lack of pressurization in the main cargo hold. The rear-end loading door was a neat device that not only provided the ramp, but could also form an extension to the rails along the sides of the hold, carrying the ten-ton load gantry crane. The floor was of reinforced titanium.

Following time-honored tradition, even this mammoth machine could be used on rough strips. Such extraordinary performance was made possible by an extraordinary landing gear. In each of the two fuselage fairings were three tandem wheels, for a total of twelve, to spread the load; and the tire pressure could be controlled during flight.

An Antonov An-22 prototype (SSSR-56391) on take-off. (Boris Vdovienko)

Comparison with Il-86
LENGTH 58m (190ft)
SPAN 64m (211ft

Antonov An-22 SSSR-09344 offloading relief supplies at Moscow-Sheremetyevo in April 1992. (Malcolm Nason)

Arctic Ice Stations

Back To The Ice Floes

The pioneering work performed by the historic Papanin expedition of 1937 (see pages 28-31) has been well documented and is widely known. Less familiar to western students of Soviet work in the Arctic Ocean is the series of more than thirty Polar Stations (Severny Polius, or North Pole Station) that have been established on the Arctic ice since 1950.

Polar Station SP-2 (Papanin's was recognized as SP-1) was established on 1 April 1950. Commanded by M.M. Somov, Doctor of Geographic Sciences, **Polar Aviation** support was provided by veteran Arctic pilots M.V. Vodopyanov and E.P. Mazuruk, together with V.M. Perov and M.A. Tutlov, using **Lisunov Li-2s** — the trusty DC-3 still indispensable. **SP-2** was more of a reconnaissance survey, but the ice stations that followed were complex stations, with difficult living conditions. With Mazuruk still in command, the Arctic Aviation Service had a tremendous task in maintaining the supply lines to the drifting ice floes. For E.G. Petrov's **SP-4**, helicopters were used for the first time.

During the mid-1950s, the program gained momentum. When **SP-5** began its drift in 1955, a regular aviation link with the mainland was flown by a small fleet of specially equipped aircraft that included **Ilyushin Il-14s** and the ubiquitous **Antonov An-2s**. In addition to servicing the station, the aircraft also carried scientists on missions deep into the Arctic Ocean Ice deserts. On 21-23 March 1958, V.K. Kokkinski made a remarkable visit to Polar Station SP-6, flying an **Ilyushin Il-18** four-engined turboprop, no less, from Moscow via Irkutsk, Petropavlovsk-Kamchatksky, and Tiksi. But the main workhorse of the Arctic supply route was the Ilyushin Il-14, which transported thousands of tons of cargo and scientists, notably to **SP-9**, located at some points of their drift 1,600km (1,000mi) from the mainland.

Aeroflot Takes Over

Polar Aviation was transferred to **Aeroflot** on 3 January 1960, but for the Polar aviators, it was `business as usual'. In summer 1962, the **Antonov An-12** and **Mil Mi-4**, as well as the ubiquitous An-2, supported the **Sever-62** (North-62) expedition. This was followed by the high-latitude **Sever-65**, in which more than 5,000 landings were made on the Arctic ice fields transporting more than 2,000 tons of cargo.

In 1968, in a truly heroic sortie, Arctic helicopter pilots rescued a crew from the **Ineyi**, a hydrographic vessel in distress in the East Siberian Sea, where it had encountered a hurricane. The helicopters battled giant waves and 100km/h (65mph) winds over thousands of miles of ocean, at night, to save the crew.

And so the work went on, with Il-14s, An-12s, and **Mil Mi-2s**, supporting `North 69' (**SP-16**, **17**, **18**), and delivering and setting up 70 automatic weather stations on the drifting floes. In 1971, under the direction of **Mark Shevelev** (who had been Dr Otto Schmidt's aviation man in the pioneer years of the Northern Sea Route Administration) the Arctic Aviation Service of Aeroflot was subdivided into three groups, the North European, based at Arkhangelsk; the Yamal-Tyumen; and the Tamyr-Krasnoyarsk. In 1975, the high-latitude **Sever-75** was supported by the Aeroflot Noril'sk station while in 1976/77, **Kamov Ka-15** helicopter crews based on the atomic-powered icebreakers **Lenin** and **Arktika** participated in an expedition to Yamal.

On 17 August 1977, the *Arktika* reached the North Pole, supported by Arctic pilots, who reached the ship in nine hours flying and spent two hours in reconnaissance. In June of the following year, when Captain Myshevsky completed the sea passage from Arkhangelsk to Magadan, via the Arctic Ocean, he was guided through the treacherous and ever-changing ice packs and floes from four aviation bases at Tiksi, Murmansk, Igarka, and Kalimo-Idigarsk, flying **Antonov An-24s** and **An-26s**, Ilyushin Il-14s, and Mil Mi-2s. They carried 360 tons of supplies and equipment, and made 710 landings on the ice. For Polar Station **SP-23** alone, 100 tons of cargo, as well as the complete expedition itself, were transported. In March 1980, work continued with **SP-32**, and the **Ilyushin Il-76** began work in the Arctic, followed later by the **Antonov An-72**.

(Below) Ilyushin Il-14D at Ice Station 9.
(Right) Inspecting the engine of a ski-equipped Lisunov Li-2, during a series of ferry flights to Ice Station 10, 1,000km (600mi) north of the Siberian Arctic coast, in 1962. (Photos: Boris Vdovienko)

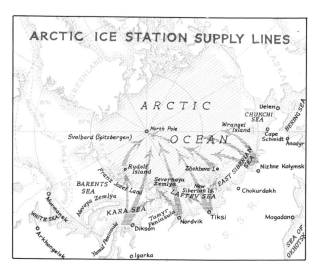

Ice Floe Air Service

(Top) Aerial support for Ice Station 10: Kamov Ka-15 on the left, Lisunov Li-2 — the `old faithful' on the right.

(Top) The ice-breaker Lenin at Ice Station 10, with a Kamov Ka-15 in attendance. (**All photos : Boris Vdovienko**)

(Center) Members of the scientific team of Ice Station 10, measuring the ice thickness — typically many meters — with their ski-equipped Lisunov Li-2 flying laboratory.

(Above) Ski-equipped Lisunov Li-2 alights on the strip at Ice Station 10, April 1962.

(Top) Ilyushin Il-14D at Ice Station 11 in 1962.

(Center) The ski landing gear of a Lisunov Li-2 at Ice Station 10. The station was managed by Comrade Kamarov, and was unofficially called Kamarovka — a satirical reference also to the Russian for mosquito, kamar, where even that insect fears to fly.

(Below) Determined not to be left out of the act, an Antonov An-2 (SSSR- 04351), far away from its more familiar cornfields of the Black Earth of Central Russia and the Ukraine, plays its part on the White Ice of Ice Station 10, April 1962.

(Below) Ilyushin Il-14D at Ice Station 10 in April 1962. This picture well illustrates the airfield conditions on the Arctic ice — and the improvised unloading ramp.

Antarctica

Preparations

By the time the Soviet Union had established its fifth scientific station on the Arctic ice floes in 1955, it was ready to join nations at the other end of the world, in Antarctica, the Last Continent. The first expedition was mounted on 30 November of that year, commanded by the Director of Geographic Sciences, M.M. Somova, 133 years after a Russian sea captain, P.G. von Bellingshausen, had been the first to set eyes on the Antarctic mainland. With Somova was an aviation detachment, under the command of E.E. Cherevechnova, who made the initial flights from the base that was to become **Mirnyy**, and who had the first taste of the harsh conditions of operating from the huge icy land mass.

During the next two years, two more bases were established, with P.P. Moskalenko and B.C. Ossipov in charge of aviation. In 1958-1959, the airmen encountered temperatures of -70ºC but managed to deliver much-needed supplies from Mirnyy to the new scientific station **Novolazarevskaya**, a distance of 3,600km (2,240mi). In December 1958, an aircrew commanded by V.M. Petrov, from Novolazarevskaya, was able to rescue the crew and passengers of a Belgian aircraft that had made an emergency landing, well out of reach by land from the Belgian Roi Baudouin base about 500km (300mi) away.

Historic Flights

In 1961, an important milestone was reached in Soviet Antarctic exploration. Headed by the veteran of the Polar Aviation Directorate, M.E. Shevelev, two large turboprop aircraft flew from Moscow to Mirnyy. An **Ilyushin Il-18** (A.S. Polyakov) and an **Antonov An-12** (B.S. Osipov) left Moscow on 15 December and arrived on Christmas Day, returning on 25 January to arrive triumphantly from a 52,800km (32,800mi) round trip on 2 February 1962. The two aircraft were able to deliver supplies and instruments. The An-12 showed its prowess on skis, while the Il-18 made a round trip to McMurdo Sound to help save an Australian mechanic who had become ill.

Encouraged by the success of these flights, two more Ilyushin Il-18s made the long trip to the Antarctic in 1963, carrying members of the 9th Soviet Expedition. Flights were also made inland to the **Vostok** station, established on the top of Dome Charlie, the gigantic icecap of East Antarctica, where the record low temperature of -89ºC was recorded on 21 July 1983. Vostok is 3,488 meters (11,440ft) above sea level, and the ice thickness is 200m (650ft) more than that. It is

1,420km (880mi) from the main Mirnyy base on the coast, and can claim to have a runway that is as thick as it is long. By 1975, the Soviet Union had six permanent scientific stations and some other temporary satellites in Antarctica.

In 1973, the diesel-electric boat *Ob*, bringing the winter shift to Antartica, was lost. The *Nabarin*, supported by Mil Mi-2 and Mi-8 helicopters and Antonov An-2s (they are everywhere!) rescued 57 men and 6 tons of precious cargo for the Molodezhnaya and Mirnyy stations.

Communication between the four main ones, Mirnyy, **Molodezhnaya**, Novolazarevskaya, and Vostok, was maintained by a small fleet of aircraft that included five helicopters — **Mil Mi-4s** in the early years, then half a dozen of

Crew of the Ilyushin Il-18, before taking off for the Antarctic in 1963.

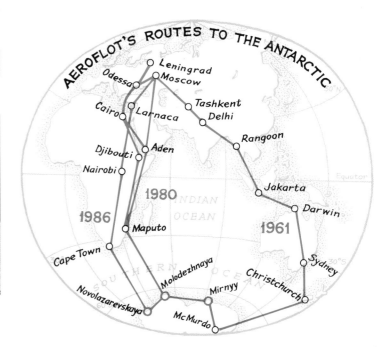

the larger **Mil Mi-6s** and **Mi-8s**, with up to ten **Ilyushin Il-14Ms**, even a couple of **Antonov An-2s**, based at Molodezhnaya and Mirnyy. These aircraft also provided links to the bases of other nationalities, U.S., British, French, and Australian, in an area where the formalities of international bureaucracy could be dispensed with, politics and their encumbrances having been cast aside by the Antarctic Treaty.

New Route

In 1980, a new route was forged to Antarctica. Previously (see map) the Soviet aircraft had flown the same path as the American and Australian flights, from Christchurch, New Zealand (which boasts the only ticket counter with Antarctica on the destination board); but this had entailed a long flight through Asia. Now, with a special version of the Ilyushin Il-18, the Il-18D, under the command of B.D. Grubly, Moscow was connected by a shorter route, through Africa (see map) made possible by the ability of the Il-18D to cover the longer distance from Maputo to Molodezhnaya — 5,000km (3,100mi) with no en route alternates. This flight, in support of the 25th Antarctic Expedition, made the outbound journey from 10-13 February and returned from 19-23 February. The 45,600km (28,380mi) round trip was made in 78hr 54min flying time.

Pilot (right-hand seat) of an Ilyushin Il-18.
(Both photos: Boris Vdovienko)

The Last Continent

A Very Special Flight

In the interests of time and economy of effort in delivering supplies to the Arctic Expeditions, and in spite of the now regular annual trips by the Ilyushin 18Ds, a decision was made in 1985 to use a bigger aircraft, a real heavy lifter, the **Ilyushin 76TD**, weighing in at a 190,000kg (420,000lb) — say 200 tons at take-off — and able to carry a 50-ton payload over a distance of 3,650km (2,270mi). Already equipped as a specialized freighter, with winches and ramps, and able to use the so-called unprepared strips, i.e. without concrete or paving, the one destined to make this historic trip was fitted with 90 seats, plus kitchen, medical, and life-saving equipment. On 18 February 1986, the Il-76TD took off from Moscow, and flew by a slightly different African route direct to Novolazarevskaya, then to Molodezhnaya, and arrived back home on 4 March 1986.

And Very Special Landings

While the thickness of the ice that formed the runway at Novolazerevskaya may not have reached the astonishing proportions of Vostok (see opposite page), it was, however, a slick surface, and all of the 3,000 meters (10,000ft, or almost two miles) length was needed for the Il-76TD to slow to a stop after touching down. Molodezhnaya, on the other hand, presented a different problem. The runway was long enough, again 3,000 meters; and wide enough — 90 meters (300ft). But the composition of the runway was not of ice, it was of snow, 82 meters thick. When properly prepared this was all right for most aircraft; but the Ilyushin Il-76 weighed 200 tons.

The ground staff at Molodezhnaya must have heard the story of the English gardener who, when asked by an American tourist how he had produced such a perfect lawn, suggested that it may have been the result of mowing it once a week, and rolling it once a week . . . for 500 years. Overcoming difficulties of alternate melting during long summer days of unbroken sunshine and crusting of surfaces with repeated freezing, the ground staff rolled and rolled and rolled the runway . . . for a whole year. The Il-76 landed and took off successfully.

(Top right) The Il-76TD on the long, solid ice, runway at Novolazarevskaya, Antartica. The bases's name betrays a wry sense of humor: the 'old' Lazarevskaya is a sunny resort on the Black Sea coast.

(Bottom right) To prepare for the big freighter, the ground crew at the base rolled the packed snow runway for a whole year.

(Left) The Il-76TD unloads at Molodezhnaya, Antarctica. (All: Vasily Karpy)

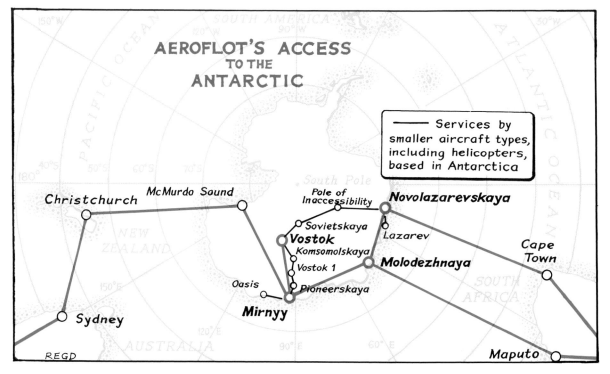

AEROFLOT'S ACCESS TO THE ANTARCTIC

——— Services by smaller aircraft types, including helicopters, based in Antarctica

Siberian School Bus

Antonovs Everywhere

Not content with providing normal air service to small communities, supporting the Arctic ice stations, surveying fishing grounds, agricultural work of all kinds, supporting railroad construction, and laying out oil-pipe lines, the **Antonov An-2** demonstrated its almost unlimited flexibility and versatility by being a school bus in places where wheeled vehicles did not dare to venture.

In this picture-essay — once again the product of **Boris Vdovienko's** peripatetic camera — an **An-2V** is seen at the tiny community of Laboroveya, in the Poluostrov Yamal (the Yamal Peninsula), just north of the Arctic Circle in northwestern Siberia. Invited by the Aeroflot pilot from their `yaranga' houses in the treeless tundra, the children are taken to the secondary school at Katrovozh, near Salekhard, the `big city' of the Yamal Nenets Autonomous District.

On board the An-2, the children appear somewhat apprehensive at the prospect of attending school at Katrovozh, near the 'big city' of Salekhard.

Anna Maximovna, teacher of the secondary school at Katrovozh, near Salekhard, keeps a watchful eye on the children en route to start the term. (All photos: Boris Vdovienko)

(Top) Summer homes in the Yamal Nenets district of northwestern Siberia. The tents, of slender tree trunks and animal skins, are called yaranga. Normal transport, even in the unfrozen brief summer, is by sled, but the ubiquitous Antonov An-2, seen here to the right, has added a new dimension to travel.

(Center) The Antonov An-2 pilot invites a family to send the children to school.

(Bottom) Children from the Yamal Nenets village of Laborovaya are shipped out to the awaiting Antonov An-2V, to attend secondary school.

An-2s in the Far East

Antonovs For Ever

In an area of Siberia much larger than the United States, where no railways exist and roads are a rare luxury, the Antonov An-2 is the only link with civilization itself. Many hundreds of the versatile 12-seater carry people to work, to school, to the shops, and to visit friends and relatives. The maps and the photographs on this page provide a glimpse of such aerial bus services in the **Far East Region** of **Aeroflot**.

The arrival of the Antonov An-2 at Khailinko, in northern Kamchatka. (Boris Vdovienko)

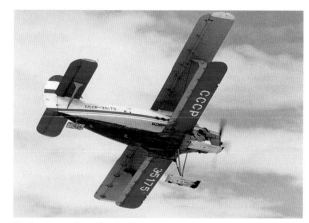

In the areas of Russia where the snows seem to be ever-present, aircraft are painted red for better visibility. (Paul Duffy)

The local bus service at Novo Kurovka, a small village northwest of Khabarovsk. (R.E.G. Davies).

The maintenance shed at Nikolayevesk-na-Amure — inclined to be draughty in winter. (R.E.G. Davies)

Aeroflot's charming terminal buidling at Nikolayevesk-na-Amure. The friendly airport bus awaits. (R.E.G. Davies)

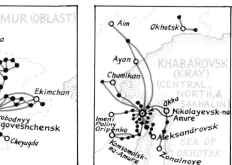
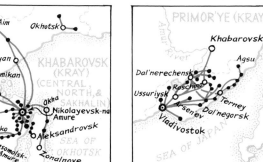

Four of the local Antonov An-2 networks in the Far East Region of the Soviet Union, where 120 towns and villages are served by about the same number of aircraft. More than 60 such networks link about 2,000 communities throughout the vast U.S.S.R., now the CIS.

Airline Helicopters

Reviving a Tradition

Back in the days of Tsarist Russia, **Igor Sikorsky** had made some experiments with helicopter designs, and was to revive his ambitions to pioneer vertical lift flights in America where he had emigrated at the outbreak of Revolution in St Petersburg in 1917. Not until the late 1940s did the helicopter spin its way upwards again in the Soviet Union, and not until the late 1950s was it put into commercial operation.

By this time, commercial helicopters had been innovatively introduced in the United States, to operate subsidized mail and passenger services in Los Angeles, New York, and Chicago; in Belgium, where a vigorous hub was established in Brussels for international services; and sporadically in Great Britain, for mail and passenger services. Interestingly, in the Soviet Union, though for different reasons, the program of helicopter operational development never became a prominent part of the scheduled passenger air network. But Aeroflot helicopters did carve important niches in areas where even the An-2 could not reach adequately.

Mikhail Mil, father of the famous series of Soviet helicopters, surveying the scene in 1959. (Boris Vdovienko)

Routes in the Crimea

Aeroflot's first helicopter services were in the Crimea, where mountainous terrain on the popular coastal vacation area prevented the establishment of airports with long paved runways; and even the laying down of strips for the Antonov An-2. On 15 December 1958, a **Mil Mi-4** eight-seater made the first flight from the main airport at Simferopol to Yalta, one of the delightful destinations of what may be termed the Crimean Riviera. This was followed shortly afterwards by a similar service on the Black Sea coast of the Russian Caucasus, from the main airport at Adler to the big resort of Sochi. Mi-4s from Adler also connected to Gagra, Khosta, Lazarevskaya, and Gelendzhik.

City Services

In 1960, further helicopter routes were opened. On 2 March, Mi-4s began a shuttle service from the Caspian oil capital of Baku to Neftune Kamne, an artificial island offshore and site of highly productive oil wells. On 19 July a helicopter station opened at Khodinka (Frunze) airfield, where Aeroflot's central bus terminal had been established on Leningradski prospekt, only four miles from Red Square. Mil Mi-4s carried passengers to Sheremetyevo Airport, and on 1 November a similar connection was made to Vnukovo and Bykovo Airports. Moscow's fourth airport, Domodedovo, was added the next year.

For about a year, in 1964-65, the Mi-4 was also used for an

*A Mil Mi-2 on Chkalov (formerly Udd) Island, in the Bay of Sakhalin. On the left can be seen the tiny pole, erected as a commemorative monument by **Vadim Romanuk**, helicopter mechanic and founder of the local air museum. This was before the erection of the permanent monument (see page 32). (R.E.G. Davies)*

A Mil Mi-4 (SSSR-35277) alights on the roof of the main Post Office building in the center of Moscow. The helicopter mail service lasted about two years in 1964-65, but was terminated because a certain `important lady' complained about the noise. (Boris Vdovienko)

experimental postal service, carrying mails directly from the roof of the post office in the center of Moscow to the airports. Such services had been tried as early as 1939, in Philadelphia, U.S.A., using a Kellett autogiro, but lasted only about one year. The Aeroflot services were rumored to have been terminated because the wife of a prominent political figure complained of the noise.

A Public Utility

Although helicopter services were tried in Australia, Canada, Italy, Pakistan, and Japan during the 1960s, none was sustained for very long, simply because helicopters are very expensive to operate. In the United States, where the three big city helicopter companies had been augmented by a fourth, at San Francisco, these too went into decline, partly because the Civil Aeronautics Board withdrew subsidy in 1965, and partly because of well-publicized fatal accidents. All were finished by 1979.

In the Soviet Union, on the other hand, where profit-and-loss statements were non-existent, and all air services were provided as a public utility, helicopter services continued to flourish in any region of the far-flung territory where they were needed: delivering mail in the northern tundra to outlying communities of the Arctic, or to inaccessible places in the mountains of Tadjikistan or Kirghizia, or to villages in northern Kamchatka, where even the An-2 was vulnerable. The use of helicopters is dictated by operational necessity, not economic feasibility, judged by western criteria; and they are often to be found in the regional timetables of Aeroflot, deployed interchangeably with other feeder aircraft.

Mil Mi-2

8 SEATS ■ 205km/h (125mph)

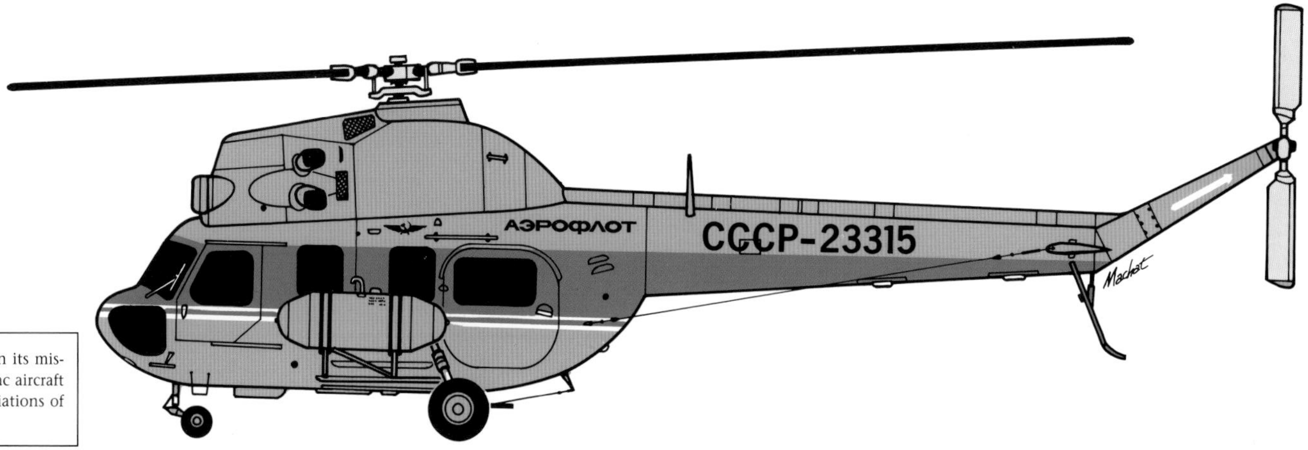

The Mi-2 appeared in a wide variety of color schemes depending on its mission. Agricultural sprayers were generally a gloss olive green; Medevac aircraft were red and white; and passenger versions appeared in several variations of orange and blue finishes, one of which is shown here.

Izotov (2x 400shp) ■ MTOW 3,500kg (7,700lb) ■ Normal Range 240km (148mi) ■ Length 12m(39ft) ■ Rotor Diameter 15m(48ft)

First of the Mils

The **Mil Mi-1**, of orthodox helicopter design, with a single main rotor and anti-torque rotor mounted on a tail boom, was the first Soviet helicopter to go into series production. As the first of the long line, making its first flight in 1948, it went through the teething troubles of all infants, and its early years were almost in the nature of experimental research. Most Mi-1s had three-bladed rotors, and during the development period, the life of both the blades and the rotor head were considerably improved, while the overhaul of the Ivchenko engines went from TBOs of about 150 up to more than 1,000. They were used mainly by the Soviet Air Force, but Aeroflot began to take delivery in May 1954, using them for agriculture, forest patrol, ambulance, and other aerial work, and occasionally for carrying passengers in mountainous areas.

The Mil Mi-4

Carrying only three passengers besides the pilot, the Mil Mi-1's work load was limited. By 1952, in response to a specification, directly from the Kremlin, for a larger machine, Mil produced the **Mi-4** (there was no Mi-3; and the Mi-2, curiously, came later), in competition with Yakovlev's Yak-24 design. It too had early problems, but necessity was the mother of invention. Four-bladed rotors made from a steel tube/wooden rib/plywood-and-fabric combination gave way to all-metal construction, including honeycomb sections. Magnesium corrosion led to replacement by aluminum parts. But when all was done, a good aircraft emerged and, as noted on the opposite page, the Mi-4 had the honor to open the first regularly scheduled helicopter airline service in the Soviet Union, carrying between eight and eleven passengers on each flight.

The Mil Mi-2

Mikhail Mil had already taken advantage of the light weight of turbine engines when he produced the Mil Mi-6, world's largest helicopter at the time, in the autumn of 1957. He then turned his attention to sharpening the performance of the smaller craft. In essence, he used two smaller and lighter turbine engines to make a new version of the Mi-1. By placing the engines above the fuselage, there was room enough for eight passengers. This was almost as much as the larger Mil Mi-4 could carry, so that essentially the **Mil Mi-2** was able to replace both of the older types.

True, the passenger cabin was a little more cramped. The Mi-2's 4.47m (14ft 8in) length was a foot longer than the Mi-4's; but its 1.2m (4ft) width and 1.4m (4ft 7in) height were almost two feet narrower and more than a foot shorter, respectively. But this did not seem to matter, as helicopter journeys are invariably of short duration, and the clientele does not need either to stand up or to move about.

Equally, the Mi-2's range was inferior to that of both predecessors; but this could be improved by supplementary tanks, if necessary. In compensation, the Mi-2's speed was 25 percent more than the Mi-4's and 50 percent more than the Mi-1's.

Rotor-blade technology was impressive. Of bonded construction entirely, the three-bladed main rotor was equipped with leading-edge electro-thermal de-icing, with a 2,000-hour or more life. The anti-torque tail rotor had only two blades. Altogether, the Mil Mi-2 emerged as a thoroughly reliable, modern aircraft of advanced construction, and it took its place in Aeroflot's inventory from 1967 onwards as a standard type which has stood the acid test of time and stringent operational conditions.

THE SMALLER MIL HELICOPTERS

First Flight Date	First Aeroflot Service	Aircraft Type	Dimensions-m(ft)		Speed km/h (mph)	Seats	MTOW kg (lb)	Normal Range km (mi)	No. Built
			Fuselage Length	Rotor Diam.					
Sep 1948	May 1954	Mi-1	12.1 (39.9)	14.5 (47.7)	135 (73)	3	2,500 (5,500)	350 (180)	2,000?
Aug 1952	1954	Mi-4	17.8 (55.1)	21.0 (68.11)	160 (86)	8-11	7,350 (16,200)	520 (320)	3,500+
1961	1967	Mi-2	11.9 (39.2)	14.5 (47.7)	205 (127)	8	3,500 (7,715)	240 (145)	2,800+

THE LARGER MIL HELICOPTERS

First Flight Date	First Aeroflot Service	Aircraft Type	Dimensions-m(ft)		Speed km/h (mph)	Seats	MTOW kg (lb)	Normal Range km (mi)	No. Built
			Fuselage Length	Rotor Diam.					
1961	1967	Mi-8	18.3 (60.1)	21.3 (69.10)	200 (125)	28	12,000 (26,450)	360 (223)	6,000+
1957	1961	Mi-6	33.2 (108.10)	35.0 (114.10)	250 (155)	65	42,500 (93,700)	1,050 (650)	850+
1960	1967	Mi-10	32.9 (107.9)	35.0 (114.10)	180 (112)	28	43,450 (95,790)	400 (250)	60+

"We Built A Railroad"

The Beginning

Throughout the history of the Soviet Union, the extension of the railroad system has always been a constant economic objective, to provide the logistics connection between the sources of wealth, particularly mineral wealth, and especially in the far reaches of the Asian territories. Gradually, branches of line sprouted from the **Trans-Siberian Railway**, often linking it with northerly ports on the great rivers, the Ob, the Yenesei, and the Lena. Of these, the most remote was the Lena, whose source is close to Lake Baikal, but which flows northeast through what was, until recently, largely uncharted territory.

By 1950, a line had reached Bratsk, site of a huge hydro-electric station under construction, and during the next decade, this was extended to Ust' Kut, on the Lena. For the first time, albeit only during the May-October summer season, when the Lena was ice-free, the historic trading center of Yakutsk, surrounded by newly-established satellite mining sites of great wealth, was linked with Moscow by a modern surface transport system.

Birth of the BAM

On 8 July 1974, the Supreme Soviet officially declared the creation of a railroad construction program of great magnitude. The **Baikal-Amur Magistral** (Main Line, or Artery), or the **BAM**, was to parallel the Trans-Siberian Railway over about 3,500km (2,200mi) of its eastern length. This action took place at a time when relations between the Soviet Union and China were cool, and the BAM was widely perceived as a defensive measure against the possible cutting of the Trans-Sib by an attacking force. But the BAM also opened up vast possibilities for improving the access to the riches of Siberian mineral wealth.

Preliminary surveys had started on 30 April 1974, using **Mil Mi-2** and **Mi-8** helicopters. But progress at first was handicapped by the onset of an early winter — in August! Housing for the workers was incomplete, and one of the first tasks for the growing armada of supporting aircraft was to bring 2,500 tons of heating equipment to the first construction sites. The first workers arrived on the Ulkan River on 28 October 1974, and in the following year, in a Soviet equivalent of ``Go West Young Man,'' teams of Komsomol (Young Communist Workers League) headed east in their thousands.

Rail-Air Cooperation

Aviation, including the resources of **Aeroflot**, supported BAM during the entire period of its construction, with main-line connections to cities on the trans-Siberian Railway, and countless sorties by feeder aircraft, fixed wing and rotary wing. Other than the 3,500km (2,175mi) of track, the mainly Komsomol teams built 2,237 bridges, established 60 cities, some of them now large centers, as well as many villages. Hundreds of thousands of passenger flights were made, and supplies for the 22 special construction trains and 37 mechanized columns, and the hundreds of bridging and tunneling units, were carried largely by air, until the BAM line was progressively completed.

The preliminary surveying for the BAM Railroad was carried out largely with the help of helicopters, such as this Mil Mi-4 in the early 1970s. (Both photos: Vladimir Kuznetzov)

This map shows how Aeroflot, from bases strategically situated along the Trans-Siberian Railway, was able to maintain an aerial supply network to the working parties who built the BAM railroad.

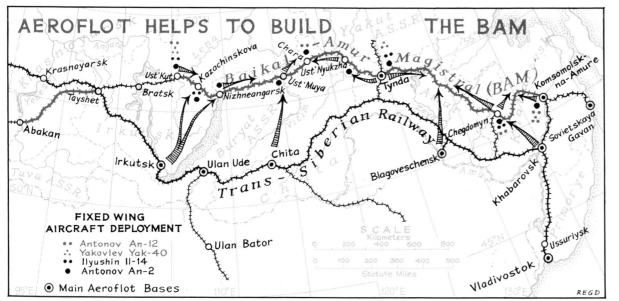

AEROFLOT HELPS TO BUILD THE BAM

Krasnoyarsk
Ust'Kut
Kazochinskova
Chara
Baikal—Amur Magistral (BAM)
Ust'Nyukzha
Bratsk
Ust'Muya
Nizhneangarsk
Tynda
Komsomolsk na-Amure
Tayshet
Abakan
Irkutsk
Ulan Ude
Chita
Chegdomyn
Sovietskaya Gavan
Trans-Siberian Railway
Blagoveschensk
Khabarovsk
Ulan Bator
Ussuriysk
Vladivostok

FIXED WING AIRCRAFT DEPLOYMENT
- Antonov An-12
- Yakovlev Yak-40
- Ilyushin Il-14
- Antonov An-2

◉ Main Aeroflot Bases

SCALE
Kilometers
200 400 600 800
100 200 300 400 500
Statute Miles

REGD

One of the legacies of the fine work done by hundreds of aircraft, including squadrons of helicopters, was the foundation of small cities along the route of the BAM, outgrowths of the first labor encampments that housed the construction teams.

Mil Mi-8

28 SEATS ■ 200km/h (125mph)

The Thoroughbred

Rather as the Mil Design Bureau had developed the Mi-1 into the far superior Mi-2 by conversion to turbine power, so, in 1960, it turned its attention to doing the same with the Mi-4. The **Mil Mi-8** first flew in 1961, and by the following year had been further improved with a five-blade rotor. It could carry 28 passengers — about the same as a DC-3/Li-2 — and for freight use, its rear fuselage was fitted with clam-shell doors.

Such a combination of characteristics made the Mi-8 into a thoroughbred aircraft, reliable and versatile. For example, during the construction of the **BAM Railroad** during a typical year, 1976, seventeen construction organizations together employed helicopters for almost 22,000 flying hours. Almost exactly half of these were with Mil Mi-8s.

Helicopter Capital of the World

The Tyumen region of Russia, with its world's largest deposits of natural gas, and one of the world's largest producers of crude oil, has been remarkable for its extensive use of heavy-lift helicopters for pipe-laying and as flying cranes for building tall towers for electricity transmission lines. Thus, the Mi-8 was quickly found to be an essential maid-of-all-work. The Tyumen sub-division of **Aeroflot** (or **Tyumen Aviatrans**, **T.A.T**. under the new reorganization) lists 450 helicopters in its fleet inventory of 660 aircraft. No less than 360 of the rotorcraft are Mil Mi-8s. Other regions of Aeroflot do not boast such numbers, but more than 1,000 Mi-8s are to be found east of the Urals alone.

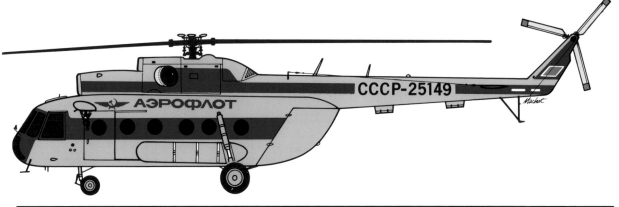

Izotov TV-2-117 (2 x 1,500shp) ■ MTOW 12,000kg (26,450lb) ■ Normal Range 360km (223mi)

A Mil Mi-8 comes in to land at North Pole Station 27, at a latitude of 83°N, in 1980.

A Mil Mi-8 (SSSR-22703) in the harsh tundra terrain near Dikson, in northern Siberia.

Holiday-makers disembark from a Mil Mi-8 at the helicopter pad at Yalta. (Boris Vdovienko)

A Mil Mi-8 on an improvised `pad' of oil pipes on the Yamal Peninsula, in northwest Siberia.

The good ship Inniy, *stuck in the Arctic ice, but with a Mil Mi-8 available to prove that all is not lost. (Photos: Vasily Karpy)*

Kamov Virtuosity

Contra-Rotation

Rather overshadowed by the preponderance of the Mil helicopters in service throughout the Soviet Union, and sometimes forgotten as world-wide interest tended to concentrate on the Mil giants (see pages 80-81), the generally smaller Kamovs deserve attention. Just as Mil perfected the techniques of single main rotor-plus-anti-torque tail rotor combinations, so did **Nikolai Kamov** solve the mechanical complexities of coaxial contrarotating main rotors, thus eliminating the need for any anti-torque device.

Getting under way with his first designs after the end of the Second World War, Kamov's first light helicopters were for the Soviet Army, for observation and reconnaissance. But as time went on, opportunities for civilian use arose.

The Kamov Ka-15, Ka-18, and Ka-25

As with subsequent designs, the first effective Kamov helicopter, the **Ka-15**, first produced in 1952, had two contrarotating rotors, each with three blades. The Ka-15 demonstrated a brisk performance, and it went into service with **Aeroflot** in a variety of working roles: crop-spraying, powerline patrol, gas pipeline patrol, and ambulance work.

The slightly larger **Ka-18** incorporated an improved fuselage structure, which was slightly longer, and with modified twin vertical stabilizers, but had the same rotors as the Ka-15. In the Ka-18, however, the rotor blades could easily be removed individually, and this made the aircraft especially useful for reconnaissance in the Arctic Ocean, where the convenience of storage space on the depot ships was at a premium.

A further stage of adaptability was achieved in the new **Ka-25** which made its first appearance in 1961. This had the novel arrangement by which the individual rotor blades could be folded, under power, so as to be aligned together while not in use; such mechanical ingenuity was a great credit to the Kamov design team. Also, the Ka-25K featured a small cabin underneath the main flight deck. This contained a backward-facing seat, for controlling operations when the helicopter was being used as a flying crane.

The Kamov Ka-26

All aircraft manufacturers have problems with reconciling conflicting requirements from different customers. In Kamov's case, these appear to have been stringent demands for versatility both from the State Scientific Institute and from Aeroflot. The former wanted a helicopter that could out-per-

(Top) A Kamov Ka-32, on fish-spotting patrol, hovers over its depot ship, the Kherluf Bidstrup, in the Sea of Okhotsk.

(Bottom) Reminiscent of the Los Angeles freeways and the control thereof, this Kamov Ka-26 keeps an eye on the traffic in Vladivostok. (Vladimir Kuznetzov)

form the previous Kamovs in such activities as mapping, geological survey, fish-spotting, fire-fighting, and ice reconnaissance; Aeroflot needed one for normal passengers, mail, and freight, as well as for general agricultural use, and gas and oil pipeline patrolling. To quote John Stroud: ``What Kamov produced was a most ingenious multi-purpose helicopter capable of almost any task except feeding itself.''

The **Kamov Ka-26** was larger than the Ka-15 and Ka-18 but smaller than the Ka-25. But it was far more efficient than any previous design. Like the Ka-25, it was twin-engined, but unlike it, the tail unit was supported by twin booms, rather than by an extension of the fuselage. Its unique feature was what can only be described as the come-apartness of the fuselage. The rear half of what would normally be a complete fuselage could be interchanged, according to the requirements: a small cabin for up to seven passengers, a pallet for cargo, or apparatus for crop-spraying, including a large hopper. This could spray dry chemicals as an alternative to liquid spraying throughout extended spray-bars, and the downwash of the rotors served to disperse the powder or granules in a uniform manner.

Later versions of the Ka-26 improved the performance and capability. The **Ka-226**, for example (fitted with Allison engines) could carry a chemical load of almost 1,000kg (compared with the 530kg of the Ka-26) on a 1 1/2-hour mission, with full reserves. Throughout the development of the versatile Kamovs, the accent was always on economy of operations — for even under the Soviet system, considerable accountability was often exercised. To borrow a sporting term, in this respect, the Kamov Ka-26 was the top seed.

THE KAMOV CONTRA-ROTATING FAMILY

First Flight Date	First Aeroflot Service	Aircraft Type	Dimensions-m(ft)		Speed km/h (mph)	Seats	MTOW kg (lb)	Normal Range km (mi)	No. Built
			Fuselage Length	Rotor Diam.					
1952	1955	Ka-15	6.2 (20.5)	10.0 (32.8)	125 (78)	2	1,410 (3,100)	390 (240)	300+
1957	1959	Ka-18	7.0 (23.1)	10.0 (32.8)	115 (72)	4	1,480 (3,260)	165 (102)	200+
1965	1967	Ka-26	7.75 (25.5)	13 (42.8)	110 (70)	6	3,250 (7,165)	400 (250)	600+
1980	1983	Ka-32	11.3 (37.1)	15.9 (52.2)	230 (143)	16	11,000 (24,250)	800 (500)	200+

Sheer Versatility

The pictures and drawings on this page summarize the amazing diversity of the range of helicopters that have been put into use by **Aeroflot**, ranging from the diminutive 20-foot-long **Kamov Ka-18** to the 108-foot-long **Mil Mi-10**. They can carry everything, from band-aids to buses, paramedics to pipelines. They have — unlike their opposite numbers in the West — taken their place alongside the fixed-wing aircraft, wherever they are needed, for carrying people from inaccessible villages, where even the Antonov An-2 dares not land (i.e. cliff faces or swamps), and for hauling large and ungainly cargoes like transmission towers for electric power lines. With these fine aircraft, the helicopter design bureaux of the Soviet Union have secured their place in aeronautical development history.

(Top right) A Kamov Ka-25K (SSSSR-21110). (J.M.G. Gradidge via John Stroud) (Right) A Mil Mi-10 transports an electricity transmission tower. A large percentage of the nationwide high-tension electricity powerline grid of the Soviet Union was constructed with the help of flying cranes. (V. Grebnev) (Top left) The Mil Mi-26T, developed from the Mi-6, with more powerful engines to drive and eight-bladed rotor, is the champion heavy-lifter, able to lift vertically a load of twenty tons. (R.E.G. Davies) (Bottom left) A Kamov Ka-26 (SSSR-19529) on ambulance duty. (V. Grebnev)

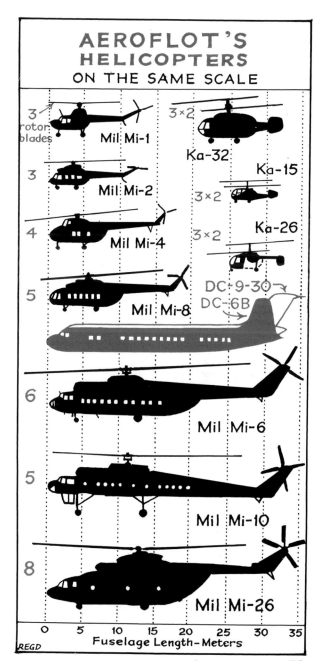

AEROFLOT'S HELICOPTERS
ON THE SAME SCALE

3 rotor blades — Mil Mi-1
3×2 — Ka-32
3 — Mil Mi-2
Ka-15
3×2 —
4 — Mil Mi-4
3×2 — Ka-26
5 — Mil Mi-8
DC-9-30
DC-6B
6 — Mil Mi-6
5 — Mil Mi-10
8 — Mil Mi-26

REGD

0   5   10   15   20   25   30   35
Fuselage Length—Meters

Heavy Lifters

The Mil Mi-6

When, late in 1957, the **Mil Mi-6** made its first flight, the reaction was justifiably one of awe. It was as long as an Ilyushin Il-18 and weighed almost as much. John Stroud, never inclined to use superlatives, described it as ``truly enormous.'' Each of the five rotor blades was 17m (55ft 9in) long, and, as with previous Mils, they had electro-thermal leading edge de-icing. Small, removable wings were fitted to the middle section of the fuselage. Two Soloviev D-25V turbine engines, rated at 5,500shp take-off power, enabled the Mi-6 to carry a load of 12,000kg (26,500lb) — this alone is the all-up weight of a DC-3.

Its rugged floor could accommodate trucks, drilling rigs, tanks, any large or bulky object. Its electric winch could handle a slung load of 9,000kg (almost ten tons) and in a fire-fighting role, it could carry 14,000kg (15 tons) of water. It was used almost exclusively in specialized air-lifting roles, but could carry 75 passengers if necessary. Deliveries began to **Aeroflot** in 1961, and it was first used in Turkmenistan on 10 August of that year. The airline had about 100 of these impressive aircraft by the late 1960s, and about half of these were allocated to the oil and gas fields of West Siberia.

(Above) The two-ton capacity crane inside the Mil Mi-26, for heavy-duty in the oilfields of the Tyumen region.
(Below) A Mil Mi-10 (SSSR-04103), carrying a bus. (Vdovienko)

The Mil Mi-10

A direct development of the Mi-6, the **Mil Mi-10** had the same enormous rotor and transmission, with a re-designed fuselage of about the same length, with long landing gear legs to make room for a platform underneath the fuselage and supported by hydraulic grips attached to the gear legs. If the Mi-6 could carry a small truck, the Mi-10 could carry a bus. To assist the crews in maneuvering at touch-down, the flight deck had closed circuit television monitors. The **Mi-10K** (Korotkonogyi, or Short-Legged) version featured a special cabin under the nose, with rearward-facing controls for coordination with the winching crew. At Tyumen, base airfield for the region containing the world's largest reserves of oil and gas, the demand is matched by the supply of helicopter strength (see page 77) of which the Mil Mi-10s, fitted with both internal and external extra tankage, can carry out missions of up to 5 1/2 hours duration. In the desolate areas of

Heroic Mission

If ever a case was to be made for the advantages of helicopter operations over those of fixed wing aircraft — and many were made in the U.S.S.R. in many diverse industrial activities, in the oilfields, the cotton fields, and the fishing grounds — it was made, under the most tragic circumstances, in 1986. On 26 April of that year, a nuclear reactor at **Chernobyl**, in the northern Ukraine, exploded with devastating effect, spreading a radioactive cloud over the area and for hundreds of miles around.

With a Hind military helicopter, with its gyro-stabilized gunsight, acting as a pathfinder for precise observation of the 1200°C `target', the molten reactor, Mi-6s and Mi-26s plugged the lethal opening laid bare in the concrete structure. After several unsuccessful attempts to solve a problem that had a hundred unknown factors, by dropping graphite, sand/boron, gravel, lead composite, and concrete, the Mi-6s dropped a total of 250 tons of prefabricated 14-ton cubes, containing special filtering/ventilation units to shut off the radiation emission.

Ground staff, clad in lead-lined suits, and teams of helicopter pilots carried out this elaborate plan. The cost was high as everyone involved risked their lives by the deliberate exposure to the dangers of radiation. Many were affected and one, **Anatoly Grishchenko**, died as a result. But the reactor was capped, and the world breathed a sigh of relief.

Most of this brave work was performed by the Soviet Army's helicopters, flown by some of the top test pilots. But **Aeroflot** played its part, supplying some observation Mi-6 and Mi-8 helicopters, and Antonov An-24s for inspection of the radiation-affected area.

taiga and tundra, with little surface communication, and opportunities for airfield construction rare, such vertical lift performance is priceless.

The Mil Mi-26

This development of the Mil Mi-6 also calls for superlatives. The Lotarev D-136 turbine engines develop 11,240shp, so as to drive on eight-bladed rotor (the Mi-6 had five). This enables the **Mil Mi-26** to lift 20,000kg (20 tons). Inside the roomy fuselage — the size of that of a Lockheed C-130 — is a gantry crane able to carry two tons along the available space.

The Kamov Ka-32

While not aspiring to the dimensions of the mighty Mils, Kamov did not allow the grass to grow under its rotor blades. It produced, in the early 1980s, the **Ka-32**, a larger version of the multi-purpose Ka-26, about the same size and of the same capability and performance than the Mil Mi-8, but of the Kamov traditional technology and design, and with the advantage of two decades of developmental experience.

(Top) The supplementary control cabin of the giant Mil Mi-10. Rearward facing, the pilot has direct control of the helicopter, working in unison with the winch controller. (photos: R.E.G. Davies)
(Bottom) This picture of the Kamov Ka-32 (with another hovering behind) illustrates the contrarotating rotorhead mechanism. (V. Grebnev)

Mil Mi-6P

Mi-10K

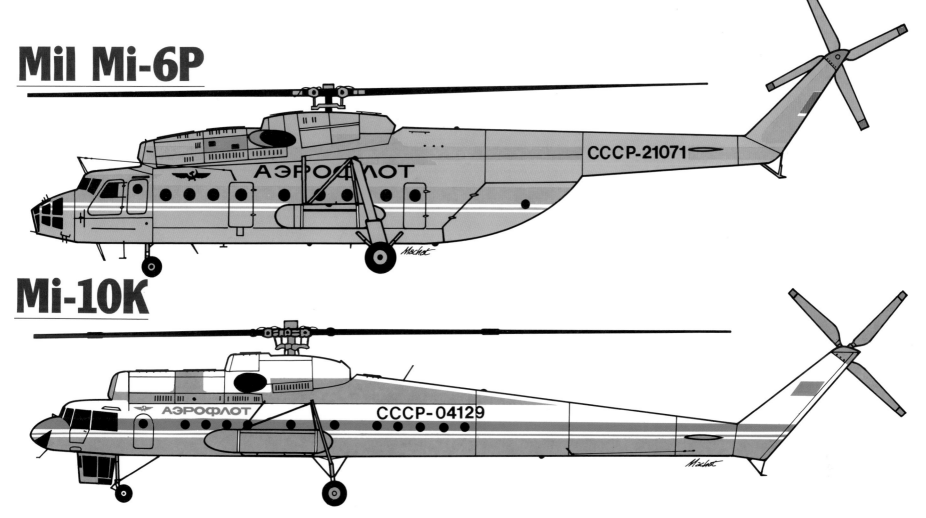

CCCP-21071

АЭРОФЛОТ

CCCP-04129

АЭРОФЛОТ

The dimensions and performance of these two large heli-copters, together with those of the Mil Mi-26, are tabulated on page 75. Their size is dramatically illustrated by comparison with two well-known western fixed-wing aircraft on page 79.

(Right) This picture of the huge rotorhead of the Mil Mi-6, indicates the extent of the engineering of this large helicopter.
(Far right) The enormous Mil V-12 used two sets of Mi-6 engines, gearboxes and lifting rotors, mounted on stub wings. First flown in July 1968, it never entered service although it was extensively demonstrated in Aeroflot titles (photos: Boris Vdovienko)

Seventy Years of Aviation Aid to Agriculture

Making the Case

Certain entomologists realized the possible applications of aircraft as aids to agriculture very early in the history of powered flight; B. Rosinski, as early as 1913; N. Yatsky, in 1919; and N.N. Bogdanov-Katkov, in 1921. Also, in 1921, N.D. Fedotov suggested the use of aircraft for crop-spraying with insecticide. In 1922, a group of pilots presented a paper to the National Colegium of Agriculture of the R.S.F.S.R., and with the help of Professor V. F. Boldyrev, a special commission was formed to study the subject and to carry out experiments. During the summer, 32 experimental flights were made, in which 4.5 hectares were treated per flying hour, and these experiments continued during the next two years.

The techniques were put to the test in 1925. Under P.A. Sviridyenko's direction, aircraft were sent to combat a plague of locusts in the flood plains of the Kuma River, in the northern Caucasus region, and during the next four years, similar operations were carried out in Daghestan, Tadjikistan, Kazakhstan, the Ukraine, and other districts in European Russia; and even as far off as Lake Baikal. A total of 111,000 hectares was treated.

Getting Under Way

In 1930, the wholesale practical application of aviation to agriculture began. An all-Soviet joint-stock company was formed, with a fleet of eleven **Polikarpov U-2** aircraft; and 60,000 hectares were worked during that year. In 1931, the fleet had increased to 65 and the work in corresponding measure. Authority passed, in 1932, to **Vsesoyuznyi Naychno-Issledovatyelskiy Institut Selskokhozyastvennoy I Lecnoy Aviatsiy (NIISKHA)** (the **All-Soviet Scientific Research Institute for Farming and Forestry Aviation**,

which set up branches in Chimkent, Krasnodar, and Leningrad. Finally, in 1934, the responsibility for agriculture aviation passed to the Civil Aviation Fleet **Aeroflot**), and during the next few years activity grew until by 1940, almost a million hectares were covered by agricultural aircraft.

Post-War Expansion

As shown in the table on this page, aircraft were deployed widely after the end of the Second World War for agricultural work. The workload increased from 4 to 50 million hectares in the 15 years from 1951 to 1965. It doubled again during the next 15 years, reaching a peak of 108 million hectares in 1980. Nevertheless, during the next Five-Year Plan, 463 million hectares were covered, or 40 percent of the total agricultural work. Of this, about 40 percent was in Russia, 20 percent in Kazakhstan, 18 percent in the Ukraine, and 15 percent in North Caucasus.

GROWTH OF CROP-DUSTING/SPRAYING (MILLIONS OF HECTARES, 1940-1965)

Type of Work	1940	1951	1955	1960	1965	1980
Insecticide Spraying for Agriculture and forest	0.90	3.00	6.29	13.70	26.84	54
Weed spraying		0.02	0.15	1.50	9.69	20
Fertilization	0.01	0.93	3.10	4.10	16.76	31
Defoliation and desiccation (forestry)		0.22	0.38	0.80	1.75	3
TOTAL	1.91	4.17	9.92	20.10	50.04	108

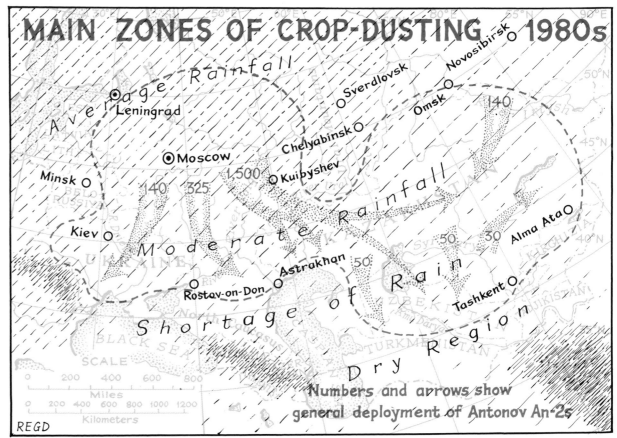

MAIN ZONES OF CROP-DUSTING 1980s

Average Rainfall

Moderate Rainfall

Shortage of Rain

Dry Region

Numbers and arrows show general deployment of Antonov An-2s

SCALE
Miles
Kilometers

REGD

King of the Crop Sprayers

Productivity

During the peak period of chemical spraying, more than 3,000 aircraft are put to use, although the number is declining as ecological concerns have reduced the activity in some areas. Ninety-five percent of the work is performed by the **Antonov An-2**, for which, in this application, the much-used word 'workhorse' is perfectly apt. The remainder, specialized work in small gardens, vineyards, and small fields, is done by helicopters.

The productivity is impressive. In pollination work, for example, the An-2s can cover 400 times as much area as by manual applications; and for crop-spraying, the factors in at least 600- fold.

Double Duty

To fly the crop-sprayers, hour after hour, day after day, is demanding on the pilots, who must exercise strict control and discipline, with no margin for error. The An-2s fly at an altitude of three meters (10ft), and each crew makes between 30 and 50 flights per day, each flight lasting between four and 15 minutes.

Seventy percent of Aeroflot captains start flying in agricultural aviation, working their way up from the grass roots — almost literally. Many an Ilyushin Il-86 or Il-62 captain will look back on his agricultural apprenticeship with a certain affection, which is also directed at the veteran biplane, the **Annachik**, or, as it is sometimes called, by the name that it inherited from the Polikarpov U-2, the **Kukuruzhnik.**

View of a typical landing strip, about 300 meters (1,000 feet) long, in a collective farm district near Novgorod. (R.E.G. Davies)

Antonov An-2, preparing for a day's crop-spraying. (V. Grebnev)

Pilot's-eye view of a field being dusted with fertilizer, from the cockpit of an Antonov An-2. (R.E.G. Davies)

During the summer months, upwards of 2,500 Antonov An-2s are engaged in crop-dusting and -spraying, and other agricultural work throughout Russia and the former Soviet republics. This one is spraying cotton in Tadjikistan. (V. Grebnev)

Ilyushin Il-76

50 TONS ■ 750km/h (470mph)

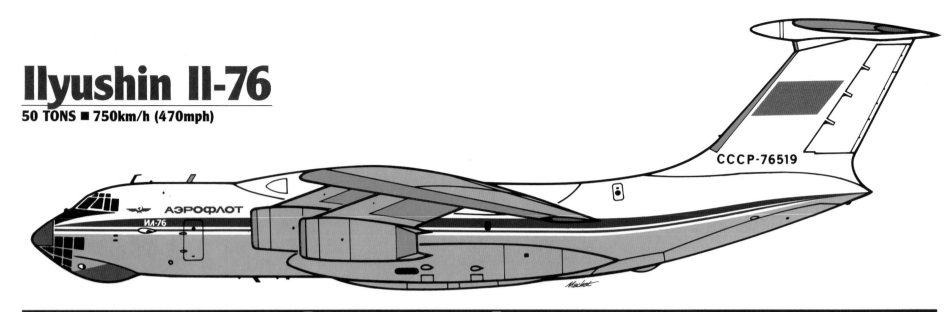

Soloviev D-30KP (4 x 12,000kg st, 26,455lb st) ■ MTOW 170,000kg (375,000lb) ■ Normal Range 3,650km (2,190mi)

The Second Big Freighter

The **Antonov An-22** (see page 67) had captured the aviation world's attention during the mid-1960s, with its impressive size and the ability to carry 80 tons of cargo. When the Ilyushin Il-76 made its maiden flight at Moscow's almost-downtown Khodinka airfield on 25 March 1971, it did not attract quite as much publicity, possibly because it did not beat any records in sheer size. Its all-up weight was about 44 tons less than the big Antonov's, but it was nevertheless just as impressive, and appears to have been more popular with the operators, as far more Il-76s are to be seen the length and breadth of Russia and the former Soviet republics than its larger rival.

The big freighter went into series production for civil use as the Il-76T in 1975, and deliveries began to **Aeroflot** in 1976. Like the Antonov series of heavy lifters, the Il-76 had a pronounced anhedral wing, and — also like the An-22 (and the Lockheed C-141) — it had superb short-field and rough-field performance, thanks to the manner in which the total weight of the aircraft was distributed among the multiple-wheeled landing gear. Sixteen main wheels are mounted in fuselage pods, and are arranged in banks of tandem axles, four abreast on each side. The Il-76 can carry 40 tons, but habitually carries loads of around 20 tons over ranges of about 7,000km (4,000mi), i.e. nonstop from Moscow to Khabarovsk or Yakutsk. It can moreover make this performance to and from airfields with runways about 1,700 meters (one mile) in length.

Universal Popularity

Such versatility makes it almost indispensable for long-range cargo operations, especially as its 24-meter (almost 80ft) -long cargo hold is more than 3m (10ft) high and wide. Every main traffic center of Aeroflot, and especially the big air traffic centers in Siberia, enjoys regular air cargo connections with all corners of the system, from Murmansk to Vladivostok; and it is especially welcomed at Yakutsk, which is not served by rail, and where road and river traffic is burdensome and restricted to a short season. A longer range variant, the Il-76TD, went into production in the early 1980s.

The Ilyushin Il-76's finest hour, however, was almost certainly when it made a flight to Antarctica in 1986, and repeated the performance in 1987 and 1989. For this operation, it was able to alight on packed snow and on slick ice, both challenges to airmanship and aircraft integrity. These remarkable long-distance heavy-lift sorties are described on page 71.

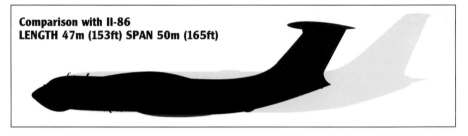

Comparison with Il-86
LENGTH 47m (153ft) SPAN 50m (165ft)

An Ilyushin Il-76TD (SSSR-76478) with red fuselage trim and outer wing panels. (Paul Bannwarth)

Yakolev Yak-42

120 SEATS ■ 740km/h (400mph)

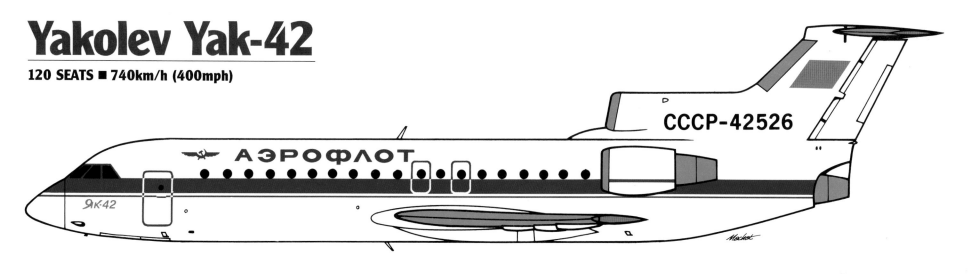

CCCP-42526

Lotarev D-36 (3 x 6,500kg st, 14,330lb st) ■ MTOW 56,500kg (124,560lb) ■ Normal Range 2,200km (1,320mi)

Early Promise

Soviet aircraft that traditionally attracted attention in the West, notably at such shop windows as the Paris Air Show, did so because they were bigger or faster than had ever been seen before. The **Yakovlev Yak-42** was different. When it first flew on 7 March 1975 (as a 100-seater), and when **Aeroflot** ordered 200 of the new trijet in June 1977, the world sat up and took notice; because at last, it was suspected, the Soviet Union had produced an airliner that could compare with equivalent western types, not only in performance, but also in operating efficiency.

Although Aeroflot discussed the possibility of the 120-seat Yak-42 being a replacement for a wide range of obsolescent types, from the Antonov An-24 to the Ilyushin Il-18, it was directed mainly to supersede the Tupolev Tu-134 80-seat twin. Certainly, the figures look promising. The 120-seat six-abreast Yak-42 was only five tons heavier than the four-abreast Tu-134, and was not much bigger. It needed only two crew members, instead of the three or four of the Tupolev. It had good short-field performance, could use rough airstrips, and had the additional features of built-in airstairs and baggage racks on each side of the door entrances. It seemed to fit halfway between the Tupolev Tu-134 twin and the Tupolev Tu-154 trijet, and a great future seemed assured.

The Pace Slackens

The Yakovlev Yak-42 entered service with Aeroflot in November 1980, on routes such as Moscow-Kostroma and Leningrad-Helsinki. Later on, it was introduced as a back-up to the heavy air corridor traffic to the Caucasus; and it operated to Prague, both from Kiev and Lvov.

The introduction of the Yak-42 was marred by many technical problems and, following an in-flight structural failure of the tailplane, the type was withdrawn from service in the early 1980s. After more than 2,300 design changes, it re-entered Aeroflot service in the late 1980s and quickly gained an impressive reputation for reliability, efficiency, and economy.

In 1990, the longer range 120-seat Yak-42D was introduced, and is probably one of the most comfortable Russian-built aircraft in the Aeroflot fleet. By June 1992, 115 Yak-42s and 50 Yak-42Ds had been delivered to Aeroflot.

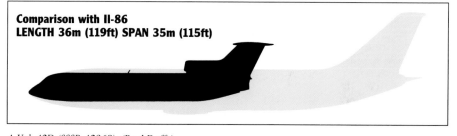

Comparison with Il-86
LENGTH 36m (119ft) SPAN 35m (115ft)

A Yak-42D (SSSR-42368). (Paul Duffy)

World Airline Status

Slow But Steady

For several decades, Aeroflot was not its own master; indeed, under the Soviet system, it probably never was; but in later years, as the Cold War thawed, it acquired more autonomy and could influence the course of its own route expansion and aircraft development. In the international arena, almost a decade was to pass after the end of the Second World War before an Aeroflot aircraft was seen in western Europe, when an **Ilyushin Il-12** resumed service to Stockholm in 1954. Subsequently, progress to other continents was slow.

Back in the 1920s, **Dobrolet** had made connections to Mongolia and Afghanistan, and experimental flights had been made to China. Now, in 1955, as the Soviet Union formed a close alliance with Mao's People's Republic, Aeroflot opened a link with Peking (Beijing); and the next year resumed flights to Kabul. More far-reaching tentacles reached out, with **Tupolev Tu-104** service to India in 1958, to Jakarta in 1962, and **Tupolev Tu-114** service to Japan in 1967. Vietnam

PROGRESS TOWARDS A GLOBAL NETWORK

Continent or Major Country	First Destination	First Service Date	Aircraft Type
Western Europe	Stockholm	11 Nov 1940	Li-2
China	Peking (Beijing)	1 Jan 1955	Il-14
Southern Asia	Delhi-Bombay	14 Aug 1958	Tu-104
North Africa	Cairo	5 Dec 1958	Tu-104
South Polar Region*	Mirnyy	15 Dec 1961	Il-18 An-12
Southeast Asia	Jakarta	31 Jan 1962	Tu-104
West Africa	Conakry	11 Sep 1962	Il-18
Caribbean	Havana	7 Jan 1963	Tu-114
Middle East	Damascus	23 May 1963	Il-18
Canada	Montreal	4 Nov 1966	Tu-114
Japan	Tokyo	19 Apr 1967	Tu-114
East Africa	Mogadishu-Dar es Salaam	1 Jan 1968	Il-62
U.S.A. (East Coast)	New York	15 Jul 1968	Il-62
Central Africa	Bangui	1 Nov 1969	Il-62
South America	Santiago	4 Nov 1972	Il-62
North Polar Region	Longyearbyen	11 Sep 1975	Il-18
U.S.A. (West Coast)	San Francisco	19 May 1991	Il-62M

Occasional flights only

came on stream in 1970.

Next continent was Africa, with an **Ilyushin Il-18** service to Cairo in 1958; then to West Africa, to Guinea, in 1962. During the period of the rise of African nationalism and the collapse of colonialism, the Soviet Union was anxious to capitalize (if that is the right word) on the situation; and Aeroflot was often the emissary, opening up links with **Moscow** throughout the 1970s and 1980s.

To The New World

These routes in the Eastern Hemisphere had been undertaken mainly with the Tupolev Tu-104 and the Ilyushin Il-18. Not until the introduction of the big turboprop Tu-114 in 1961 did Aeroflot feel confident enough, and the Soviet Union feel proud enough, to span the Atlantic. Service to Havana started in 1963 and to Canada in 1966. When the **Ilyushin Il-62** was ready, Aeroflot was able to claim some slots at New York's Kennedy International Airport.

And just as it had made its first landfall in North America in Fidel Castro's Cuba, so it repeated the pattern by opening the first service to South America when Chile voted in a Marxist government, and Aeroflot promptly began to fly to Santiago, via Gander and Havana, in 1972. Eleven years later it started service to Buenos Aires; and later on to Nicaragua, where the left-wing Sandanistas had ousted the Somosas.

Political Ups and Downs

While in most parts of the world, politics did not interfere with, although they sometimes helped, sometimes hindered, Aeroflot's ambitions to forge a global network. The relationship with the United States was so precariously balanced that the smooth continuance of scheduled air service between New York (and Washington, from 5 April 1974) and Moscow was never assured. In December 1981, all pretense of tolerance was thrown aside when martial law was declared in Poland, and one of the knee-jerk reactions of the Reagan administration was to terminate Aeroflot's service to the U.S.A. Less than two years later, on 15 September, even the Aeroflot offices in the U.S. were closed down after a Korean airliner had been shot down by Soviet jets off the coast of Kamchatka.

Other countries had also imposed a ban after the `Flight 007' incident, but in time the political climate eased and Aeroflot continued to build its route system. Not until 29 April 1986, however, was Aeroflot able to resume service to the States, after Presidents Reagan and Gorbachev had met in Geneva in the fall of the previous year. By 7 December 1987,

when Mikhail made a state visit to Washington, the Ilyushin Il-62M was not even remarked upon by the press. Aeroflot was part of the scene.

Polar Specialist

Not all of Aeroflot's routes and services were politically motivated or necessarily linked with political strategy. The same could be said for the airlines of other nations, although it is arguable that Aeroflot was, as a branch of the Soviet Civil Air Administration, more directly the instrument of policy than were some other flag carriers or `chosen instruments'. The pioneering of some routes, however, while having certain political undertones, were just as much examples of the true spirit of airline enterprise and development.

On 10 September 1975, for example, Aeroflot opened a twice-monthly service to Longyearbyen, in Spitzbergen (Svalbard), a Norwegian territory of the Arctic on which there were two Soviet-operated coal mines. Questions were occasionally raised as to why the U.S.S.R., with all its extensive wealth of coal within its own borders, should need a couple of mines in Spitzbergen. Such suspicions aside, it did give Aeroflot, along with S.A.S., the privilege of operating to the most northerly airport in the world open to the public.

At the other end of the globe, on the opposite polar axis, Aeroflot was also active, having made its first flight to Antarctica as early as 1961 (see pages 70-71). The Soviet national air carrier thus carried the flag to every continent except Australia, and operated both to the Arctic and the Antarctic — though service to Mirnyy and Molodezhnaya was not exactly frequent, roughly once or twice a year.

Round-The-World

Aeroflot was eventually to join the ranks of those airlines that offered service completely around the world — or nearly enough to qualify for that claim. On 19 May 1991, from its well-established far eastern terminal of Khabarovsk, an Ilyushin Il-62M started service to San Francisco, via Anchorage. On 29 March 1992, this route was augmented by a direct flight, also via Anchorage, from Moscow.

Pan American Airways used to be proud of its round-the-world flights but Juan Trippe and his successors never did fill the domestic gap across the U.S.A. until it purchased National Airlines in 1978. The supreme irony was that, at the end of the same year when Aeroflot achieved round-the-world status, Pan American Airways, one of the world's great airlines, closed its offices and terminated all its services.

A Global Network

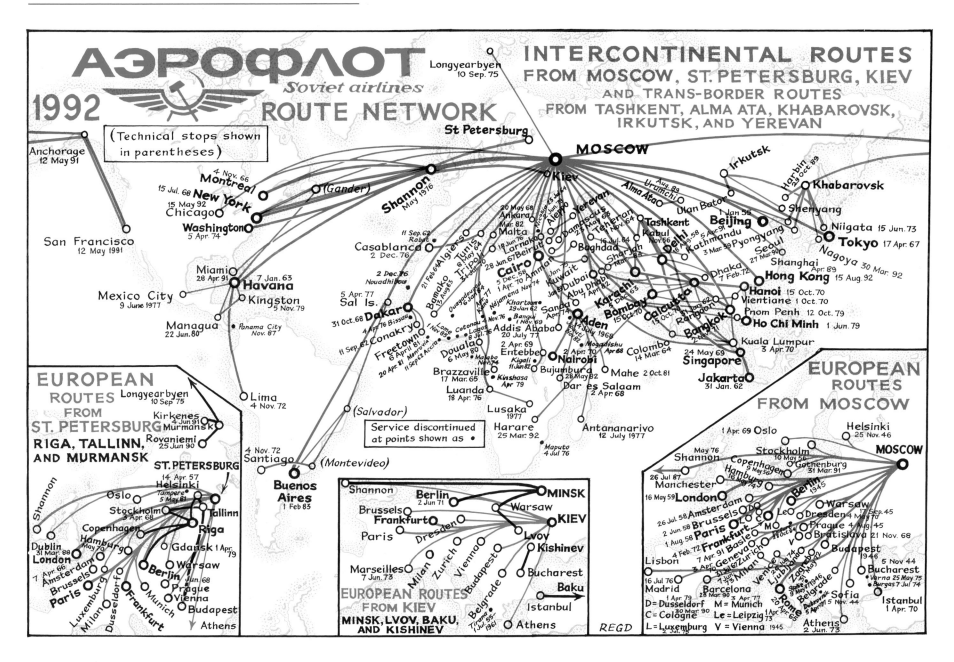

АЭРОФЛОТ
Soviet airlines

1992 ROUTE NETWORK

INTERCONTINENTAL ROUTES
FROM MOSCOW, ST. PETERSBURG, KIEV
AND TRANS-BORDER ROUTES
FROM TASHKENT, ALMA ATA, KHABAROVSK,
IRKUTSK, AND YEREVAN

(Technical stops shown in parentheses)

Service discontinued at points shown as •

EUROPEAN ROUTES FROM ST. PETERSBURG
RIGA, TALLINN, AND MURMANSK

EUROPEAN ROUTES FROM KIEV
MINSK, LVOV, BAKU, AND KISHINEV

EUROPEAN ROUTES FROM MOSCOW

D = Dusseldorf   M = Munich
C = Cologne   Le = Leipzig
L = Luxemburg   V = Vienna

REGD

The First Soviet Airbus

Long Gestation

By the time the Soviet Aircraft industry got under way with its first wide-bodied airliner, the Boeing 747 had already entered service. News filtered through to the West during summer 1971 that the Ilyushin Design Bureau, with Genrikh Novozhilov taking over from Sergei Ilyushin's design leadership, was working on a four-engined wide-bodied airliner, with podded engines on the wing. The 350-seat **Ilyushin Il-86** had two aisles, permitting eight- or nine-abreast seating, and like most large Soviet aircraft, had a multiple-wheeled landing gear, 14 altogether, with main wheels mounted on three tandem-mounted pairs of four. The center one of the three was mounted in the fuselage, like the long-range Douglas DC-10's. This was — again following Soviet design custom — intended to provide soft-field, but not necessarily short-field performance. When delivered, the Il-86 normally needed about 2,500m (8,000ft) of paved runway for airline service.

Five years elapsed before the first flight, on 22 December 1976, at Khodinka, only a few kilometers from Red Square. This was almost like a new big jet making its maiden flight from London's Hyde Park or New York's Central Park — or even down Washington's Mall. Production was at Voronezh.

The first **Aeroflot** scheduled Ilyushin Il-86 service was in December 1980, from Moscow to Alma Ata, capital of Kazakhstan, and the destination city of the only Soviet supersonic airline service. Right from the start, the aircraft had never been promoted as a long-range airliner and it was compared unfavorably with western wide-bodied types. But with state-supplied fuel and with no competitive pressure, this was not an issue for Aeroflot's operational requirements.

Virtue Out of Necessity

As time went on, with most of Aeroflot's transatlantic flights of necessity stopping at Shannon, the spirit of free enterprise and innovative minds generated opportunities for cooperation between Aer Rianta, the Irish airport authority, and Aeroflot, to their mutual advantage. Aeroflot set up its own fuel 'farm' and thus avoided having to pay out scarce hard currency. Aeroflot paid for airport charges with fuel, which

Shannon then sold to other carriers, including, ironically, U.S. military VIP flights. Soviet travelers also liked the duty-free shopping amenities, and Aeroflot and the airport authorities in Russia invited the Irish to set up similar facilities in Moscow and Leningrad. Ilyushin Il-86s began to call at Shannon in the mid-1980s and Aeroflot became the airport's biggest customer. In 1990, the Soviet airline began to take advantage of liberal international regulations as the airline world deregulated, and began to promote Ireland as a destination from the United States. Far from being a necessary evil, Shannon has become an Aeroflot asset.

ILYUSHIN IL-86 CARRY-ON BAGGAGE CONVENIENCE

Standard Overhead Racks

Lower Level Luggage Compartment

Passenger Entrance

The Il-86's carry-on baggage arrangements are excellent. Passengers can deposit their 'not wanted on voyage' items on the 'left-luggage' shelves.

WIDE-BODIED AIRLINERS COMPARED

First Flight Date	First Service Date	Aircraft Type	Dimensions-m(ft) Length	Dimensions-m(ft) Span	Speed km/h (mph)	Seats	MTOW kg (lb)	Normal Range km (mi)	First Airline	No. Built
9 Feb 1969	22 Jan 1970	Boeing 747-100	70 (231)	60 (196)	875 (540)	450	333,390 (710,000)	8,800 (5,500)	Pan American	712[1]
29 Apr 1988	8 Feb 1989	Boeing 747-400	70 (231)	64 (211)	875 (540)	470	394,630 (870,000)	11,000 (6,900)	Northwest	200*
29 Aug 1970	5 Aug 1971	MDD[2] DC-10-10	55 (181)	47 (155)	920 (575)	360	206,385 (445,000)	4,500 (2,800)	American Airlines	122
10 Jan 1990	20 Dec 1990	MDD MD-11	61 (201)	52 (170)	875 (540)	276	276,690 (610,000)	9,270 (5,760)	Finnair	50*
16 Nov 1970	15 Apr 1972	Lockheed TriStar 1	54 (178)	47 (155)	795 (495)	270	945,000 (430,00)	4,800 (3,000)	Eastern	200[3]
16 Oct 1978	7 May 1979	Lockheed TriStar 500	50 (164)	50 (164)	780 (485)	240	231,330 (510,000)	6,935 (4,300)	British Airways	50
28 Oct 1972	23 May 1974	Airbus A300	54 (177)	45 (147)	875 (540)	265	171,500 (378,535)	2,560 (1,600)	Air France	375*
3 Apr 1982	12 Apr 1983	Airbus A310	47 (153)	44 (144)	875 (540)	230	164,000 (361,560)	5,100 (3,200)	Lufthansa	210*
22 Dec 1976	26 Dec 1980	Ilyushin Il-86	60 (195)	48 (157)	900 (560)	350	208,000 (458,560)	2,500 (1,550)	Aeroflot	120*

Notes: [1] Includes all -100/-200/300s. [2] McDonnell Douglas, [3] includes all versions, * production continues.

An Il-86 (SSSR-86119) being towed past five others at Moscow-Sheremetyevo. (Paul Duffy)

Ilyushin Il-86

350 SEATS ■ 900km/h (540mph)

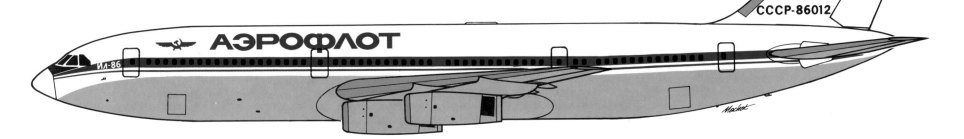

Kuznetsov NK-86 (4 x 13,000kg st, 28,660lb st) ■ MTOW 208,000kg (458,560lb) ■ Normal Range 2,500km (1,500mi)

Made For The Market

The Il-86 had some good features, apart from substantially improved cabin and galley furnishings — even the seats were more comfortable than those that had served **Aeroflot** since time immemorial. The passenger entrance was through doors in the fuselage lower level up self-contained collapsible steps. Immediately on entering, passengers could take advantage of one of the airliner's best features, and one that other manufacturers could well copy. This was a downstairs luggage compartment, where all excess carry-on baggage — and Russians always travel with excess — could be deposited, in a `not-needed-on-voyage' aerial equivalent of shipping practice. Incidentally, anticipating extremes of temperature at such destinations as Yakutsk, plastic wing covers were made for the Il-86.

The critics of the Soviet aircraft industry concentrated on its wide-bodied candidate's lack of range. It could not carry a full payload across the Atlantic, unless it stopped at Shannon and Gander — a necessity that had been dispensed with as long ago as 1957, with the introduction of the Bristol Britannia and the Douglas DC-7C. The critics should have put themselves in the shoes of the Ilyushin market researcher. Not a single intercontinental long-range route required the services of an airliner bigger than the Ilyushin Il-62M. The density of traffic on routes such as Moscow-New York, or Moscow-Tokyo did not come close to that on routes such as London-New York or Los Angeles-Tokyo, and could certainly not justify a 350-seat airliner. And Ilyushin had no illusions about the slim chances of breaking into the world market against Boeing, McDonnell Douglas, Lockheed, and Airbus.

Domestically, the requirement was quite different. Only two major cities in the far east, Khabarovsk and Vladivostok, were far enough away from the big cities of European Russian and Ukraine to demand an aircraft larger than the Il-62M. The main markets from Moscow, Leningrad, and Kiev were to the Black Sea and Caucasian resorts, and to destinations such as Novosibirsk, Tashkent, and Krasnoyarsk — within Il-86 range. Whatever the shortcomings of the Ilyushin wide-bodied airliner for long ranges, it was just right for Aeroflot.

One of the best features of the Il-86 is the lower level baggage compartment, where passengers can stow carry-on items that are not needed during the journey. (R.E.G. Davies)

LENGTH 60m (195ft) SPAN 48m (157ft)

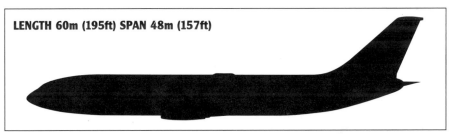

World's Biggest

The Mostest

Sheer size has always fascinated people in all walks of life. The tallest building, the longest bridge, the biggest ship, the highest mountain, the longest river; all these have excited a natural curiosity, and though the world's natural wonders are unchanging, mankind has constantly tried to build things bigger, even if they are not better. The Russians have shared this urge and attempted, none too successfully, to build outsize aircraft during the 1930s. After the Second World War, the banner for bigness was taken up by the Ukraine, whose Antonov Design Bureau produced a fine series of large freighter aircraft.

The pictures and the diagrams on this and the following page tell their own story. Except for its six-engined cousin (see below), the **Antonov An-124 Ruslan**, tipping the scales at more than 400 tons, is, by a comfortable margin — 55 tons — the world's largest aircraft to be produced in quantity.

Standard payload for the An-124 is 150 tons. On one occasion, it carried 171 tons to an altitude of 10,750m (35,260ft), or the normal cruising height of most long-range airliners—about seven miles. To help load such weights, the freight hold is equipped with two overhead traveling cranes, each one able to lift ten tons. Heavy duty floors, roller-tracks, and winches match this capability, which, incidentally, makes the giant freighter virtually self-supporting.

The An-124 has an upward-hinging front loading door, and a rear-loading ventral door. Both are equipped with heavy duty ramps, and the aircraft can be tilted to the fore or to the aft to assist the loading procedures.

As Antonov built them bigger, it just added wheels to accommodate the heavy loads and to maintain the low wheel loading for use on soft surfaces, including packed snow. The An-124 has 24 wheels; five pairs mounted in tandem in fuselage pods on each side, and two twin nose-gear wheels.

The Mriya

Exceeding the American Lockheed C-5A in all departments, the Ruslan was unchallenged in the Guinness Book of Records throughout the 1980s — until the last month of 1988. An even larger aircraft, a stretched-fuselage modification of the An-124 the **Antonov An-225 Mriya** (Dream), with a larger wing to add two extra engines, was produced specifically to carry the Soviet Space Shuttle Buran. The Ruslan had only been able to carry the huge SS20 missile (or the fuselage sections of almost any airliner). With Antonov's two giant machines, the store of superlatives is almost exhausted. Fortunately for the world, the Cold War has ended, the Arms Race is over, and the need for quantities of giant air freighters has declined. Only one Mriya has been completed. However, this aircraft is of considerable general interest and is included in this book if only to escape criticism for omitting it by applying too strictly the qualifying definition.

(Top) On one special flight, on 6-7 May 1987, the Antonov An-124 circumnavigated the U.S.S.R., flying a closed circuit distance of 20,151km (12,524mi)—slightly more than halfway round the earth at the equator; the flight took 25hr 30min.

(Center) Before 1991, all civil aircraft in the Soviet Union—and many non-civil—were required to wear Aeroflot colors or did so under a `flag of convenience'. Although many An-124s appeared in Aeroflot colors, none was part of the airline's fleet. This Ruslan (SSSR-82008) is operated jointly by the manufacturer and U.K. cargo airline AirFoyle. (Malcolm Nason)

(Bottom) The Antonov An-225 Mriya, world's biggest aircraft, carrys the space shuttle Buran.

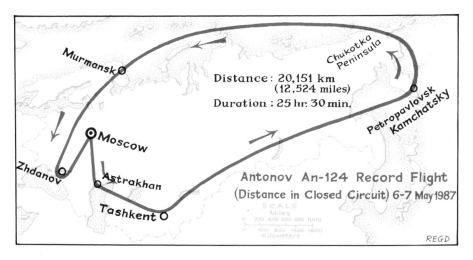

Distance: 20,151 km (12,524 miles)
Duration: 25 hr. 30 min.

Antonov An-124 Record Flight (Distance in Closed Circuit) 6-7 May 1987

Antonov An-124

150 TONS ■ 800km/h (500mph)

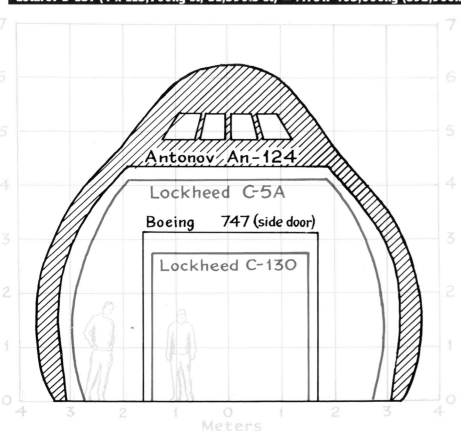

Lotarev D-18T (4 x 113,700kg st, 51,590lb st) ■ MTOW 405,000kg (892,900lb) ■ Normal Range 4,500km (2,700mi)

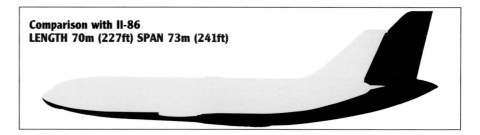

Comparison with Il-86
LENGTH 70m (227ft) SPAN 73m (241ft)

THE HEAVY FREIGHTERS

First Flight Date	Aircraft Type	Dimensions-m(ft)		Speed km/h (mph)	Max Payload (tons)	Engines			MTOW (tons)	Normal Range km (mi)	No. Built
		Length	Span			No	Type	ehp (or thrust)			
23 Aug 1954	Lockheed C-130 (L-100)	34 (113)	40 (133)	480 (300)	23	4	Allison 501-D22A	4,500	70	2,500 (1,500)	2,000*
27 Feb 1965	Antonov An-22	58 (190)	64 (211)	600 (380)	88	4	Kuznetzov NK-12MA	15,000	250	5,000 (3,125)	55
30 Jun 1968	Lockheed C-5A	75 (248)	68 (229)	830 (515)	118	4	GE TF39	19,500 (43,000)	379	5,500 (3,400)	81
30 Nov 1971	Boeing 747-200F	70 (231)	60 (196)	940 (590)	112	4	P & W JT9D	24,830 (54,750)	377	8,000 (5,000)	69
26 Dec 1982	Antonov An-124	69 (227)	73 (241)	865 (537)	150	4	Lotarev D-18T	23,450 (51,600)	405	4,500 (2,800)	45*
21 Dec 1988	Antonov An-225	84 (276)	88 (290)	750 (470)	250	6	Lotarev D-18T	23,450 (51,600)	600	4,500 (2,800)	1

*Notes: Boeing 747-200F may also be powered with Rolls-Royce RB211 and GE CF6 engines; An-22 production total does not include prototypes. *Production continues*

Into The Nineties

Metamorphosis

After **Mikhail Gorbachev** launched the policies of glasnost and perestroika in the mid-1980s, the Soviet Union was never the same again. The fires of communist revolutionary spirit, long dampened, were extinguished as the smoldering embers of independence broke into flames when **Boris Yeltsin** led the final overthrow of communist power in 1991. In the capitals of the autonomous republics, political and social instincts combined to proclaim regional identities and to break away from the perceived domination of centralized Moscow control. But in a country that stretched almost halfway around the earth, complete balkanization would have led to chaos, and recognizing practical and economic realities, eleven of the states of the Union of Soviet Socialist Republics (U.S.S.R.) were proclaimed the **Commonwealth of Independent States (CIS)** on 22 December 1991.

Problems of Fragmentation

The three Baltic republics had already reclaimed their independence. The remaining twelve states came to grips with the challenge to replace a 70-year-old economic system. The 29 local regions (other than the four Moscow entities and the three Baltics of Aeroflot) took steps to go their own way.

The sheer magnitude of sharing out some 11,000 aircraft and more than 600,000 staff was an awesome prospect. Nevertheless, aircraft, ground installations, airfields and airports, navigational services, and personnel of the old Aeroflot giant would be reidentified with the new regional airlines, with the transfers amounting almost literally to no more than the signing of documents. At the time of the publication of this book, however, only a handful of aircraft have been painted in the new color schemes of the independent companies.

The New Aeroflot

Even before the creation of the CIS, the decision was made in Moscow that the Aeroflot name should remain as that of the official flag carrier of Russia's international air routes. Effectively, it simply adopted the fleet of Sheremetyevo II, Moscow's main international airport, formerly one of the 36 regional subdivisions. Of the 103 aircraft, 28 were long-range Ilyushin Il-62s and 18 were Ilyushin Il-86 Airbuses

The new Russian International Airlines was no longer inhibited by an obligation to operate only Soviet-built aircraft, although Aeroflot Soviet Airlines remained as the legal name until 23 July 1992. As described on page 93, it leased a small fleet of **Airbus A310s**. A new era had begun.

Designed specifically for Arctic and Antarctic operations, the Antonov An-74 is derived from the An-72 light transport. With a crew of five, it has more fuel capacity, advanced avionics, and provision for a wheel/ski landing gear.

Superficially similar to the Il-86, the 300-seat Ilyushin Il-96 long-range wide-body is a new design. First flown on 28 September 1988, it should enter service with Aeroflot early in 1993. Powered by four Soloviev PS-90A turbofans, the stretched fuselage 350-seat Il-96M with Pratt & Whitney PW2037 engines is due to make its first flight in March 1993. (photos: Paul Duffy)

The twin-turbofan 200-seat Tu-204 first flew on 2 January 1989. Initial versions have Soloviev PS-90ATs, a Rolls-Royce RB211-535E4-powered variant first flew on 14 August 1992. Its sponsor, BRAVIA (British Russian Aviation Co), expects CIS certification (with CIS-built avionics) by the end of 1993 and international certification with Western avionics in mid-1995.

Following two prototypes (the second, SSSR-54001, is illustrated), the first production Il-114 turboprop made its first flight at Tashkent on 7 August 1992. Designed as an An-24 replacement and first flown on 29 March 1990, the 60-seat Il-114 was scheduled to enter service with the Uzbeki Civil Air Department (formerly a division of Aeroflot) by the end of 1992. (photos: Jean-Luc Altherr)

Airbus A310-300

193 SEATS ■ 875km/h (540mph)

This color scheme was used during the latter months of 1992 on the Airbus A310. Selection of a permanent insignia for the whole Aeroflot fleet has yet to be decided.

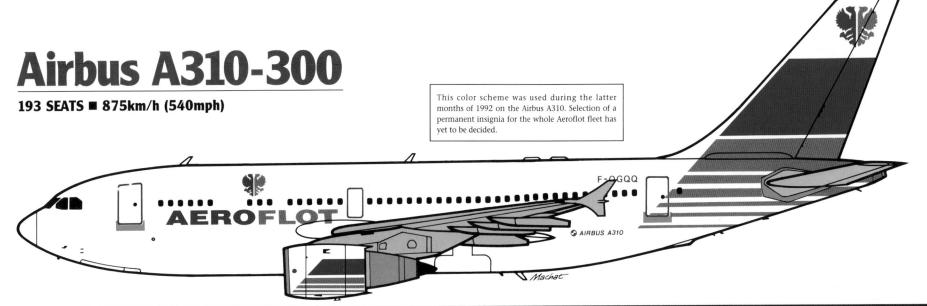

F-OGQQ

AEROFLOT

AIRBUS A310

Machat

General Electric CF6-80C2A8 (2 x 26,760kg st, 59,000lb st) ■ MTOW 164,000kg (361,560lb) ■ Normal Range 6,550km (4,050mi)

Development History

The first truly European airliner project, the wide-bodied 250/280-seat **Airbus A300B** made its maiden flight on 28 October 1972, and entered service with Air France in May 1974. After a slow start, the order book began to fill up after the twin had proved its economic worth and operational reliability. To compete effectively with US manufacturers, Airbus built up a family of twin-jet derivatives of the A300B, each incorporating the most modern technology.

Launched in spring 1979, the 200/220-seat **A310-200** (originally called A300B10), designed for short-to-medium-range routes, featured a two-crew digital or so-called `glass cockpit' and an advanced wing. A long-range version, the **A310-300**, which incorporated an additional fuel tank in the tailplane, made its first flight on 8 July 1985 and proved to be a popular choice with airlines as ETOPS (Extended-range Twin-engine Operations), pioneered by Airbus, became commonplace.

Aeroflot's First Western Jetliner

Although much improved over the original model, the Il-62M's long-range nonstop capability was limited (see page 55) and Aeroflot turned to the West to solve the problem. In October 1989, it announced its intention to order five A310-300s (plus five options) and confirmed its plan on the following January 24, with deliveries between November 1991 and June 1992. Following guarantees by the Russian government to the French creditors, the first aircraft was handed over on 2 July 1992.

Following a period of crew familiarization (some pilots had already been trained in anticipation of the lease arrangement), the A310 entered service with Aeroflot on 4 August 1992 on European routes. Eleven days later it flew the inaugural service from Moscow to Hong Kong.

The five Aeroflot A310-308s were originally painted at Toulouse with Aeroflot's blue-winged hammer-and-sickle logo on the forward fuselage as shown in this photo of F-OGQR (the fourth aircraft delivered to Aeroflot). Before handover to Aeroflot, a small Russian flag was applied to the tip of the rudder, but the third aircraft (F-OGQQ Tchaikovski), illustrated in Mike Machat's sideview above, adopted the new double-eagle logo of Aeroflot-Russian International Airlines. (photograph: Airbus Industrie)

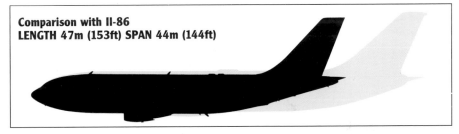

Comparison with Il-86
LENGTH 47m (153ft) SPAN 44m (144ft)

Metamorphosis

Many Aeroflot fleet figures have been quoted, ranging from "about 3,500" to "as many as 8,000". The following data have been compiled from consultation with regional administrations.

THE AEROFLOT FLEET 1991

Type	Number	Type	Number
Mainline Jets		**Freighters**	
Ilyushin Il-62/62M	180	Antonov An-12	150
Ilyushin Il-86	90	Antonov An-26	450
Tupolev Tu-134	450	Antonov An-74	10
Tupolev Tu-154/154M	600	Ilyushin Il-18	20
Yakovlev Yak-42	150	Ilyushin Il-76	200
total	1,470	total	830
Feeder Jets			
Yakovlev Yak-40	750	**Feeder Pistons**	
		Antonov An-2	3,000
Mainline Turboprops			
Ilyushin Il-18	10	**Helicopters**	
		Kamov Ka-26/Ka-32	200
Feeder Turboprops		Mil Mi-2	1,000
Antonov An-24	750	Mil Mi-8/Mi-17	2,000
Antonov An-28	50	Mil Mi-6/Mi-10/Mi-26	200
Let L410	650	total	3,400
total	1,450		
TOTAL (derived from best estimates)		**10,800-11,000**	

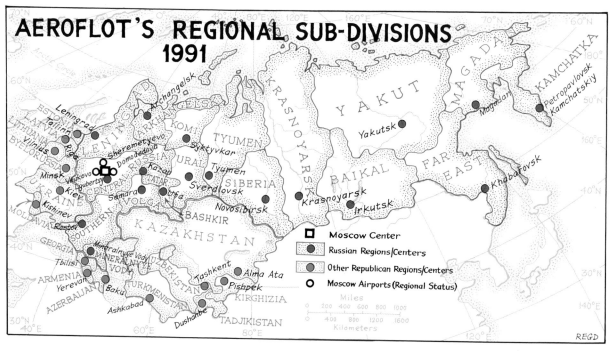

AEROFLOT'S REGIONAL SUB-DIVISIONS 1991

□ Moscow Center
● Russian Regions/Centers
● Other Republican Regions/Centers
○ Moscow Airports (Regional Status)

REGD

THE NEW CIS AIRLINES

Independent Companies

Aerolicht (ALAK) ....Moscow-DME
Aerosher Express ....Moscow-SVO
Air Russia (Aeroflot/British Airways) ....Moscow-DME
Air Transport School ....Zhukovskiy
AJT Air/(Asian Joint Transport) ....Moscow-VKO
ANTK (Tupolev Aviation Complex) ....Zhukovskiy
ASA (American St Petersburg Airlines) ......St Petersburg
ASDA ....Moscow
Aveko ....Nikolaev
Avial ....Moscow-DME
Bosfor-V ....Vladivostok
Elf Air ....Zhukovskiy
Ecological Concern Rescue Service ....St Petersburg
Interfreight ....Moscow
KMZ (Antonov Machine Works) ....Kiev
Liana ....Nikolaev
LII (Gromov Flight Research Centre) ....Zhukovskiy
ORBI ....Tblisi
PO Transport Aviation ....Moscow
Polair ....Moscow
Polet ....Omsk

`Progress' Factory ....Samara
Russia (Avia Ross) ....Moscow
Saiakhat ....Alma Ata
SGA ....Moscow
SPA Aero ....Ekaterinburg
Sterkh ....Mirnec
Soyuz ....Moscow
Taiga-1 ....Moscow
Ukrainian Air Leasing ....Kiev
VolgaDniepr ....Ulyanovsk
Yak Air Service ....Moscow

Not all of the above were issued with operating licences or had started operations by the end of 1992.

State/Government Companies

(Former Aeroflot directorates are shown in bold type)
**Aeroflot - Russian International
Airlines** (CUMVS) ....Moscow-SVO
Aerovolga ....Kazan
Air Ukraine ....Kiev
Archangelsk CAD ....Archangelsk
Armenian Airlines ....Yerevan

Azerbaijan Airlines (AZAL) ....Baku
Baikalavia ....Irkutsk
Bashkir Airlines ....Ufa
Belarus CAD ....Minsk
Domodedevo PO ....Moscow-DME
Far Eastern Avia ....Khabarovsk
Georgian CAD ....Tbilisi
Goniiga State Scientific
and Research Institute ....Moscow-SVO
**Independent United
Air Detachment** ....Moscow-VKO
Kazakh CAD ....Alma Ata
Kirghizi CAD ....Bishkek
Komi Avia ....Syktyvkar
Krasnoyarskavia ....Krasnoyarsk
Leningrad ACA ....St Petersburg
Magadan Avia ....Magadan
Mineralvodskoe PO ....Mineralnyevody
Moldavian CAD ....Kishinev
Nerungri Sakha Corp ....Yakutsk
NPO PANKH ....Krasnodar
Sibavia ....Novosibirsk

Southern Airlines ....Rostov-on-Don
Tadzhik CAD ....Dushanbe
Tatarstan Airlines ....Kazan
Tyumenavia Trans ....Tyumen
Transaero ....Moscow-SVO
Turkmenavia ....Ashkhabad
Ugats ....Moscow-Bykovo
Urals CAD ....Ekaterinburg
Uzbeki CAD ....Tashkent
Vnukovo CAD ....Moscow-VKO
Yakutavia ....Yakutsk

Notes: ACA: Association of Civil Aviation, CAD: Civil Air Department, PANKH: Aerial Work Detachment, PO: Production Association

DME = Domodedevo
SVO = Sheremetyevo
VKO = Vnukovo

Like No Other

Industrial Giant

In the early 1990s, the world witnessed the dissolution of a political and industrial empire. In the production of many mineral and agricultural resources, it was among the world's leaders. Though marked by a uniformity of design, Soviet manufacturing continuously revealed impressive statistics of volume production. This demanded concentrated labor and equipment, concentrated into big cities. In this respect, the Soviet Union was no different from the United States, Europe, or Japan.

Urban Concentrations

By 1990, the U.S.S.R. had 52 cities with more than half a million inhabitants each. About half of these had populations of more than a million. Leningrad had five million, and Moscow's eleven ranked it among the top half dozen conurbations in the world. Thirty of the 52 are in Russia, a reminder that the new regime is still a powerful force in the industrial world. Nine are in Ukraine, which, of the breakaway republics, alone has a balanced economy of world stature.

Of great significance to **Aeroflot** is the geographical distribution of the urban concentrations. Of the 52 big cities, only 15 are more than 2,000km (1,250mi) and only three are more than 4,000km (2,500mi) from Moscow. The domestic market for a long-range Ilyushin Il-86 is thus very small.

Conversely, only three major cities are within 400km (250mi) of Moscow, and only Gorki (Nizhni Novgorod) has more than one million people. It was the destination for Dobrolet's first service in 1923, but is hardly a natural air route in the jet age. St Petersburg (Leningrad), is connected to Moscow by a good railway service, with future high-speed rail potential.

Aeroflot's Challenge and Achievement

Aeroflot, therefore, has always provided air service on a bewildering permutation of medium-haul routes that comprise the majority of the city pairs. This accounts for the preponderance of **Tupolev Tu-154s** (see page opposite) which are deployed mainly throughout an area roughly the size of the U.S. (see map and page 62) and also the bulk of the capacity on the trans-Siberian and trans-Turkestan trunk arteries.

Equally praiseworthy, however, has been Aeroflot's dedication in providing countless local services to thousands of otherwise isolated communities. The ubiquitous **Antonov An-2**, a humble piston-engined biplane, made an outstanding contribution to the welfare of the Soviet peoples, from the Baltic Sea to the Pacific Ocean.

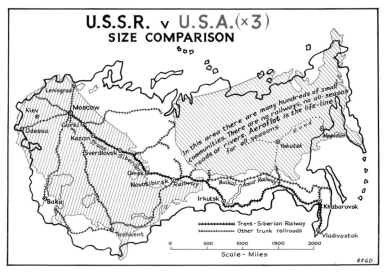

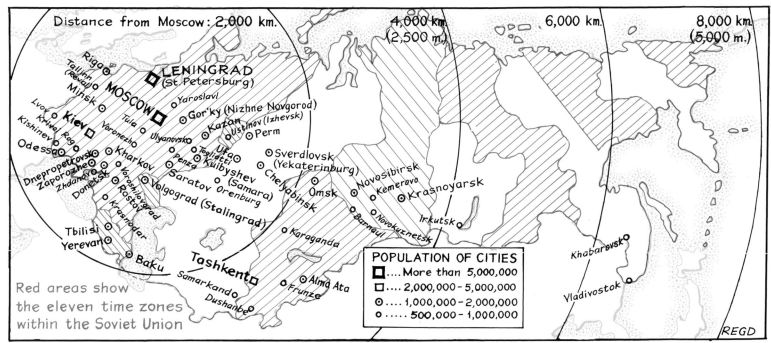

Red areas show the eleven time zones within the Soviet Union

POPULATION OF CITIES
- ☐ .... More than 5,000,000
- ☐ .... 2,000,000 - 5,000,000
- ⊙ .... 1,000,000 - 2,000,000
- ○ ..... 500,000 - 1,000,000

BIBLIOGRAPHY

Books about Aeroflot, and even those relating to Soviet aviation or air transport, are difficult to obtain, none of them having enjoyed wide circulation. Notably, however, three were published about two decades ago, and deserve much commendation as pioneer works:

Soviet Transport Aircraft Since 1945 by John Stroud (Putnam, London, 1965) is all that seasoned readers of Stroud's work could expect;

Aeroflot — Soviet Air Transport Since 1923 by Hugh MacDonald (Putnam, London, 1975) assembled every detail of Aeroflot that was practically possible at the time — when almost every avenue of research was closed;

Russian Aircraft Since 1940 by Jean Alexander (Putnam, London, 1975) is a good complement to Stroud's groundbreaking effort.

More recently,
Aircraft of the Soviet Union by Bill Gunston (Osprey,London, 1983) is an invaluable and encyclopaedic reference by an indefatigable aviation writer, while

Soviet S.S.T. by Howard Moon (Orion, New York, 1989) analyzes one of the most controversial transport aircraft produced in the Soviet Union.

Russian Lindbergh by Georgy Baidukov, Edited by Von Hardesty (Smithsonian Press, Washington, D.C., 1991; first published by Molodaya Guardia, Moscow, 1975) is a tribute to the great Valery Chkalov.

Soviets in the Arctic by T.A. Taraconzio (McMillan, New York, 1938) provides an authoritative insight into the work of the U.S.S.R. in exploring and developing the northern regions of Eurasia, by land, sea, and air.

Life on the Ice Floe by I.V. Papanin (J. Messner, New York, 1939) is the diary of the dramatic four-man visit to the North Pole in 1937.

Igor Sikorsky: The Russian Years by K.N. Finne (Edited by Carl J. Bobrow and Von Hardesty) (Smithsonian Institution Press, Washington, D.C., 1987, first published in Belgrade, Yugoslavia, 1930) reveals a first-hand glimpse of the Il'ya Muromets, the world's first transport aircraft.

Some English language books have been published in the Soviet Union, including:

Wings Over the Arctic by Mikhail V. Vodopyanov (Foreign Languages Publishing House, Moscow, 1948), a delightful account of bush flying for Aeroflot in the early days and of sorties into the Arctic, including the Papanin Polar Expedition, for which Vodopyanov was the Chief Pilot.

Many books have been published in the Soviet Union on all aspects of aviation. These include (the titles have been translated for readers' convenience):

The First Flights Across the Arctic by Georgy Baidukov (Dyetskaya Literatura, Moscow, 1967)

Civil Aviation of the U.S.S.R. (Chief Editor: G.F. Bezborodov) (Ministry of Civil Aviation, Moscow, 1967)

History of Civil Aviation in the U.S.S.R. (Chief Editor: Boris Bugayev) (Air Transport, Moscow, 1967)

History of Aircraft Construction in the Soviet Union Two volumes, by V.B. Shavrov (Machinostroyenie, Moscow, 1986-1988)

Soviet Aircraft Constructors by A.N. Gonoma (Voyenoye ledatelstvo, 1990)

Ilyushin Aircraft (Edited by G.V. Novozhilov) (Machinostroyenie, Moscow, 1983 and reprinted 1990)

Soviet Aircraft Constructors by A.N. Ponomaryev (Voyenoye Izdatelstvo, Moscow, 1990)

Over the Arctic and the Antarctic by A.A. Lebedev and I.P. Mazuruk (MISL, Moscow, 1991)

Brief Historical Sketches of Eastern Siberia and the Far East, 1923-1945 by E.V. Altunin (Irkutsk University, 1990)

Wings of the North by Altunin (Magadan Publishers, Magadan, 1976).

Wings of Siberia by Altunin (Eastern Siberian Publishers, Irkutsk, 1988).

Waiting for Take-Off by V. Danilenko (Khabarovsk Publishers,Khabarovsk, 1990)

Wings Over Yakutia by E.V. Maximov and U.N. Zyev (Yakutsk Publishers, 1986)

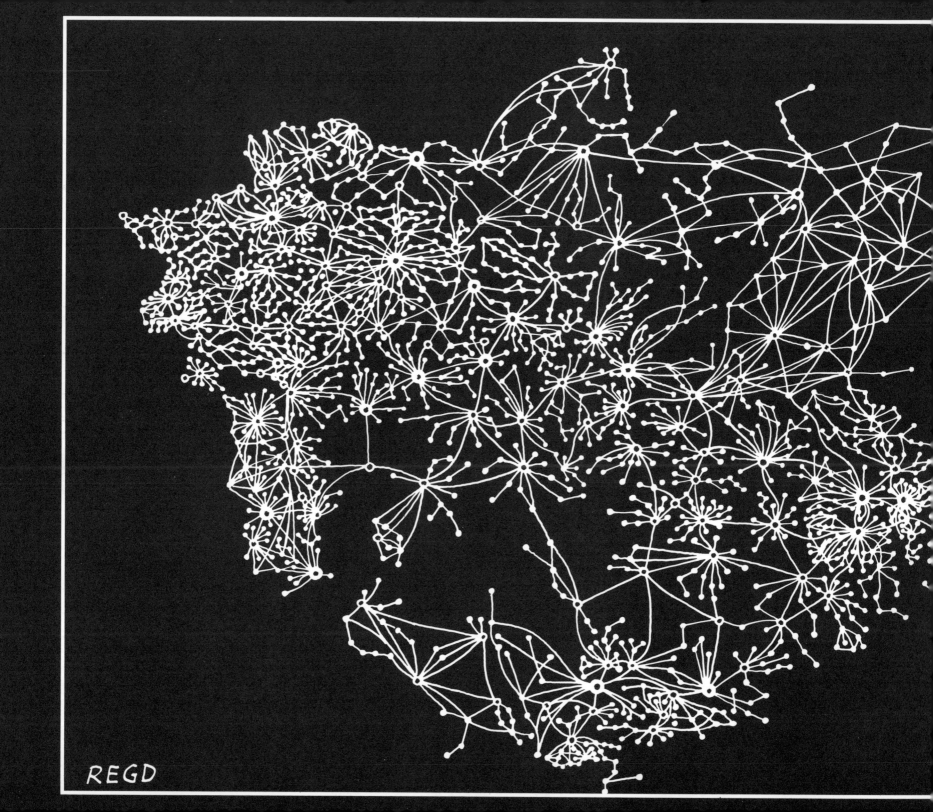

REGD